Panic

The Social Construction
of the Street Gang Problem

Richard C. McCorkle
University of Nevada, Las Vegas

Terance D. Miethe
University of Nevada, Las Vegas

Prentice
Hall

Upper Saddle River, New Jersey 07458

Library of Congress Cataloging-in-Publication Data

McCorkle, richard C., 1954-
  Panic : the social construction of the street gang problem / Richard C. McCorkle,
Terance D. Miethe.
    p. cm.
  Includes bibliographical references and index.
  ISBN 0-13-094458-0
    1. Gangs--Government policy--United States. 2. Gangs--United States--Public opinion.
3. Gangs--Press coverage--United States. 4. Gangs--Government policy--Nevada. 5.
Gangs--Nevada--Public opinion. 6. Gang prevention--Nevada. 7. Public opinion--United
States. 8. Public opinion--Nevada. I. Miethe, Terance D. II. Title.

HV6446.M38 2001
364.1'06'60973--dc21   2001036196

Publisher: Jeff Johnston
Executive Assistant: Brenda Rock
Executive Acquisitions Editor: Kim Davies
Assistant Editor: Sarah Holle
Managing Editor: Mary Carnis
Production Management: Naomi Sysak
Production Editor: Naomi Sysak
Interior Design: Naomi Sysak
Production Liaison: Adele M. Kupchik
**Director of Production
  and Manufacturing:** Bruce Johnson
Manufacturing Buyer: Cathleen Petersen
Cover Design Coordinator: Miguel Ortiz
Formatting: Naomi Sysak

Electronic Art Creation: Mark Ammerman
Marketing Manager: Ramona Sherman
Marketing Assistant: Adam Kloza
Printer/Binder: R.R. Donnelley, Harrisonburg, VA
Copyeditor: Natalia Morgan
Proofreader: Julie Boddorf
Cover Design: Scott Garrison
Cover Photograph: Kent Knudson/PhotoLink
Cover Printer: Phoenix

Pearson Education LTD.
Pearson Education Australia PTY, Limited
Pearson Education Singapore, Pte. Ltd.
Pearson Education North Asia, Ltd.
Pearson Education Canada, Ltd.
Pearson Educación de Mexico, S.A. de C.V.
Pearson Education—Japan
Pearson Education Malaysia, Pte. Ltd.

10 9 8 7 6 5 4 3 2 1
ISBN: 0-13-094458-0

Contents

Section II
The Gang Panic in Nevada 123

Preface

Criminal justice policy is rarely founded on a bedrock of facts. It is far more likely to be assembled amidst a swirl of distorted media images, interest group claims, polling figures, and political posturing. Not surprising, policy outcomes often appear unreasoned and generally fail to make much of a dent in the crime problem. Examples abound:

- Federal legislation is passed providing funding for 100,000 new police officers, though no one knows what calculations, if any, were performed to arrive at this figure. (Why not, for example, 500,000 new police?) Assuming that number was not simply pulled out of the air, several decades of research have demonstrated we cannot reduce crime by putting more officers on the street.[1]

- We pass laws providing harsher penalties for crack cocaine offenses than powder cocaine offenses—even though the substances are pharmacologically indistinguishable.

- Though statistics show that most of those admitted to prisons have either been sentenced for drug use or a crime directly related to their addiction, we provide drug treatment for only 1 in 10 prisoners during incarceration.[2]

- The "three strikes and you're out" provisions, intended to provide long or life imprisonment for repeat offenders, inevitably incarcerate individuals well beyond the age when they would be a threat to society.[3]

- To expedite executions and maximize deterrence, jurisdictions across the country have ruled to limit the number of appeals in death penalty cases. Seemingly ignored, however, is the disturbing number of death row inmates exonerated during their appellate processes over the past two decades, or the lack of any evidence that a swifter application of the death sentence might be more likely to deter a potential murderer.

The list goes on.

To some extent, groundless and ineffectual crime policies should be expected: policy agendas and initiatives are, after all, affected more by politics than careful thought or empirical evidence. The policymaking process is driven by the activities of certain groups or organizations attempting to bring some aspect of the crime problem to public awareness. Assertions made in the process may or may not correspond to the facts. This does not necessarily involve deliberate distortion or exaggeration. The social reality of crime is extremely complex; perceptions are filtered and shaped by political ideologies, organizational cultures and interests, and situational imperatives. It is most certainly the case, however, that those groups or organizations motivated to have "discovered" some aspect of the crime problem are also those that stand to profit most. For having succeeded in placing the problem on the policy agenda, their policy initiatives will be adopted, providing the additional resources to address the condition. But given that those initiatives were based on distorted claims, they will have a minimal impact on the overall crime problem.

This book deals with the "discovery" of the street gang problem in the United States during the 1980s. In these pages we argue that gangs came to be defined as a major social problem, not because of any actual increased threat, but because of the claims and activities of certain organizations, including (and primarily) law enforcement, the media, and members of the academic community. The result has been a proliferation of ineffectual gang policies, idle criminal statutes, and a squandering of taxpayer dollars. Although it speaks broadly to the issue, this book focuses on events, organizations, and processes that surrounded the gang panic in Nevada during the late 1980s and early 1990s. Since the policy process in Nevada is not unlike that in other states, this book will provide critical insights into the discovery of the gang problem in other parts of the country and, hopefully, impress others to reexamine the nature of the gang threat in other jurisdictions.

ACKNOWLEDGMENTS

The research reported in this book was funded by National Institute of Justice grant #94-IJ-CX-0053.

We wish to thank the following reviewers: Dr. Ronald J. Graham, Fresno City College, Fresno, California; George Knox, Chicago State University, Chicago Illinois; Bruce Scott, Mineral Area College, Park Hills, Missouri; Tom O'Connor, North Carolina Wesleyan College, Rocky Mount, North Carolina; Jerry Loar, Walters State Community College, Morristown, Tennessee; and Roger Levesque, Indiana University, Bloomington, Indiana.

Notes

1. David H. Bayley. 1994. *Police for the Future*. New York: Oxford University Press; Malcom K. Sparrow, Mark H. Moore, and David M. Kennedy. 1990. *Beyond 911: A New Era for Policing*. New York: Basic Books; George Kelling, and Catherine M. Coles. 1996. *Fixing Broken Windows: Restoring Order and Reducing Crime in Our Communities*. New York: Martin Kessler Books.
2. Steven Belenko. 1998. *Behind Bars: Substance Abuse and America's Prison Population*. National Center on Addiction and Substance Abuse. Columbia University.
3. Michael R. Gottfredson and Travis Hirschi. 1995. "National Crime Control Policies." *Society*. Vol. 32, pp. 30–37.

SECTION I

Gangs as Moral Panics

Prior to the 1980s, there was no gang problem in the United States, at least not one given much attention by police or the media. Indeed, in a very real sense, the country did not even have a crime problem prior to the 1960s. Of course, even during the post-World War II years of comparative innocence and order, individual crimes were committed. But there was nothing approaching the near obsession with crime we find in the culture today; for most people, crime was not a topic of great concern. Americans did not, for example, have to suffer interruptions of their evening meal to respond to some telephone surveyor's question about how safe they felt when walking alone in their neighborhood at night. Front doors were opened without first finding out who was on the other side. Families and neighbors mingled outdoors on warm evenings, congregating on stoops and lawn chairs to chat, without having to worry about a spray of gunfire from a passing car. People flocked to downtown restaurants and theaters, unconcerned about confrontations with drug-hungry addicts or packs of turf-conscious gang members.

This sense of security was, however, shattered in the 1960s. A crime wave gripped the nation, one seemingly so grave as to threaten the very foundation of society itself. Slowly, the country began to divide itself into three camps. One camp was filled with *them*. Members of this camp were assumed to be greedy, predatory, devoid of moral scruples, and undeterred by the penalties of law. Over the years, the threat from *them* appeared to take different forms; sometimes it was serial killers or pedophiles, at other times child abductors or satanists, at still other times political extremists or crazed postal workers.

In a second camp was *us*, the law-abiding public. This camp was essentially a pool of potential victims, driven by fear to buy dead bolts and burglar alarms, distrust neighbors, and avoid public areas, particularly after dark.

Finally, there were the *pundits* and *protectors*. In this third camp were hordes of print and broadcast journalists, providing *us* with lurid coverage of the latest carnage, police progress in battling *them*, and editorials lamenting the deterioration of law and order on our streets. Social scientists were also in this camp. Learned men and women devoting their careers to studying and understanding *them*, their scholarly pursuits also informed public policy toward *them*. In this third camp were also a growing number of criminal justice workers. Most visible and powerful were the police, the front-line soldiers in the war against *them*.

Our image and reaction to crime over the past thirty years has been significantly shaped by the reports and opinions from those in this third camp. Often what we hear from the *pundits* and *protectors* about crime is inaccurate; in fact, the threat from *them* is deliberately exaggerated and distorted to make *us* more afraid. This is particularly true regarding street gangs, a new threat from *them* discovered by law enforcement in the 1980s.

Introduction and Overview

As the new millennium approached, the American public had achieved new levels of optimism about several important issues. Take the state of the economy, for example: A Gallup poll conducted in 1998 revealed that nearly two-thirds of Americans regarded the country's economy as "good" or "excellent," a sharp turnaround since the early 1990s.[1] That same poll indicated that the number of Americans positive about their own economic futures was at an all-time high. Nearly three-quarters of the public said they were currently satisfied with the way things were going in the country.[2]

At the same time, the poll reflected that most Americans believed the country was in a moral tailspin. Nearly half reported being "pessimistic" about the moral and ethical standards in the country (another one-third was "uncertain," itself a revealing statistic).[3] The beliefs, traditions, and institutions that once inspired, ordered, and restrained were viewed by most as having withered under the relentless assault of modernism and the culture of individual expression. Seven out of ten Americans favored allowing daily spoken prayers of some kind in the nation's classrooms; a slightly higher percentage would support a proposal to allow the Ten Commandments to be posted in schools.[4] Declining moral standards were felt to be behind the string of recent shootings in the nation's schools, tragedies a majority of Americans believe indicate that something is "seriously wrong" in the country.[5]

In the context of what is widely perceived as social and moral degeneration, the public's perception of crime is understandably affected. Consider that, despite nearly a decade of declining crime rates, most Americans believe that crime actually *increased* during the 1990s.[6] And though fear of crime has diminished somewhat recently, most Americans report feeling more threatened by crime today than they were five years ago.[7] At the same time, however, most believe that crime in their own neighborhoods has *decreased*; nearly 75 percent of Americans say they would feel safe walking alone in their neighborhood at night.[8]

In the minds of most Americans, then, it is the world beyond their neighborhood that has grown increasingly dangerous. That assessment is not generally the result of personal experience, although certainly some people are victimized in areas away from their homes. Instead, images of crime are shaped primarily by our exposure to popular culture, a shared set of knowledge transmitted through the mass media. From news media which provide round-the-clock, national coverage of events, Americans learn what lies beyond the edges of their own neighborhoods. What they see is a world in which murder and rape seem as common as burglary and vandalism, a world where serial killers lurk in the shadows, waiting for the right moment to strike, a world where satanic cults kidnap, abuse, and murder children, a world in which vast and sinister criminal organizations use 10-year-olds to peddle crack on street corners. No wonder so many are so afraid.

Most Americans' perception of the criminal justice system is similarly influenced by what they read, hear, and see in the mass media. Among the most pervasive images conveyed is that of the police as crime fighters: front-line soldiers in the war on crime, battling daily to keep criminals "out there" and away from our neighborhoods, homes, and families. On occasion, media dispatches from the front report a crack in the "blue wall": criminals of one form or another are claimed to have overrun defensive positions and are invading our communities. Police generals present statistics to demonstrate the threat, fleshed out by tales of criminal atrocities, issue dire prognostications, and appeal for additional resources to mount a counter-offensive. In response to the menace to public safety, the size and authority of the criminal justice apparatus are expanded and public safety ostensibly restored.

THE EMERGENCE OF THE GANG THREAT

During the 1980s, police in many parts of the country began reporting a sharp rise in street gang activity. Media coverage of gangs exploded. Newspapers, television, and films were suddenly awash with images of gun-toting, drug-dealing, hat-to-the-back gangstas. With this hue and cry came a massive mobilization of resources. Federal, state, and local funds were allocated to create antigang units in law enforcement and prosecution agencies. Sophisticated, nationwide identification and tracking systems were developed to monitor gang activity and facilitate information sharing by law enforcement agencies. Tough antigang legislation was passed in many jurisdictions which created new criminal codes (e.g., the drive-by shooting) and/or harsher penalties for gang-related offenses. Millions of dollars were funneled into universities and think-tanks to conduct research on the extent, cause, and consequences of the gang "epidemic." Gang "experts"—typically, police officers and former gang members—began to crisscross the country giving seminars to groups of concerned citizens and public officials. In public schools across the country, gang awareness and resistance techniques were incorporated into the curriculum, gang-related clothing banned from campuses, and teachers instructed on how to identify gang members and spot concealed weapons. Despite all this activity, as we approach the new millennium we are informed that the gang threat has yet to peak.

How afraid should the public be of gangs? Do the images and rhetoric surrounding street gangs accurately reflect the nature and extent of the threat? Has the response to gangs been commensurate with the actual threat posed by these bands of young males? Is it possible that, at least in certain parts of the country, the gang problem has been exaggerated, distorted, and exploited by those seeking to further organizational interests, sell newspapers, attract viewers, and sometimes even advance personal careers?

We attempt to answer these questions in this book and, by so doing, hope to offer a different perspective on the gang problem in this country. Before proceeding, however, we would like to make one thing clear: We do not dismiss the threat posed by gangs. Street gangs do exist, as they have for generations, and in certain cities at certain times they have been responsible for a considerable number of crimes against persons, property, and the public order. We suggest, however, that the current threat posed by gangs—in many jurisdictions, at least—may be less real than imagined: Stereotypical, stylized images of highly organized street gangs, armed to the teeth, corrupting and enlisting innocent youth in order to dominate illicit drug markets are largely hype. We argue that law enforcement officials have figured prominently in the creation and promotion of such stereotypes, marketing this threat to the public in order to protect and advance the interests of their respective police organizations. The media has sensationalized the problem in order to attract customers and advertisers. And some criminologists, but certainly not all, have given undue focus to gangs as a result of a rigid adherence to theoretical perspectives regarding the onset and progression of criminal behavior.

STRUCTURE OF THE BOOK

Section I provides a framework for the observations and arguments contained in later chapters. In Chapter One we review the two competing perspectives on how social problems emerge. Under *objectivism*, a condition becomes defined as a social problem because it poses a significant threat to the lives or wellbeing of substantial numbers of people. The competing perspective is *constructionism*. Constructionists contend that social problems are defined not simply on the basis of the threat a condition may represent. Instead, they argue social problems should be viewed as *products*, derived from the claims and assertions of groups and individuals with respect to some actual or reputed condition. Access to policymakers, institutional resources, rhetoric—these factors are much more important than the condition itself in determining what will be defined as a social problem. Because there is any number of conditions that could conceivably be defined as social problems, competition among claims-makers in public arenas is stiff. To distinguish a condition from the pool, claims-makers engage in exaggeration and distortion. Under certain circumstances, such claims can spark a "moral panic" in which public fears and state interventions greatly exceed the threat posed by the condition itself (e.g., the communist scare of the 1930s, satanic cults in the 1980s, etc.). We argue that the response to gangs, in some parts of the country, constitutes a moral panic.

To place the current gang panic in context, Chapter Two provides an overview of criminal gangs in American history. Gangs are hardly a new problem: Since at least the early 19th century, bands of young criminal males have been recognized as a threat to the community.

Chapter Three describes how the politicization of crime over the past several decades, and zealous claims-making by law enforcement bureaucrats, has resulted in dramatic increases in the size and power of law enforcement. The claims-making by law enforcement officials has necessarily entailed a focus on particular groups within society (e.g., drug dealers, car thieves, serial killers, etc.) and has not always corresponded to the threat actually posed by such groups. Undoubtedly, distorted and exaggerated claims are motivated, at least in part, by a genuine desire on the part of the police to protect the community. Perhaps police believe it is sometimes necessary to inflate a threat in order to make the public pay attention. But as with other government bureaucracies, police claims-making is also motivated by the need to protect and to further organizational interests in environments where resources are often scarce. The gang threat, we argue, has well served the interests of law enforcement.

The media's coverage of gangs and crime is the subject of Chapter Four. Crime news is one of the principal components of news reporting, though it generally provides the public with little accurate information about the crime problem or the criminal justice system. This is particularly true regarding the media's coverage of gangs. Coverage is typically inflammatory and sensationalized, equates gangs with violent crime, and portrays gangs as dominating illegal drug markets. This distorted coverage of gangs is largely the result of the manner in which news is produced: Reporters rely almost exclusively on law enforcement for information about gangs (and crime in general). This dependence on law enforcement for crime information allows the police to shape public images of gangs and gang policy.

Though police are the primary definers of crime in society, criminologists (most of whom are sociologists) are also important sources of information. In Chapter Five, we discuss the part that sociologists have played in generating the intense concern which has surrounded street gangs over the past two decades.

Sociology, generally speaking, locates the roots of crime in the individual's experiences with peer groups and social institutions. Thus, it should not be surprising that some sociologists make such a fuss over gangs. In this chapter, we provide an overview of the two major schools of sociological criminology and note the role each ascribes to gangs in the onset and progression of criminal behavior. We then attempt to show how profound changes in the urban landscape over the past two decades (i.e., the emergence of an urban underclass) have influenced the theoretical debate surrounding gangs and how the current perspective has provided fuel for the gang panic.

Section II describes the findings of a three-year study, funded by the National Institute of Justice, examining the legal, political, and organizational response to the "discovery" of a gang problem in Nevada. When we began the study in 1995, we did so holding certain assumptions about gangs and gang activity, derived from a close reading of the scholarly literature and also, like most of the public, from simply having watched portrayals of gangs in the news and entertainment media. Several months into the project it was becoming increasing clear that many of those assumptions were inaccurate, at least in the state of Nevada, and what had occurred in the state was a moral panic.

In Chapter Six and Chapter Seven, we describe the discovery and evolution of the gang problem in two of Nevada's largest cities, Las Vegas and Reno. Through law enforcement reports and a media frenzy, during the 1980s the public was informed that there had been an explosion in the number of gangs and gang members in their communities. Local media regularly carried stories, the source of which was almost exclusively police officials, that gangs were controlling illegal drug markets and responsible for much of the violent crime. By examining court records, we were able to evaluate law enforcement claims regarding the extent and nature of the gang problem in both cities. Did gangs dominate local drug markets? How much of the two cities' violent crime was actually committed by gang members? The answers to these questions are presented in these chapters.

The panic that swept across the state inevitably arrived in the state legislature, the topic of Chapter Eight. Over the course of four years, a raft of gang bills was introduced before the state senate and assembly, many of which eventually became law. Much of that legislation was initiated by law enforcement; indeed, they prepared the drafts for what was to become the most comprehensive piece of gang legislation passed in the state, and arguably the entire country. Through newspaper accounts, records from legislative hearings, and interviews with key state political figures, we were able to reconstruct the events surrounding the passage of legislation during the gang panic. As will be shown, these new laws were constructed based on the images of gangs and gang activity supplied by law enforcement and the media. In later chapters we show that, since their enactment, most of these laws have been used only infrequently, and some not at all.

Chapter Nine deals with the prosecutorial response to gangs in Las Vegas and Reno. Recognizing an opportunity to crack down on gangs, garner public support for political careers, and/or increase organizational resources, prosecutors in both jurisdictions during the 1980s began a war on street gangs. Prosecutors claimed in public hearings and in the local press that gangs were sophisticated organizations, driven by profit and unrestrained by conscience. Gang crime was different, and to fight it effectively they claimed would require specialized gang prosecution units, low case loads, and start-to-finish attention to all gang cases moving the system. We describe the prosecutorial response to gangs in Las Vegas and Reno in this chapter. We also evaluate the claims made by prosecutors during the years following the discovery of the gang problem. Using case files provided to us by the district attorney's offices in both jurisdictions, we were also able to determine if gang criminals and gang crime were, as had been claimed, different from run-of-the-mill criminals and their offenses.

In Section III, we summarize the major findings of our study and draw some conclusions about the moral panic that occurred. Generalizations from this study to other parts of the country can only be speculative; claims regarding the prevalence and activity of gangs are undoubtedly affected by the unique political and economic environments in which law enforcement agencies and the media operate. The conditions in one jurisdiction may exert pressure to overestimate the problem; in another, circumstances may dictate a denial of a gang problem at all. Still, we believe that at least some of the claims being made about gangs by law enforcement, the media, and some gang scholars are simply not consistent with the facts. We discuss these inconsistencies in this section

Notes

1. The Gallup Organization. 1998. Gallup Social and Economic Indicators. "Trend: Economic Rating." November 6–9.
2. The Gallup Organization. 1999. Gallup Social and Economic Indicators. "General Mood of the Country." February 12–13.
3. The Gallup Organization. 1999. Gallup Social and Economic Indicators. "Politics and Moral Values." February 4–8.
4. The Gallup Organization. 1999. Poll Releases. "Most Americans support prayer in the public schools." July 9.
5. The Gallup Organization. 1999. Poll Releases. "Public views Littleton tragedy as sign of deeper problems in the country." April 23.
6. The Gallup Organization. 1998. Poll Releases. "As confidence in police arises, American's fear of crime diminishes." November 24.
7. The Gallup Organization. 1998. Gallup Social and Economic Indicators. "Crime Issues." October 23–25.
8. The Gallup Organization. 1999. Gallup Social and Economic Indicators. "Crime Issues." October 23–25.

chapter 1

Conditions, Social Problems, and Moral Panics

◀▶◀▶

In September 1994, during a ceremony announcing National Gang Violence Prevention Week, President Clinton stated that "the problem of gang violence is among the most profound we as a people have ever faced."[1] Many would agree. Since the 1980s, law enforcement, the media, and many criminologists have issued warnings that the threat of street gangs in the country is serious, growing rapidly, and unlikely to abate until we are prepared to invest significant resources prevention, intervention, and control efforts. How did the gang problem come to represent so great a threat? How, and by whom, was the gang problem "discovered"?

How does any condition, for that matter, come to be recognized by the public as a social problem? Folk wisdom supplies us with two explanations.[2] The first locates the cause of the problem in the deterioration of society, specifically the decline in traditional values and structures. Though part of a general trend in the 20th century, since the 1960s the erosion of the moral fabric and traditional institutions of society is said to have accelerated, and a degenerate popular culture has rushed in to fill the void. This is the explanation offered by William Bennett and his colleagues for the persistent high levels of crime over the past three decades.

> Widespread moral poverty is the inevitable result of the enfeebled condition—in some places in our society, the near-complete collapse—of our character forming institutions. In a free society, families, schools, and churches have primary responsibility for shaping the moral sensibilities of the young. . . As the hand of family, church, and school loosens, the grip of popular culture grows stronger.[3]

Those who adhere to this line of thinking believe that things are bad and getting worse, and steps must be taken soon to arrest, and hopefully, reverse the trend. The suggested remedies include stiffening laws to require greater personal responsibility, instituting character education into the public school curriculum, and a renewal of religious faith.

A second folk wisdom explanation for social problems emphasizes not decline, but progress. Society, once naive, has become more enlightened, more sophisticated, and now recognizes conditions once concealed, tolerated, or neglected. Moreover, society now has the means (i.e., the resources and institutions) to address the problem. Consider spousal abuse as an example. Long considered a private matter, family violence is now recognized and responded to as criminal behavior, in certain instances even a federal offense.[4]

OBJECTIVIST VERSUS CONSTRUCTIONIST VIEWS OF SOCIAL PROBLEMS

According to Joel Best, both folk wisdom explanations assume that our concern reflects the real danger posed by the problem.[5] As such, these explanations are similar to the standard sociological explanations for social problems in which problems are equated with troublesome conditions and defined in terms of objective social conditions. Social problems textbooks are filled with discussions of the causes and consequences of certain issues or conditions (poverty, urban decay, discrimination, etc.) that are taken as objectively given and posing a significant threat to the quality or length of life of a substantial number of people.[6]

This sociological explanation is commonly referred to as the *objectivist approach* to social problems. The objectivist approach ignores or minimizes the subjective nature of social problems and assumes that empirical measures of a condition (i.e., statistics and figures) accurately reflect the objective threat it poses. The objectivist model is a variant of sociology's functionalist paradigm, in that it views social problems as largely the product of dysfunctions of the social system, social disorganization, role and value conflicts, and norm violations.[7]

The challenge to the objectivist approach to social problems comes from the *constructionist* (sometimes referred to as *subjectivist* or *relativist*). Rather than the causes and consequences of social conditions, the constructionist approach focuses on the causes and consequences of the *concern* about a social problem.[8] Accordingly, a condition does not become a social problem simply because of the objective threat it poses to human life and the social fabric. In fact, it is not necessary that a threat even exist.

> To the constructionist, social problems do not exist "objectively" in the same sense that a rock, a frog, or a tree exists: instead, they are *constructed by* the human mind, *called into being* or *constituted by* the definitional process. The objective existence of a harmful condition does not, by itself or in and of itself, constitute a social problem. Merely because a disease kills the members of society does not mean that it constitutes a social problem among these people; if they do not conceptualize or define the disease as a problem, according to the constructionist, to these people it

◆◆ _____

OBJECTIVIST vs. CONSTRUCTIONIST PERSPECTIVES ON SOCIAL PROBLEMS

Objectivist

A particular condition in society exists and constitutes a social problem because it threatens the quality or length of life of a substantial number of people.

Constructionist

A social problem is a product of claims-making activities by groups regarding the existence of and threat posed by a certain condition. The objective threat posed by a condition is far less important than the persuasiveness of the claims made by activist groups with respect to a putative condition.

_____

is not a social problem. . . Indeed, to the subjectivist, a given objective condition need not even exist to be defined as a problem—witness the persecution of witches in Renaissance Europe and Colonial America.[9]

In short, social problems are what people think to be social problems; if they don't see a problem, for all intents and purposes the problem doesn't exist. Thus according to the constructionist, before a condition is defined as a social problem, it must first be brought to the people's attention. Someone or some group must persuade the public that the condition exists and that it poses a significant threat to them. Consequently, sociologists Malcolm Spector and John Kituse argue that a social problem may best be understood as a product derived from the "activities of individuals or groups making assertions of grievances and claims with respect to some putative condition."[10] What is thus important is not the actual nature of the condition, but rather what these individuals *say* about that condition.

THE ROLE OF CLAIMS-MAKERS IN DEFINING SOCIAL PROBLEMS

There is an incredibly large number of conditions that could conceivably be identified and responded to as social problems. Most will remain outside the public's awareness. A fraction are presented by groups of individuals—claims-makers—who attempt to persuade the public, and perhaps more importantly policy-makers, that a particular condition is deserving of the collective designation of a social problem. The zeal of these claims-makers can be explained by recognizing that "a problem to some is a benefit to others."[11] Political scientist Murray Edelman reminds us that, although the motives of claims-makers are often sincere, "those who recognize that the attachment of a favored course of action to a problem will get them what they want can easily persuade themselves of the rationality and morality of their rhetorical appeals as part of the process of persuading others."[12] The designation of a condition as a social problem provides claims-makers with the influence and resources to address the condition; it also provides them with jobs, promotions, and status.

These kinds of rewards do not come easily. While the number of conditions and claims-makers is quite large, the public arenas in which social problems are framed and funded have limited capacities: Government, the media, political organizations, and other institutions can only accommodate a certain number of issues at any given time. This conflict between the number of potential social problems and the limited public space for addressing them generates tremendous competition among activists.[13] To distinguish themselves from the crowd, claims-makers present their issues in terms of symbolic representations that distort and dramatize their respective conditions.[14]

One popular method of presenting a condition is through *narrative stories*. The condition takes on story form, depicted as having been good or under control but now bad and out of control, followed by dire predictions of crisis if action is not immediately taken. It is important not only that the condition has grown more severe, but also that it now is affecting populations once untouched.[15] Claims-makers construct the narrative in such a way as to make their skills and suggested course of action necessary to a happy ending to the story. To mobilize anger, activists also frequently employ *synecdoches* or *atrocity tales*, offering up one atypical, extreme case or incident to represent the condition. *Metaphors*—disease or wars being the most popular—are also used to describe the condition and prescribe an appropriate response.

Yet another rhetorical device used by claims-makers is the linking or *convergence* of one form of behavior with another form that is widely accepted as even more dangerous, fueling what Hall and his colleagues refer to as part of a "signification spiral."

> Convergence occurs when two or more activities are linked in the process of signification as to implicitly or explicitly draw parallels between them. Thus the image of "student hooliganism" links the student protest to the separate problem of hooliganism—whose stereotypical characteristics are already part of socially available knowledge . . . In both cases, the net effect is amplification, not in the real events being described but in their threat potential for society.[16]

Phillip Jenkins notes examples of convergence in the controversy surrounding the serial killer panic in the early 1980s.[17] Claims regarding the threat of serial murder, perhaps the most dangerous and pathologically predatory of behaviors, were made even more ominous by linking serial killing to satanism, sexual deviance, pedophilia, racial bias, and misogynism. There is nothing worse than a serial killer except, for example, a satanic or child serial killer.

Whenever possible, claims-makers also attempt to frame a condition as representing a particular threat to children. During the 1980s, concerns about dangers to children were intensified as a result of claims, generally unsubstantiated, as to the extent to which they were victims of molestation, incest, child pornography, kidnaping, and even harmful rock lyrics.[18] Children are innocent, vulnerable, and represent the future. Consequently, claims "expressing concern for protecting children is" according to Philip Jenkins "usually a sure and risk-free way of garnering public support."[19]

The *manipulation of numbers* is a powerful strategy in the promotion of social problems. Statistics that measure the scope and growth of the problem "strengthen a claimant's argument because they can be offered (and are usually accepted) as facts, as correct, indisputable, more than the claims-maker's mere opinion."[20] But measuring a social problem is not like measuring physical objects; it involves decisions about the construction of categories, where to draw the line, and what is and what is not to be included in the measurement; in other words, someone decides what to count and how to count them.[21] In the measurement of a particular condition, claims-makers have tremendous incentive to fudge the numbers. When in doubt, they will generally chose more liberal measurement strategies. In the heat of competition for attention and resources, claims-makers "tend to use big numbers" when describing a condition, because, after all, "big numbers are better than little numbers."[22] In fact, if claims-makers were to offer up accurate numbers, they would run the risk that the condition they are promoting may be judged as really not that serious and thus undeserving of attention. Joel Best reminds us that since the numbers offered by claims-makers are done so to persuade, "their numbers need to be understood for what they are—part of the rhetoric of claims-making."[23] Whatever statistics are offered should thus be taken with a grain of salt.

PUBLIC BUREAUCRATS AS CLAIMS-MAKERS

Claims-makers can be insiders or outsiders.[24] Outsiders usually seek recognition of some new social problem and can be either individuals or groups seeking to gain recognition of the social problem and as well as the problem's owner. Most claims-makers, however, are insiders and fall into one of three types.

1. Lobbying organizations, several of which exert tremendous influence on public policy at levels of government, for instance the National Rifle Association (NRA) or the American Association for Retired Persons (AARP)

2. Professional or specialist organizations charged with handling a particular problem, such as American Medical Association (AMA)

3. Official agencies, government bureaucracies struggling to protect and
    expand organizational status and resources. Usually, claims from
    government bureaucracies concern "new wrinkles" in existing and
    accepted acknowledged social problems.

In the public arenas where conditions are presented, bureaucratic representatives enjoy a huge advantage. One favoring circumstance is their greater, direct access to lawmakers.[25] Day in and day out, high-level bureaucrats interact with elected officials, building the kinds of interpersonal relationships that provide influence in decision-making. Despite the traditional assumption that politicians set policy and bureaucrats simply implement a line of prescribed action, the skills and knowledge of bureaucrats put them in a critical policy-making role.[26] Politicians, as we all know, come and go: The rule of civil servants is considerably longer. Elected officials thus naturally lean heavily on agency executives for analysis and advice.

A second advantage enjoyed by bureaucracies is that they are already organized with a fraction of their budgets permanently allocated to lobbying efforts.[27] There are none of the costs of start-ups or delays in activism experienced by nascent claims-making groups. Because of access and present funding, political scientist Francis Rourke suggests these bureaucracies "sometimes come close to enjoying monopoly power over the course of public policy."[28] Indeed, it is within bureaucracies that most legislation and programs originate.[29]

Because of their position and power, some political observers have long harbored a concern that government bureaucracies might become a "power elite," serving the interest of the organization and its members rather than the public at large. Nonetheless, the perception that bureaucracies are run by disinterested, public-spirited experts runs deep among the public. William Niskanen, suggests, however, to anyone seeking to understand public policy formation that "the beginning of wisdom is the recognition that bureaucrats are people who are, at least, not entirely motivated by the general welfare or the interests of the state."[30] At the upper levels of the bureaucracy, executives have a strong desire to extend the scope of their influence to enhance their status and careers.[31] They are also under considerable pressure to maximize the agency's budget in order to appease and reward subordinates through increased salaries, promotions, and contracts.[32] This budget maximization is not seen as in conflict with the public interest; in the bureaucrat's mind, the public simply receives more of a valued service.

Bureaucracies expand by demonstrating a need. Through aggressive political activism, bureaucrats attempt to frame a particular condition such that the public and elected officials perceive it as significant problem and accept their proposed initiatives as the appropriate response. Their stiffest competition for resources comes not from the private or professional organizations who enter these political arenas, but from other bureaucracies which, having defined the condition in a different manner, propose an alternative course of action. The intensity of the claims-making by bureaucrats varies according to budget cycles, the availability of public funds, and the entrepreneurism of the organizational leadership.

CLAIMS-MAKING AND MORAL PANICS

There is nothing inherently malicious about claims-making. Indeed, one could argue that, in most instances, the ends do justify the means: The public good is protected and enhanced. However, the exaggeration and distortion that is inherent in claims-making can, under certain conditions, produce a form of social problem known as a *moral panic*. This concept was popularized by Stanley Cohen, who used it to characterize the reactions of the media, the public, and law enforcement to youth disturbances in Britain during the 1960s. Cohen defined a moral panic as

> A condition, episode, person or group of persons emerges to become defined as a threat to societal values and interests; its nature is presented in a stylized and stereo-typical fashion by the mass media; the moral barricades are manned by editors, bishops, politicians and other right thinking people; socially accredited experts pronounce their diagnoses and solutions; ways of coping are evolved or . . . resorted to; the condition then disappears, submerges or deteriorates and becomes visible.[33]

Implicit in the term moral panic is the existence of a threat to something sacred or fundamental to society. That threat is not, as Kenneth Thompson has noted, "something mundane—such as economic output or educational standards—but a threat to the social order itself or an idealized (ideological) conception of it."[34] Such a threat is far more likely to be perceived during times of widespread anxiety, moral malaise, and uncertainty about the future. In this context moral panics are more likely to occur.

Though overlapping with social problems, moral panics can be distinguished by three characteristics.[35] First, in moral panics there is necessarily a focus on the behavior (real or imagined) of certain individuals within the community. These groups are transformed into *folk devils*, stripped of all favorable characteristics and ascribed exclusively negative ones.

> All moral panics, by their very nature, identify, denounce, and attempt to root out folk devils. A condition that generates such widespread public concern must have had a personal agent responsible for its inception and maintenance. Such evil does not arise by happenstance or out of thin air; there must be a circle of evil individuals who are engaged in undermining society as we know it. In short, folk devils are *deviants*; they are engaged in wrongdoing; their actions are harmful to society; they are selfish and evil; they must be stopped, their actions neutralized.[36]

◆◆

A "moral panic" is a form of collective behavior characterized by a sudden and disproportional response toward a certain group, perceived as a threat to the social and moral order.

Though there are sometimes folk devils in social problems, they are not essential. In many troubling conditions, no specific set of deviant actors can be targeted as being responsible (e.g., poverty). On the other hand, scapegoats are a necessary component of moral panics.

A second difference between a moral panic and a social problem is the discrepancy between the concern directed toward a condition and the objective threat that it poses. In social problems, the response to a condition may be more in line with the real world, concrete threat that it is alleged to pose. A gap between a condition's objective threat and the fear or concern it generates is an essential element of a moral panic.

Lastly, the concept of a moral panic implies fluctuations in the levels of concern over a given condition over time. A threatening condition is "discovered," concern reaches a fever pitch, and then subsides, sometimes—but not always—flaring up again.

Those who study moral panics have proposed several explanations or models to account for the social phenomenon.[37] In one model, the spark that ignites the panic originates within the general public with a widespread concern about a particular group of individuals and their behavior. In this *grassroots model*, the media, politicians, and social control agencies react to the growing fear or concern among the public towards a condition. The Salem witchcraft trials in Massachusetts during the 1600s provides a good example of this kind of sponta-neous uprising. A more recent example of the grassroots model is the rumor, voiced by many African-Americans, that the Central Intelligence Agency (CIA) conspired with Columbian drug lords to distribute crack cocaine in minority communities to raise money for covert operations.[38]

Under the *elite-engineered model*, the dominant economic group within society deliberately and consciously generates a moral panic to divert attention from the real, more objectively dangerous, problems of society and maintain their privileged status. Here the spark for the panic originates not with the public, but in society's upper crust. Stuart Hall and his colleagues argue, for example, that during the 1970s the ruling elite in Britain created a short-lived panic in order to direct the public's attention from double-digit inflation, high unemployment, and a deepening recession.[39] Through its control of the media and influence on government officials, the elite were able to manufacture an epidemic of street muggings (when no significant increases were recorded) in order to convince the public that the real enemy was not British capitalism, but criminals and a lack of law enforcement.

The most commonly used perspective in moral panics is the *interest-group model*. Accordingly, most panics are said to emanate not from the ruling elite, but from the middle rungs of power (the "insider" claims-making groups). In the interest-group model, "professional associations, police departments, the media, religious groups, educational organizations, may have an independent stake in bringing an issue to the fore—focusing media attention on it or transforming the slant of news stories covering it" and suggesting responses that would enhance their own particular status or interests.[40] Again, we should not view these claims-makers as being exclusively motivated by organizational or personal interests; they "may sincerely *believe* that their efforts will advance a noble cause—one in which they sincerely believe."[41] As a rule, however, advancing a cause simultaneously advances the interests of the claims-making organization.

THREE EXAMPLES OF MORAL PANICS

The Satanic Panic of the 1980s

During the 1970s, rumors regarding "satanic cults" emerged following reports of cattle mutilations in the western states. Lips, ears, tongues, udders, and genitals were removed with surgical precision, often with little trace of any blood having been shed. The suspicion grew that these cattle were being used by satanic cults as part of their blood rituals. By the mid-1980s, the fear of satanic cults was no longer restricted to concerns about livestock. These cults were allegedly responsible for abducting vast numbers of children and involving them in satanic rituals that included their sexual abuse, mutilation, brainwashing, and even murder.[42] These charges received national attention in 1983–1984 during the McMartin preschool case in southern California (62-year-old Peggy McMartin Buckey, her son, and five other child-care workers were accused, but later acquitted, of performing sexual acts on 360 children over a period of five years). Dozens of other "ritual abuse" cases followed. Soon there were claims of a national and clandestine network of Satan worshipers who were engaged in the pornography business, prostitution, and drug dealing. Such occultists had reportedly even infiltrated the ranks of educators, the police, politicians, and other legitimate and respected occupations. Some claimed that there were as many as 10 million cult members—1 out of every 25 Americans!

Satanists were reportedly at the center of the "stolen children" panic that gripped the country in the early 1980s, responsible for the missing children whose images appeared on milk cartons, shopping bags, and highway billboards during those years. From 50,000 to 60,000 children every year were reportedly being kidnapped and murdered each year as objects in demonic rites (though some placed the figure as high as 2 million). Television talk show host Geraldo Rivera summarized the scale of the threat posed by satanic cults during those years:

> . . . the murders of unbaptized infants, child sexual abuse in daycare, rape, ritual abuse of children, drug trafficking, arson, pornography, kidnaping, vandalism, church desecration, corpse theft, sexual trafficking of children and heinous mutilation, dismemberment and sacrifices of humans and animals. [They are] responsible for the deaths of more than 60,000 Americans each year, including missing and runaway youth.[43]

According to Jeffrey Victor, author of *Satanic Panic*, the shocking—and unsubstantiated—claims surrounding the threat of these satanists came from several sources, including some fundamentalist preachers, child protective organizations (e.g., Believe the Children, the Cult Awareness Network), and mental health professionals (the latter linked child ritual abuse to the controversial diagnosis of multiple personality disorder.[44] However, most influential in creation of the panic were the police charged with responding to reports or signs of occult crime—the "cult cops," initially, only a few police with expertise in occult crime. They traveled the country conducting police training seminars, lecturing at gatherings of concerned citizens, and working as private consultants. However, according to former law enforcement officer and cult critic Robert Hicks, by the late 1980s their numbers, organization, and influence had grown considerably.

> Now cult cops appear everywhere: officers attend a few cult seminars, return to their departments, and organize portfolios of Satanalia so that they themselves can give seminars to teachers, parents, and enforcers; they join informal networks of other cult cops, then parade their own consciousness-raising seminars by inventing *mise-en-scène* replete with Black Mass artifacts, books adorned with garish pentagrams, and resurrected photos of Anton LaVey's 1966–67 Church of Satan featuring nude women as altars. News reporters follow the seminars, giving them wide coverage and quoting alarmed citizens, their consciousness appropriately raised in response to the cult cops' glib and slick ideology.[45]

Cult cops urged communities to recognize and respond to the threat posed by satanists. Parents were pressed to look through their teen's belongings for signs of cult involvement, to screen their kid's friends, activities, and music. To those who might respond by saying that there was no evidence of satanic activity in their community, cult cops would argue that this simply indicated the sophistication of local satanists: The more abductions, abuse, and ritualized murders an occult commits, the fewer clues it leaves behind.[46] These officers would also add that the occult epidemic had reached its current proportions because of the public denial that these groups could exist in their communities.

◆◆

> . . . "occult crime" is very different from the menace that is sometimes portrayed, and most of the serious charges are mythical . . . It is a tiny fringe movement worthy of treatment in the least responsible and most sensaationalistic media.
>
> *Phillips Jenkins and Daniel Maier-Katkin. "Satanism: Myth and Reality in a Contemporary Moral Panic," 1992.*[47]

As the panic spread, public libraries became battlefields. Concerned groups of parents demanded that local officials pull books containing satanic themes from shelves. Heavy metal rock music was also targeted. Censorship campaigns alleged that audible and subliminal messages extorting children to commit suicide and other acts of violence were contained in the lyrics of Def Leppard, Judas Priest, Metallica, Megadeth, and other heavy metal rock bands. In the climate of suspicion and fear, vigilantism surfaced; neighbors suspected of being "closet" satanists were frequently assaulted and harassed.

While it is true that there were small circles of satanist cults, and crimes against children did occur, there was no credible evidence to link one with the other. Scholars have concluded that satanism was never more than a "tiny fringe movement" and most of the serious charges leveled at satanic cults were "mythical."[48] By the end of the 1980s, the panic had passed; cult cops had been reassigned to regular police duties; those making claims regarding the satanic threat had moved to the fringes of public debate.

The Crack Epidemic of the 1980s

About the time the Satanic panic was subsiding, reports of a new social problem were surfacing. A new form of smokable cocaine—crack—had landed on the streets of urban America, a drug so cheap and powerful that it threatened to destroy an entire generation of youth. Newspapers, magazines, and television networks carried lurid tales of crack-related violence, lethal overdoses by young sports figures on the brink of fame and fortune, and neighborhoods turned into war zones by drug turf wars. There were no casual users of crack: Compulsion, it was said, inevitably followed experimentation. Footage of crack babies—tiny, trembling, sustained by tubes and medical equipment—stirred the public's sympathy and indignation.[49] Experts were quoted as claiming these children were permanently damaged and doomed to a life of deviance and inferiority, each infant saved only at the cost of hundreds of thousands of dollars to taxpayers. Disadvantaged black youth were shunning school and minimum-wage jobs to work as runners and street-level dealers, earning as much in a day in the drug business as they could in a year at McDonalds.

In the months leading up to the 1986 elections, more than 1000 stories on crack appeared in the national press.[50] *Time* magazine called crack cocaine the "issue of the year"; *Newsweek* concluded it was the biggest news story since Vietnam and Watergate. The CBS documentary *48 Hours on Crack Street* became the most watched documentary in television history.[51] ABC News referred to crack as a "plague that was eating away at the fabric of America."[52] Not surprisingly, crack became a major issue in the 1988 presidential primaries, with candidates arguing that cocaine was destroying a generation of American youth and fueling a wave of crime, violence, prostitution, and child abuse. Crack cocaine served as the catalyst for a new War on Drugs that included beefed-up penalties for drug dealers and recreational users, federal funds for local drug enforcement initiatives, and even the creation of a Drug Czar cabinet-level post to coordinate the war effort.

According to some researchers, there is little evidence to support the kinds of claims offered by politicians, law enforcement, and the media regarding crack cocaine.[53] Data to evaluate the truthfulness of those claims is provided by the Drug Abuse Warning Network (DAWN), a monitoring project that surveys hospitals, crisis and treatment centers, and coroners across the country about drug-related emergencies and deaths. In 1986, there were only 69 cocaine-related incidents in emergency rooms a day in the United States, most of those occurring in a few large cities and involving people who had also been drinking alcohol. Moreover, in many of these situations cocaine use was probably incidental to the emergency room visit (e.g., auto accidents).

Claims regarding a drug epidemic are even less convincing in light of national surveys of drug use conducted by the National Institute of Drug Abuse (NIDA), showing that cocaine use by young adults actually peaked four years before the crack scare and has continued to decline since then. The largest increase among young adults occurred years before the crack panic, between 1972 and 1979. True, there was a large number of overdoses but, according to drug policy expert Mark Kleiman, it hardly represented a "social crisis."[54]

The existence of government studies suggesting that crack contributes to the deaths of a very small proportion of users, that an unknown but somewhat larger group becomes addicted to it, that its use is "related" to some fraction of crimes committed in groups prone to such acts, is neither a necessary nor a sufficient condition for all the attention it has received.

Craig Reinarman and Harry G. Levine, "The Crack Attack: Politics and Media in America's Latest Drug Scare."[55]

Claims that crack was instantly addictive were baseless: Smoking cocaine does not invariably lead to compulsive use. Upon closer examination, it turns out that crack babies were less victims of cocaine-indulgent mothers than overall gross neglect; women who used crack during pregnancy were also drinking alcohol, smoking cigarettes, eating junk food, and generally ignoring the fact that new life was forming inside their bodies.[56] Police claims of a link between illegal crack markets and violent crime were also distorted and exaggerated. For example, in a study of users in New York, Paul Goldstein and his colleagues concluded that most of the violence their subjects reported was "independent of drug use or drug distribution," their violence more a correlate of crack use than a cause of it.[57] Despite the often spectacular imagery, we also know that street gangs did not enjoy a monopoly over street-level sales of crack cocaine.[58] Nor did the individuals who sold crack make large sums of money. One representative study of drug sales in the District of Columbia found that the median income of dealers was only about $10,000 a year.[59]

How then are we to account for the frenzy over crack during the late 1980s? According to Craig Reinarman and Harry Levine, the crack epidemic of the 1980s began when cocaine use became visible among the poor, particularly minorities in urban areas.[60] They point out that similar drug scares have occurred throughout this nation's history. In the late 19th and early 20th centuries, for example, it was alcohol that was blamed for poverty, crime, family dissolution, and a host of other social ills. During periods throughout the 20th century, opium, marijuana, cocaine, and heroin were subjects of intense public concern and garnered an official response in no way proportional to the actual prevalence of use or the dangers of the drugs themselves. As with crack, in these previous drug panics state officials and the media consistently linked "dangerous, forbidden substances and suppressed strata in the population": alcohol and the Irish, opium and the Chinese, marijuana and Mexicans, heroin and cocaine—and now crack—with African-Americans. Reinarman and Levine conclude that the crack epidemic was "concocted by the press, politicians, and moral entrepreneurs" to attract readers and viewers, fatten bureaucratic coffers, further political careers, and promote right-wing ideological agendas.[61]

Serial Killers

Moral panics seem to come in rapid succession, and even overlap, during the 1980s. It was during that decade the country learned that it was also experiencing an "unparalleled threat" from serial killers. According to reports from the Federal Bureau of Investigation (FBI), serial killers were responsible for up to a fifth of all homicides that occurred in the United States each year, roughly 4,000–5,000 murders. Though fretfully high, these figures were reported as only part of an upward trend in serial killing, a spiral that would not abate without an ambitious and sustained national and interjurisdictional effort. In response to the claims about a serial killer epidemic, FBI status and resources were increased and new legislation passed that significantly expanded the scope of federal law enforcement powers.

Philip Jenkins, author of *Using Murder: the Social Construction of Serial Homicide*, confirms that multiple murders had been increasing since the 1960s, but argues the threat was greatly exaggerated by FBI claims-makers to promote their bureaucratic, ideological, and personal interests.[62] Most influential in constructing the serial murder epidemic was the FBI's Behavioral Science Unit (BSU). Established in the early 1970s, BSU developed expertise in profiling violent offenders and popularized the terms *serial crimes* and *serial murder*. In 1982, two of BSU's most prominent agents, John Douglas and Robert Ressler, undertook an NIJ investigation that involved interviews with 36 incarcerated multiple killers, providing taxonomies designed to be used by local law enforcement officers to reconstruct the traits of likely killers. During that time, BSU experts became concerned about the failure to note connections between crimes committed across various jurisdictions. In response, a proposal was submitted that requested the creation of the National Center for the Analysis of Violent Crime (NCAVC), as well as a data bank of unsolved crimes from different jurisdictions, the Violent Criminal Apprehension Program (VICAP). Local police would submit information about unsolved crimes to VICAP which would then be analyzed at NCAVC, all done under the auspices of the BSU unit.

Both the NCAVC and VICAP required significant resources and an expansion of federal law enforcement powers. The obstacles facing BSU were substantial. In Congress, residual suspicion remained surrounding the FBI as a result of its abuses during the Hoover years. There was also stiff opposition from state and local law enforcement, which resented federal intervention: Funding for these programs would expand the role of federal law enforcement into local homicide investigations. According to Jenkins, the threat of serial killers was sufficiently exaggerated and distorted so as to win broad support for both NCAVC and VICAP.

Together, the two types of claims-makers [law enforcement and child advocacy groups] succeeded in creating and promulgating a powerful picture of an enormous social threat, in which Americans were portrayed as being at the mercy of dozens of hundreds of monstrous random killings, each of whom might be responsible for hundreds of deaths and kidnapping.

Philip Jenkins, Using Murder, *1994*[63]

Congressional hearings on abused, exploited, and missing children in 1982 provided BSU officials their opportunity to systematically present their definition of the serial murder problem. BSU officials portrayed the threat of the serial killer as directed at children, tending to emphasize cases in which children were targeted and murderers had escaped apprehension because of their tendency to cross jurisdictional borders (reinforcing the need for NCVAC and VICAP). During these hearings, the figure of 4,000–5,000 victims was introduced. Jenkins suggests that BSU's claims regarding the serial killer problem were affirmed by several other activist groups present at the hearings, child advocacy organizations in particular.

The efforts of BSU officials to construct and promote a serial killer panic were successful. The National Center for the Analysis of Violent Crime was funded in 1984; the following year, the Violent Criminal Apprehension Program was created. According to Jenkins, it was the manipulation of numbers that proved most important in persuading the public and elected officials of the threat of multiple murders. The figures pronounced were the product of a loose definition of serial murder and the "unpardonable" interpretation of national homicide statistics. When a serious crime occurs, Jenkins reminds us, police across the country submit a Uniform Crime Report (UCR), and in the case of murder, a Supplemental Homicide Report (SHR). The SHR provides detailed information about the murder, including the circumstances (e.g., lover's quarrel, gangland killing, etc.) and the nature of the relationship between victim and offender. Homicides that cannot be filed under one of the supplied categories are classed as by *unknown* or *stranger*. By interpreting unknown circumstances and stranger homicides as the work of serial killers, BSU officials announced the idea of 4,000–5,000 victims of serial killing each year. This interpretation, Jenkins notes, is unwarranted: All that those unknown circumstances or stranger homicides mean is that, at the time the report was filled out, the police agency did not know the exact nature of the crime or simply didn't take the time to fill out the form properly. Over the course of several weeks or months, police may learn the circumstances of the homicide and the relationship of the victim to the offender. The chances of an amended report being submitted, however, are low. Nonetheless, the figures presented by BSU were virtually unchallenged at the time and, consequently, profoundly influenced public opinion and criminal justice policy.

Though it came to be defined as a serious social problem, serial killing "involves minuscule numbers of people, either as victims or perpetrators, and the likelihood of becoming a victim of this activity is extremely low."[64] Each year, about 1 percent of all homicides—fewer than 200—can be accurately characterized as serial murder. Through exaggerations and distortion, however, the FBI and BSU were able to define the problem of serial killing in such a way as to further their own organizational interests. According to Jenkins, the FBI experts

. . . successfully presented themselves as the best (or only) authorities on the topic . . . originated and popularized the high statistics about the scale of the crime, and once disseminated, these figures shaped the public perception that serial murder represented a grave social threat. . . . In terms of their underlying interests in making these claims, the federal officials stood to gain substantially in terms of their bureaucratic position because establishing the reality of a problem provided added justification for BSU . . . In terms of the agency as a whole, focusing on the social menace of this sort was likely to erode public opposition to the enhancement of FBI powers and resources, at a time when such a development was politically opportune.[65]

GANGS AS MORAL PANICS

The Mods and Rockers

Though the moral panic concept has been used to explain societal responses to a range of conditions, the first sociological application of the concept involved events surrounding British gangs during the 1960s. In the small seaside town of Clacton, on Easter 1964, hundreds of young people were milling about the streets, bored and searching for fun and excitement. The rather ordinary act of delinquency that set the panic is motion is described by Stanley Cohen, then a graduate student at the University of London:

> Easter 1964 was worse than usual. It was cold and wet, and in fact Easter Sunday was the coldest for eighty years. The shopkeepers and stall owners were irritated by the lack of business and the young people had their own boredom and irritation fanned by rumors of café owners and barmen refusing to serve some of them. A few groups started scuffling on the pavements and throwing stones at each other. The Mods and Rockers factions—a division initially based on clothing and lifestyles, later rigidified, but at that time not fully established—started separating out. Those on bikes and scooters roared up and down, windows were broken, some beach huts were wrecked and one boy fired a starting pistol into the air. The vast number of people crowding into the streets, the noise, everyone's general irritation and the actions of an unprepared and undermanned police force had the effect of making the two days unpleasant, oppressive and sometimes frightening.[66]

Cohen characterized the events following the Clacton disturbance as a panic after examining the reaction of the media, social control agencies, and activists or *moral entrepreneurs*. Media coverage of the disturbance was characterized by *exaggeration* and *distortion and prediction*. The seriousness of the events, the number taking part, and the resulting damage from the disturbance were all, according to Cohen, wildly exaggerated. The seaside village was reported as having been "invaded" by highly structured gangs on motorbikes from London; however, most of the youth involved were locals or lived nearby, were on foot rather than on motorbikes, and these reported "gangs" were, at best, simply loose collectivities or crowds. The media also took frequent liberties with the facts. For example, where one boat was overturned, the media reported "boats" were overturned. In one report, the windows of *all* the dance halls on the beach had been broken; however, there was only one dance hall on the beach and only some of its windows had been smashed. Events were further distorted in the press through the use of sensational headlines and the frequent use of words and phrases such as "riot," "orgy of destruction," "battle," "attack," and "screaming mob." Coverage regularly included predictions from local police that what happened at Clacton was sure to repeat itself again and again over the coming months if swift and severe preventative actions were not taken.

These predictions, because of the nature of the media's coverage, became a self-fulfilling prophecy. After the account of the Clacton disturbance, all kinds of youth misbehavior were interpreted as part of a wave of gang activity sweeping the country. After 1964, similar disturbances were reported in British newspapers, most of them of the same magnitude, or smaller, than those in Clacton. Each event was portrayed by the media as part of the Mods and Rockers phenomenon and warned that these kinds of gang-related disturbances were getting worse.

According to Cohen, the police played a critical role in the creation of the moral panic. In response to the events such as those in Clacton, local law enforcement agencies across Britain established and strengthened ties to better deal with the youth gang threat that was claimed to be sweeping the nation. Innovative police tactics and powers were also employed. Given the scale of the perceived threat, police determined it was necessary to suspend the principles of neutral law enforcement and civil rights. Youth who wore certain kinds of Mods and Rockers clothing or hair styles were arbitrarily stopped, questioned, and arrested. Force was used in making arrests where the suspect had not struggled or resisted. Groups congregated in a public area, even if it was a bus stop and they were simply using it for shelter from the rain, would risk arrest if they refused to move. Based on gang "profiles," certain youth were, in fact, forced out of town.

In response to police pressure and lobbying by "moral entrepreneurs" (typically, local merchants who equated youth gangs with commercial losses), members of the British Parliament recommended new laws and stiffer penalties against youth crime. There were even calls for a return to corporal punishment. Others stood to gain from the Mods and Rockers panic as well. Some enterprising businessmen, for example, began advertising consumer goods using the groups' images. Some of the very shops in which youth disturbances occurred began selling "The Latest Mod Sunglasses" and coffee bars in seaside resorts were billed as "The Top Mod Spot of the South."

Five years after the initial outbreak of the panic, the Mods and Rockers had all but disappeared. They remain "only in collective memory as folk devils of the past, to whom current horrors can be compared."[67] In Britain, other folk devils would follow—the Greasers, the student militants, the soccer hooligans, the Skinheads; in each, the claims and dynamics which characterize a moral panic would be evident.

The Panic in Phoenix, Arizona

In the late 1970s, Phoenix police began issuing warnings about a dangerous trend in gangs and gang activity.[68] By the early 1980s, the number of gangs had reputedly increased from 5 or 6 to 35; gang membership had grown from several dozen to between 3,000 and 4,000, most of them young Chicano men. Moreover, gangs were portrayed as "vicious," "drunken," "cruis[ing] the streets spoiling for blood," and connected to the threat of a more general social disorder. The Chief of Police warned that "If gangs grow, and their contempt for the law deepens, they will rule the streets" and that in Phoenix, like other cities, soon there would be entire neighborhoods living in fear of "cocky young criminals who defied their parents, civility, and the law."[69]

What accounted for this reported explosion of gangs during these years? According to sociologist Majorie Zatz, law enforcement manufactured a youth gang problem in the late 1970s as a means to acquire federal funds for a new gang crime unit, and continued to hype the threat of gangs in the 1980s to secure additional funding.[70] Public fears were fanned by law enforcement's skillful manipulation of the media, exploiting the media's penchant for violence, sensationalism, and crime "themes" by providing a regular stream of violent, random crimes committed by *alleged* gang members. The number of known gang members did increase during that period, but the police criteria for determining gang membership was often subjective and almost always culturally biased.

In an analysis of juvenile court records, Zatz found little to support law enforcement's claims of an increased threat of Chicano youth gang members. Chicano youth gang members referred to juvenile court were no more a threat to the community (i.e., no more likely to commit robbery, burglary, murder, or rape) than nongang referrals; most gang youth had been arrested for fighting—primarily among themselves—and minor property crimes. Nonetheless, the public became that Chicanos in general, and Chicano youth in particular, were a threat to their lives, property, and way of life.

The Panic in California

During the 1980s California was, by all appearances, besieged by criminal street gangs. It became nearly impossible to pick up a newspaper or magazine or turn on the televison and not be confronted by reports of gang violence and destruction. Gangs and gang members from the Golden State became the focus of intense

◆◆ _____

> It is not at all clear that Phoenix truly faced a major problem of gang-related crime. What is clear, however, is that Chicano youth gangs became defined as a serious social problem—a problem to which the media and law enforcement agencies responded vociferously and vigorously.
>
> *Majorie Zatz. "Chicago Youth Gangs and Crime: The Creation of a Moral Panic," 1987.*[71]

_____

local and national media coverage, featured on national newscasts, talk shows, newspapers, and weekly magazines such as *Time* and *Newsweek*. Major motion pictures, such as *Colors*, graphically portrayed life and death in Los Angeles gangs to Middle America. Public fear and concern grew at an alarming rate. State and local government responded by enacting a spate of antigang legislation which included increased penalties for drugs, guns, and drive-by shootings; the criminalization of "rock" (crack) houses; raising victim intimidation from a misdemeanor to a felony; and a comprehensive statute, the Street Terrorism Enforcement and Prevention Act (STEP).

According to Patrick Jackson and Cary Rudman, the response to gangs in California during this period was excessive and extreme, shaped by stereotypical portrayals of gangs provided by law enforcement and the media.

> The image of gangs that figured prominently in mass media and the discussions at public hearings was of groups who use juveniles, high-power weaponry, and motor vehicles to traffic drugs. These gangs were characterized as instrumental groups or vaguely defined youth street gangs whose overriding purpose was to make large amounts of money through the distribution and sale of crack and other drugs.[72]

Jackson and Rudman argue that the response to gangs in California was heightened by media and law enforcement reports in which gangs, violence, and drugs were coalesced. The linking of these three social problems "evoked an intense public and legislative reaction, one much greater than would likely have been the case had each been considered separately."[73] Moreover, rather than reacting to the reality of the gangs, both the public and law makers were reacting to distorted, stereotypical images of gangs provided by the media, law enforcement, and other groups.

A distinguished gang scholar, Joan Moore, has also characterized the response to gangs in Los Angeles, California, during two specific time periods, as moral panics.[74] One period was that of the famous "Zoot-Suit Riots" of the 1940s. After a young Chicano was killed in a gang-related incident in 1942, all 22 members of a gang were arrested for conspiracy to commit murder; 17 of those

◆◆◆ _____

> The evidence to date suggests that the nature of the reaction to the "gang problem" in California is similar to other instances of what has been referred to as "moral panics."
>
> *Patrick Jackson and Cary Rudman. "Moran Panic and the Response to Gangs in California."[75]*

_____

charged were eventually convicted. The media went into a frenzy, warning the public of the dangers posed by Mexican zoot-suit gangs. Police began a series of sweeps and raids, netting more than 600 young Chicanos. Anglo servicemen on leave in the city got into a series of brief but bloody clashes with anyone they believed to be a gang member; usually, the target was not even a gang member. Noting the work of social scientists studying gangs during that period, Moore concluded that "it appeared that the zoot-suit panic had very little to do with the violence and criminality of young Mexican-American men, and a lot to do with how Anglos saw Mexicans in Los Angeles."[76]

The second panic, Moore argues, occurred in the 1980s. Following a series of gang shootings, including that of a young woman in a rich university community in West Los Angeles, the media began to portray the gang problem as a crisis and out of control. Law enforcement reported that Los Angeles was now the nation's gang capital. A series of massive police sweeps were directed at "drug gangs" believed to be responsible for the increased violence. Hundreds of officers arrested, cited, or made field reports on virtually every male encountered on the streets except for those of advanced age. Few drugs were actually found, and the vast majority of those arrested (75 percent) were not even gang members.

Conclusion

A seasoned and highly respected observer of the gang problem, Walter Miller has asserted that contemporary street gangs are now "more numerous, more prevalent, and more violent . . . than anytime in the country's history."[77] Yet even among those who argue the severity of the gang problem, several scholars suggest that— in certain places, during relatively brief periods of time—society's reaction has been way out of proportion to the threat such groups actually posed. This kind of skepticism, however, is ephemeral; to our knowledge, no one has suggested that the response to street gangs more generally represents a moral panic, similar in scope and degree to that which surrounded satanists, crack cocaine, or serial killers. Instead, those who police, report on, or study street gangs claim that the threat is now at epidemic proportions and deserving of public attention and all the resources that can be mustered. Statistics, horror stories, and other rhetorical devices are marshaled in support of such claims. Is the contemporary gang problem more severe than in times past? Claims-makers would have us believe so, particularly since it is easier to generate concern for a "new" condition than a persistent one. Consequently, for claims-makers, Philip Jenkins concludes, "a certain amount of historical amnesia is necessary."[78]

Notes

1. President William J. Clinton. 1994. "Proclamation 6717: National Gang Violence Prevention Week." *Weekly Compilation of Presidential Documents*. Vol. 30 (September 10), p. 37.
2. Joel Best. 1990. *Threatened Children: Rhetoric and Concern about Child-Victims*. Chicago: University of Chicago Press.
3. William Bennett, John DiIulio, and John Walters. *Body County: Moral Poverty: How to Win America's War Against Crime and Drugs*. 1996. New York: Simon and Schuster, pp. 98–199.
4. Patricia Barnes (ed.). *Domestic Violence : From a Private Matter to a Federal Offense*. 1998. New York: Garland Publishing.
5. Best, 1990.
6. Jerome Manis. 1974. "The concept of social problems: Vox populi and sociological analysis." *Social Problems*. Vol. 21, pp. 305–315.
7. Erich Goode and Nachman Ben-Yehuda. 1994. *Moral Panics: The Social Construction of Deviance*. Cambridge, MA: Blackwell; Robert K. Merton and Robert Nisbet (eds). 1976. *Contemporary Social Problems*. New York: Harcourt Brace Jovanovich.
8. Goode and Ben-Yehuda, 1994; Best, 1990.
9. Goode and Ben-Yehuda, 1994, p. 88.
10. Malcolm Spector and John Kitsuse. 1973. "Social problems: A reformulation." *Social Problems*. Vol. 21, pp. 145–159.
11. Edelman, Murray. 1988. *Constructing the Spectacle*. Chicago: University of Chicago Press, p. 14.
12. Edelman, 1988, p. 22.
13. Stephen Hiltgartner and Charles Bosk. 1988. "The rise and fall of social problems: A public arenas model." *American Journal of Sociology*. 94, pp. 53–78.
14. Deborah Stone. 1988. *Policy Paradox and Political Reason*. Glenview, IL: Scott Forsman.
15. David A. Rochefort and Roger W. Cobb. 1994. "Problem definition: An emerging perspective." In D. Rochefort and R. Cobb (eds.), *The Politics of Problem Definition: Shaping the Policy Agenda*. Lawrence, KS: University of Kansas Press; Best, 1990; Goode and Ben-Yehuda, 1994; Stone, 1988.
16. Stuart Hall, Charles Critcher, Tony Jefferson, John Clarke, and Brian Roberts. 1978. *Policing the Crisis: Mugging the State, and Law and Order*. New York: Holmes and Meier.
17. Philip Jenkins. 1994. *Using Murder: The Social Construction of Serial Homicide*. New York: Aldine de Gruyter.
18. Best, 1990.
19. Jenkins, 1994, p. 58.
20. Best, 1990, p. 45.
21. Stone, 1988; Best, 1990.

22. Joel Best. 1989. "Dark figures and child victims: statistical claims about missing children." In J. Best (ed.), *Images of Issues: Typifying Contemporary Social Problems*. New York; Aldine de Gruyter, p. 21, p. 32.

23. Best, 1990, p. 64.

24. Best, 1990.

25. Bruce L. Benson. 1990. *The Enterprise of Law: Justice Without the State*. San Francisco: Pacific Research Institute.

26. Charles E. Lindblom. 1980. *The Policy-Making Process*. Englewood Cliffs, NJ: Prentice-Hall; Francis E. Rourke. 1984. Bureaucracy, Politics, and Public Policy. Boston: Little, Brown and Co.

27. Benson, 1990.

28. Rourke, 1984, p. 3.

29. B. Guy Peters. 1996. *American Public Policy: Promise and Performance*. Chatham, NJ: Chatham House Publishers.

30. William A. Niskanen, Jr. 1971. *Bureaucracy and Representative Government*. Chicago: Aldine de Gruyter, p. 36.

31. Rourke, 1984.

32. Niskanen, 1971.

33. Stanley Cohen. 1980. *Folk Devils and Moral Panics: The Creation of the Mods and Rockers* (second edition). New York: St. Martin's Press, p. 9.

34. Kenneth Thompson. 1998. *Moral Panics*. London: Routledge Press, p. 8.

35. Goode and Ben-Yehuda, 1994.

36. Goode and Ben-Yehuda, 1994, p. 29.

37. Goode and Ben-Yehuda, 1994.

38. Gregory Vistica and Vern Smith. 1996. "Was the CIA Involved in the Crack Epidemic? A Newspaper Links the Contras to Cocaine." *Newsweek*. Vol. 128, (September), p. 72.

39. Hall et al., 1978.

40. Goode and Ben-Yehuda, 1994, p. 139.

41. Goode and Ben-Yehuda, 1994, p. 139.

42. Phillip Jenkins and Daniel Maier-Katkin. 1992. "Satanism: Myth and reality in a contemporary moral panic." *Crime, Law and Social Change*. Vol. 17(1), pp. 53–75; Jeffrey S. Victor. 1993. *Satanic Panic : The Creation of a Contemporary Legend*. Chicago: Open Court.

43. Alan H. Peterson. 1988. *The American Focus on Satanic Crime*. South Orange, NJ: American Focus Publishing Co. (cited in foreword).

44. Victor, 1993.

45. Robert Hicks. 1991. *In Pursuit of Satan: The Police and the Occult*. Buffalo, NY: Prometheus Books, p. 34.

46. Hicks, 1991.

47. Jenkins and Maier-Katkin, 1992, p. 71, p. 72.

48. Jenkins and Maier-Katkin. 1992.

49. Mike Gray. 1998. *Drug Crazy. How We Got into this Mess and How We Can Get Out*. New York: Random House.

50. Craig Reinarman and Harry Levine. 1989. "The crack attack: Politics and media in America's latest drug scare." In Joel Best (ed.), *Images of Issues: Typifying Contemporary Social Problems*. New York: Aldine de Gruyter, 1989, pp. 115–137.

51. Steven Belenko. 1993. *Crack and the Evolution of Anti-Drug Policy*. Westport, Conn.: Greenwood Press.

52. Belenko, 1993.

53. Reinarman and Levine, 1989.

54. Mark Kleiman. 1992. *Against Excess: Drug Policy for Results*. New York: Basic Books.
55. Reinarman and Levine, 1989, p. 123.
56. Mike Gray, 1998.
57. Paul Goldstein, Patricia Belluci, Barry Spunt, and Thomas Miller. 1991. "Volume of cocaine use and violence: A comparison between men and women." *Journal of Drug Issues*. Vol. 21, pp. 345–368.
58. Malcolm Klein, Cheryl Maxson, and Lea Cunningham. 1988. *Gang Involvement in Cocaine "Rock" Trafficking*. Final Report for the National Institute of Justice. Los Angeles: University of Southern California, Social Science Research Center.
59. Peter Reuter, Robert MacCoun, and Patrick Murphy. 1990. *Money from Crime: A Study of Drug Dealing in Washington, D.C.* Santa Monica, CA: Rand.
60. Reinarman and Levine, 1989.
61. Reinarman and Levine, 1989, p. 127.
62. Jenkins, 1994.
63. Jenkins, 1994, p. 50.
64. Jenkins, 1994, p. 19.
65. Jenkins, 1994, p. 60.
66. Cohen, 1980, p. 29.
67. Cohen, 1980, p. 62.
68. Majorie Zatz. 1987. "Chicano youth gangs and crime: The creation of a moral panic." *Contemporary Crisis*. Vol. 11, pp. 129–158.
69. Cited in Zatz, 1987, p. 132.
70. Zatz, 1987, p. 151, p. 152.
71. Zatz, 1987, p. 153.
72. Patrick Jackson and Cary Rudman. 1990. "Moral panic and the response to gangs in California." In S. Cummings and D. Monti (eds). *Gangs: The Origin and Impact of Contemporary Youth Gangs in the United States*. New York: SUNY Press, p. 258.
73. Jackson and Rudman, 1990, p. 270.
74. Joan W. Moore. 1991. *Going Down to the Barrio: Homeboys and Homegirls in Change*. Philadelphia: Temple University Press.
75. Jackson and Rudman, 1990, p. 271.
76. Moore, 1991, p. 2.
77. Walter Miller. 1990. "Why the United States has failed to solve its youth gang problem." In R. Huff (ed.), *Gangs in America*. Newbury Park, CA: Sage Publications, p. 263.
78. Jenkins, 1994, p. 122.

chapter 2

Looking Back

From the kinds of claims that are currently being made, it might appear that gangs are a new problem. That is, however, hardly the case. Gangs have been a persistent problem throughout this country's history. Nor is it clear that gangs today are anymore troublesome than they have been in times past. Indeed, anyone looking closely at the underside of American history will find groups of young, unattached, usually minority, males whose presence and activities were generally perceived as a threat to the greater community. Set apart by their distinctive dress, language, and culture, heavily armed and routinely violent, boozed or drugged up, such groups have long been a source of public anxiety, media attention, and law enforcement suppression efforts.

EARLY 19TH CENTURY URBAN GANGS

The emergence of these troublesome bands of young males in the United States can be traced to a period of rapid immigration witnessed in the early 19th century. So great was the tide that by 1850, immigrants comprised more than two-thirds of the population of the largest cities in the northeast, more than three quarters of those in New York, Boston, and Chicago.[1] In New York, street gangs operated out of greengrocery stores, shabby little shops wedged in between saloons, tenements, and houses of prostitution, offering partially damaged or spoiled produce at reduced prices. These greengroceries were also fronts for illegal liquor sales, and thus were a natural hang-out for the criminal element. Perhaps the first urban gang to emerge in that city was an Irish band known as the Forty Thieves; its base of operation was Rosanna Peer's greengrocery in the Five Points District. Other gangs emerged from similar shops in Five Points, with names such as the Chichesters, the Roach Guards, the Kerryonians, the Dead Rabbits, and the Plug Uglies. Like contemporary street gangs, bands within Five Points wore distinctive

◆◇ _____

Gangs of distinctively dressed youth during the 19th century used graffiti to mark "turf" and frequently engaged in armed battles on public streets.

_____

colors for identification. The Roach Guards, for example, wore a blue stripe on their pantaloons; the Dead Rabbits—deadly enemies of the Roach Guards—wore red stripes. The Plug Uglies, a particular violent group, were known for their enormous plug hats, which they stuffed with wool and leather and pulled down around their ears in preparation for street battles. On the street, Plug Uglies projected an image just as threatening as any street gang from the Crips or Bloods today.

> The Plug Ugly walked abroad looking for trouble, with a huge bludgeon in one hand, a brickbat in the other, a pistol peeping out from his pocket and his tall hat jammed over his ears and all but obscuring his fierce eyes. He was adept at rough and tumble fighting, and wore heavy boots studded with great hobnails with which he stamped his prostrate and helpless victim.[2]

Street gangs soon spread to the Bowery District in New York, such as the Bowery Boys, the True Blue Americans, the O'Connell Guards, and the American Guards. Like the Five Points gangs, the Bowery gangs were almost exclusively recent Irish immigrants. Nonetheless, the Five Point and Bowery District Gangs regularly battled over turf, turning the busy streets into war zones, often for two or three days at a time.

> The streets of the gang area were barricaded with carts and paving stones, and the gangsters blazed away at each other with musket and pistol, or engaged in close work with knives, brickbats, bludgeons, teeth, and fists.[3]

From the sidelines, female companions supplied emotional support, ammunition, and medical aid. Sometimes they actually participated in the battles. One legendary female gangster was Hell-Cat Maggie, a fierce moll who fought alongside the Dead Rabbits, armed with teeth filed to sharp points and long artificial fingernails made of brass.[4]

Of course, these gangs also preyed on the local citizenry, engaging in street muggings and pickpocketing. As today, much of their violence was seemingly senseless, or "thrill" violence, committed for status enhancement or simply sport.

> One strolled up to an old man sipping beer and hacked open his scalp with a huge bludgeon. Asked why, the ruffian replied, "Well, I had forty-nine nicks in my stick, an' I wanted to make it an even fifty." Another Plug Ugly seized a stranger and cracked his spine in three places just to win a two-dollar bet.[5]

Though not without fear, local politicians recognized the potential of these street gangs. During the 1830s, ward and district politicians in New York City bought the greengroceries and saloons where gangs typically spent most of their time. These politicians offered gangs protection and money in exchange for muscle, enlisting gang members to vote often, disrupt polling places, and intimidate political opponents.

Even more violent gangs emerged along the docks and shipyards on the East River Side of Manhattan. While Five Point and Bowery gangs were primarily thieves and muggers, the victims of waterfront gangs were more often to be killed. These gangs pirated cargo from ships and docks, which frequently entailed murdering watchmen and innocent passers-by. Observers noted that among the Daybreak Boys, the first of the waterfront gangs, "there was scarcely a man among them who had not committed a least one murder . . . "[6] Other waterfront gangs included the Short Tails, the Border Gang, and the Swamp Angels. Because they did not enjoy the protection provided by local politicians, waterfront gangs were the targets of intense law enforcement efforts. Nonetheless, they continued to exist until after the Civil War.

Street gangs slowly emerged in other northeastern cities as well. In Philadelphia, city streets were a magnet for urban youth with little else to do. There were frequent complaints over "corner loungers" who were loud, obscene, and physically abusive of pedestrians. From these corner loungers emerged the same kinds of violent male bands observed in New York. A Philadelphia reporter, disturbed by the proliferation of graffiti on public property, described parts of the city in late 1840s as being filled with:

> . . . loafers, who brave only in gangs, herd together in squads in clubs, ornamented with such outlandish titles as "Killers," "Bouncers," "Rats," "Stingers," "Nighthawks," "Buffers," "Skinners," "Gumballs," "Smashers," "Whelps," "Flaggers" and other appropriate and verminous designations, which may be seen in any of the suburbs written in chalk or charcoal on every deadwall, fence, and stable door.[7]

Within these Philadelphia gangs there was typically a small core of hard-core sociopathic types who accounted for most of the violence attributed to gangs generally. Like today, most members were only loosely associated with the gang and had a weak commitment to gang culture.

> They were divided into three classes—beardless apprentice boys who after a hard day's work were turned loose upon the street at night, by their masters or bosses. Young men of nineteen and twenty, who fond of excitement, had assumed the name and joined the gang for the mere fun of the thing, and who would either fight for a man or knock him down, just to keep their hand in; and fellows with countenances that reminded of the brute and devil well intermingled. These last were the smallest in number, but the most ferocious of the three.[8]

Street warfare was reportedly also common among Philadelphia gangs. So frequent were gang wars that one area within the city, where opposing gangs met for combat, came to be known as the "Battlefield."[9] Random acts of violence against the citizens were also frequent. Many pedestrians were knifed as a result of unknowingly having "dissed" gang members, accidently brushing up against a gang member as they moved through crowded city streets.

Law enforcement was generally ineffective in dealing with street gangs during this period. Asbury describes this:

> A lone policeman, with more courage than judgement, tried to club his way through the mass of struggling men and arrest the ringleaders, but he was knocked down, his clothing stripped from his body, and he was fearfully beaten with his own nightstick. He crawled through the plunging mob to the sidewalk, and, naked except for a pair of cotton drawers, ran to the Metropolitan headquarters in White Street, where he gasped out of alarm and collapsed. A squad of policemen was dispatched to stop the rioting, but when they marched bravely up Center Street the gangs made common cause against them, and they were compelled to retreat after a bloody encounter in which several policemen were injured.[10]

In response to the battles in New York City, the National Guard and the regular army were called into action. Newspapers reported that "regiments of soldiers in full battle dress, marching through the streets to the scene of a gang melée, were not an uncommon sight in New York."[11]

WESTERN OUTLAW GANGS

A tremendous westward migration occurred during the second half of the 19th century, the American Frontier experiencing a more or less continuous flow of people seeking wealth, freedom, and adventure. They came not only from the eastern United States, but also from around the globe—from Peru, Chile, China, Australia, the British Isles, and continental Europe. The frontier quickly became the country's most ethnically diverse region. By 1870, roughly a third of the population in California was foreign born; in Arizona and Idaho, more than half.[12] These migrants were also overwhelming young, unattached males. This was due, in great part, to the nature of the frontier economy. Mining, lumbering, railroad construction, freight hauling, and cattle driving required physical strength and itinerancy; older men, men with families, and women generally remained in settled regions or cities.[13] The arduous journey, as well as the hardships and isolation of frontier living, were sufficient deterrents to all but the most hardy.

The exceptional conditions of life in the West bred a cluster of beliefs that nearly guaranteed high levels of violence.[14] More so that the rest of the country, those on the American frontier rejected certain aspects of the English common law of homicide and self-defense, specifically those which legally required flight or retreat in all personal confrontations that threatened to become violent. Instead, Westerners embraced the *doctrine of no duty to retreat*, giving a man the right to "stand his ground" and use lethal violence in response to physical threats. Also particularly strong on the frontier was the *imperative of self-redress*. Frontier men were nearly obsessed with male honor, carefully cultivating and vigilantly protecting their public images. A public show of disrespect (known on the street today as "dissing") demanded a quick, violent response from the target. Together with the premium placed on "reckless bravado," these values "mentally programmed westerners to commit violence. . . "[15]

The confrontations encouraged by such values were easily transformed into homicides by the ubiquitousness of firearms. The modern revolver made its appearance in 1835, allowing a shooter to fire six times without reloading. By the end of the Civil War, handguns were nearly as common as garden tools, carried openly on belts or concealed under clothing. Weapons of all kinds—from cheap revolvers to automatic rifles—were available from mail-order suppliers to anyone who could fill out a form and pay a few dollars.

As today, the likelihood of violence was greatest when these young, unattached, heavily armed males were in groups. In a historical perspective of American violence, Courtwright (1996) provides a revealing portrait of the "cowboy subculture" concomitant to the rise of the cattle industry in the latter part of the 19th century.[16] The early cowboys were young (an average of 23 or 24), Texans or Texas immigrants, typically Civil War veterans, and generally white; however, one in seven were black, ex-slaves from southern Texas. Branding calves, breaking horses, and driving cattle for months on end to railheads or northern pastures was extremely demanding, dangerous, and low-paying work. By most accounts, while at work cowboys were sober and responsible. Off work, especially after the end of a long cattle drive, they were a particularly lawless bunch. With perhaps $50–90 in each pocket, cowboys would rush en masse to the nearest town. After a shave and a bath at the barber shop, a stop at the dry-goods store for a new hat, clothes, and boots, and a hot meal, groups of cowboys would then proceed to the local salon to begin a spree of drinking, gambling, and whoring that usually ended in shooting out the street lights or "taking the town." Armed with large-bore revolvers and repeating rifles, minor arguments frequently ended in deadly confrontations. During the boom years of the 1870s, towns such as Dodge City, Abilene, Wichita, and Fort Griffin, Texas had the equivalent of anywhere from 50 to 229 homicides for every 100,000 residents.[17]

Little was done by local law enforcement to discourage these drunken, violent cowboy sprees. Town residents, businesses and banks found themselves locked on the horns of a dilemma: They deplored and feared the cowboy's excesses, but desperately needed their dollars and feared too much law and order would result in their spending those dollars elsewhere. The solution was a measured response to cowboy crime. Few were arrested, and those charged with acts of serious violence were typically allowed to plead guilty to some lesser offense. So disruptive was the lot that President Chester Arthur, in his annual address to Congress in 1881, declared that a "band of armed desperados known as 'Cowboys' was terrorizing parts of the southwest, committing acts of lawlessness which the local authorities have been unable to repress."[18] Worse, many cowboys (undoubtedly having considered their limited career prospects) became full-time outlaws. By the late 19th century, in some parts of the country the terms cowboy and outlaw actually became synonymous.[19]

There were other outlaws, arguably the most dangerous, who had known little of cattle but much of war. As Confederate soldiers drifted back to their homes after the end of the war, continued hatreds and social dislocations left many angry and alienated. As young males, they also missed the thrill of war: The dull, repetitive routines of civilian life were felt insufferable. A life of crime, on the other hand, offered the danger, risk, and glory many had become addicted to on the battlefield. In *A Dynasty of Western Outlaws*, Paul Wellman advanced the theory that the conditions of the post-Civil War period spawned a "special brand of outlawry" that in the 20th century would produce the likes of Pretty Boy Floyd, Baby Face Nelson, and Machine Gun Kelly. Throughout the 1860s and 1870s, there were "bitter resentments, an entire population of men as deadly with weapons and indifferent to death as any this country has seen."[20]

The first of many outlaw gangs to emerge during this period was led by William Clarke Quantrill. Prior to the outbreak of the Civil War, Quantrill had already begun a career of calculated lawlessness. After secession, Quantrill attempted to redefine himself as a Confederate guerilla fighter, though one operating outside of the normal chain of command. Only 26 years old, Quantrill assembled a large group of malcontents from western Missouri, and under the guise of military victory, set off on a spree of plunder and murder that lasted from 1861 until his death in 1865. As many as 450 men filled the ranks of Quantrill's Raiders, wearing uniforms consisting of large, heavily pocketed overshirts and carrying an assortment of weaponry.

> The arms of the guerillas consisted principally of Colt's Navy revolvers of forty-four caliber. Some of them carried Cavalry carbines which they had captured, a few had Sharps rifles, and there were even shotguns and old muskets among them. . . . Every guerilla carried two revolvers, most of them carried four, and many carried six, some even eight. They could fire from a revolver in each hand at the same time. The aim was never by sighting along the pistol barrel . . . but at random.[21]

Quantrill and his band thus began a campaign of terror throughout Missouri, Arkansas, and Kansas. In 1862, Quantrill's Raiders were formally outlawed by the Union. The Confederate officials also recognized their outlaw status, denying a

◆◆ _____

"Ride-by" shootings were not uncommon on the American frontier.
_____

request from Quantrill for a commission as a colonel. Denied legitimacy by the Confederacy, their crimes increased in number and cruelty. On the morning of August 21, 1863, Quantrill's Raiders stormed into Lawrence, Kansas, committing what is accepted as the most "fiendish" evil of the entire Civil War period. Wellman provides a description of the ferocity of the Lawrence Massacre, a wild-West "ride-by" more terrifying than any modern-day "drive-by":

> Suddenly the peace of the slumbering town is broken by a hideous din of gunshots and yells, and the people of Lawrence awake to a nightmare of horror. Terrified women scream, men are shot down and groan as they die. Galloping squads of fierce riders seek victims in homes, gardens, ravines, even fields of growing corn. Through the town roars a holocaust of flames, kindled by the raiders, "consuming sometimes the living-often the dead." When Quantrill and his wild retinue ride out of Lawrence hours later they leave it looted and burned, and in its streets, its ruined houses, and its environs lie 142 murdered citizens.[22]

From Kansas, Quantrill's Raiders rode to Texas, attacking several defenseless wagon trains, robbing and murdering dozens of travelers. Considered an anathema by the Confederacy, the gang's numbers began to dwindle; splinter groups developed. Most infamous was the James–Younger Gang. Eight hard-core criminals formed the nucleus of the band: Jesse and Frank James; Cole, Jim, and Bob Younger; Charlie Pitts; Clell Miller; and Bill Chadwell. The leader was Jesse, age 19, who, as a result of his guerilla experiences had "lost all moral sense of the value of human life."[23] It was Jesse James who perfected train robbery and "invented" bank robbery, borrowing heavily from Quantrill's tactics: riding into town, whopping it up, firing shots indiscriminately, forcing residents to shut themselves up behind closed doors until the gang had looted the bank and made their exit. From the James–Younger Gang and other splinter groups can be traced such notorious outlaw bands as Butch Cassidy and the Hole-in-the-Wall Gang, the Dalton Brothers Gang, and the Doolin Gang. These and other bands of cowboy-outlaws produced high levels of lawlessness and disorder throughout the 19th century West.

Law enforcement was fragmented and underfunded, making the capture of outlaw gangs difficult. Outlaws also enjoyed support from the public, which was reluctant to offer information. Their targets were largely banks and railroads, now under Yankee control. Literacy levels had greatly increased by the late 19th century, creating a market for print publications. Newspapers, detective magazines, and ten cent novellas by the thousands appeared, creative journalists transforming thieves and killers into clever, virtuous heroes. Books such as Augustus Appler's (1876) *The Guerillas of the West* and James Buel's *The Border Outlaws* (1882) went through a dozen printings or more.[24] Young boys throughout the country idolized the likes of William Quantrill and Jesse James, emulating what they had read to be the dress and mannerisms of these desperados. By the end of the 19th century, the Western outlaw enjoyed a special mystique—that of the *social bandit*.

URBAN GANGS IN THE LATE 19TH CENTURY

As Western outlaw gangs faded in the years following the Civil War, the gang problem worsened in the northeastern cities. Thousands of gangs now plagued urban areas, with nationalities other than Irish. The most infamous of the period were the Battle Row Gang, the Stable Gang, the Silver Gang, the Traveling Mike Grady Gang, the Gophers, the Gas Housers, and the Hudson Dusters. Many became infamous for their criminal specialties. The Hartley Mob, for example, robbed graves, traveling in hearses to avoid detection by police.[25] The Nineteenth Street Gang, a juvenile gang led by "Little Mike," preyed on those only slightly more vulnerable: cripples and children. Operating out of the Bowery District during the 1870s, the Dutch Mob consisted of as many as 300 pickpockets.

Perhaps the most novel approach to crime was developed by the Molasses Gang. Members of the gang would enter small shops in New York City, hold out their hats to proprietors and asked to fill the hat with Sorghum molasses. They would acknowledge their request as "crazy," but simply told owners that it was to cover a bet they had made with a friend. When the store owner filled the hat, the hat would then be placed over the proprietor's head, temporarily blinding him and allowing gang members to empty his cash register.

From the Five Point gangs emerged the Whyos Gang, by far the most violent of the post-Civil War gangs. The Whyos, so named because of the cry gang members uttered, dominated the Fourth Ward of the Lower East Side and considered the entire Manhattan area their turf.[26] The roughly 500 members of the Whyos gang hung out at a local drinking spot nicknamed the "Morgue," the scene of over 100 violent murders. Indeed, in order to gain membership, a prospective Whyos was required to kill a man. Members were so skilled and comfortable with violence that many actually began to advertise their services, along with the expected payment for particular services (see Table on following page).

After the demise of the Whyos gang in the 1890s, the Eastman gang arose.[27] Yet another Irish group, the Eastmans were notoriously violent, committing an unknown number of robberies, assaults, and murders. The weapon of choice for Edward Eastman, the gang's leader, was a sawed-off baseball bat, into which he carved a notch for each head he had cracked. At the last known count, Eastman's bat had 40 notches.

Punching	$2
Both eyes blackened	$4
Nose and jaw broke	$10
Jacked out (knocked out with a blackjack)	$15
Ear chewed off	$15
Leg or arm broke	$19
Shot in leg	$25
Stab	$25
Doing the big job	$100 and up[28]

Gang activity became the focus of considerable attention in New York City following President Lincoln's proclamation of April 1863 calling for the drafting of 300,000 men into military service. Lincoln had been granted the power to draft by Congress with the passage of the Conscription Act; the War Department announced that the draft would commence in New York City on July 11. There was tremendous opposition in the nation to the draft, in large part because it contained a clause that allowed any man drafted to be exempted if $300 were paid to the government. Most of those forced into military service would, consequently, be drawn from the ranks of the poor. On July 12th, local gangs converged on the draft office at Third and Forty-Sixth Street. Hoping to avert a full-scale riot, police rushed to form a barricade around the office. Someone in the mob suddenly raised a pistol and fired it into the air, sparking a wave of rioting and violence that to this day has not been equaled. Over the next six days, gangs looted and burned police stations, businesses, and private homes. The Governor of New York declared the city in a state of siege; several thousand federal troops were sent in to restore order, local police having been outmanned and outgunned by local gangsters. When the violence subsided, reports were that some 2,000 people had been killed, another 8,000 wounded, and property losses exceeded $5 million.[29]

Gang activity worsened following the war's end. The post-Civil War gangs also became the focus of considerable media attention. Jacob Riis, whose stories and photographs documenting lower class urban life in New York City during the period appear in *How the Other Half Lives* (1890), reported that local newspapers followed gang activity "with a sensational minuteness of detail that does its share toward keeping up its evil traditions and inflaming the ambition of its members to be as bad as the worst."[30] Nor were gang members camera shy, posing for cameras, demonstrating mugging techniques, and bragging to reporters of their crimes.

Although in many ways similar to their predecessors, late 19th century urban gangs were distinguished by their heavy drug abuse. Technological innovations and discoveries, such as morphine (1803), the hypodermic syringe, cocaine, chloral hydrate (1868), and heroin (1898) increased greatly the availability and applicability of narcotics.[31] Narcotic addiction grew, in part, because of the medical profession.[32] At the time, the medical profession's ability to cure disease and alleviate pain was crude; physicians naturally turned to narcotics for their anesthetic properties. However, proprietary medicines containing morphine, cocaine, and laudanum could be bought at any store or ordered through the mail. In addition, many soldiers from both the North and South had become addicted during the war and returned to their communities heavily addicted to morphine, and spreading addiction even further by recruiting new users.[33]

The most popular drug among late 19th century urban gangs was cocaine, a stimulant. Among certain gangs, as many as 90 percent of members may have been cocaine addicts. Their addiction served to increase public fears, the perception held that "when under the influence of the drug" these gang members "were very dangerous, for they were insensible to ordinary punishment, and were possessed of great, if artificial bravery and ferocity."[34]

Gang activity was not confined to the North. It was during the post-Civil War period that the Ku Klux Klan emerged in the South.[35] The gang was actually started by six Civil War veterans who, after returning to their Pulaski, Tennessee home, quickly grew bored and discouraged. They decided to form a club to bring mystery and excitement to their lives. Group colors were carefully chosen to symbolize the gang's goals: white for purity, red for the blood each man was prepared to shed in defense of the helpless. Conditions in the South, however, would pervert these lofty aims. Under the Reconstruction Act passed by Congress in 1867, the South was occupied by federal troops, and most residents denied the right to vote or hold public office. Local economies had been devastated by the war. White southerners perceived themselves as oppressed, and saw the Klan as a vehicle for striking back at white northern "carpetbaggers" and newly enfranchised blacks. Hundreds of groups emerged across the South, outfitted in garb popularized by the Pulaski gang, intimidating, whipping, and lynching blacks and supporters.

Drug use became associated with urban street gangs in the post-Civil War years.

EARLY 20TH CENTURY GANGS

During the later 19th and early 20th centuries, waves of immigrants from eastern and southern Europe arrived in the United States. From 1880 to 1920, more than 2 million Jewish immigrants, fleeing persecution in Russia, Germany, and Poland, were tossed into major urban areas in the Northeast. The majority crammed into Manhattan's lower East Side, living in filthy tenements "more crowded than the worst slums of Bombay."[36] With no public parks or playgrounds, and scarcely even a blade of grass, and apartments far too crowded to accommodate anyone other than family, the streets inevitably became the center of youthful activity. By the early 20th century in the Lower East Side, over 300 gang hang-outs existed in only a single square mile.[37] Less politically connected than the Irish, the earliest Jewish gangs gained a niche by providing a higher level of order to Irish-dominated gambling and prostitution markets.

The latecomers were the Italians, though they would eventually come to dominate organized criminal activity. Between 1891 and 1920, 4 million Italians entered this country, mostly poor, uneducated, tenant farmers from Sicily and southern Italy. Like earlier generations of immigrants, a small number sought to embrace the American dream by bending or breaking moral and legal codes. Never a part of the Irish-Jewish cabal, their edge was their ruthlessness. Daniel Fuch, reformed Jewish gang member and novelist, recalled that:

> The most vicious of all the gangs were easily the Italians. They were severe in their methods, seldom willing to fight with their fists or with stones, but resorting unethically to knives and guns. After all, the Irish could be said to fight almost for the fun of it; while the Jews always fought in self-defense. But the Italians were out definitely to maim or kill.[38]

The first Italian gangs to attract attention were the so-called Black Hand societies, bands of extortionists who plagued Italian businessmen. The target typically received a letter "requesting" money and a threat of dire consequences— usually a bombing—should the victim decide not to pay. The letter would be signed with a skull or black-inked hand. Often these threats were carried out; Black Hand extortionists were linked to the deaths of over 400 persons in Chicago alone between 1895 and 1925.[39]

Criminal gangs such as the Black Hand societies were comprised primarily of adults, though juvenile street gangs provided a ready pool of eager, often crimi- nally experienced, recruits. Concern about juvenile gangs had grown during the early 20th century, prompting the first scholarly study of these bands of young, immigrant males. In *The Gang* (1928), Frederick Thrasher documented 1,313 gangs in Chicago, existing primarily in socially disorganized, deteriorated neighborhoods characterized by rapid population turnover. Thrasher argued these gangs had emerged spontaneously from adolescent play groups in the slums. In response to conflict with rival groups, these gangs had grown more cohesive, fostering a collective sense of identity. Most gangs Thrasher observed, however, were neither more nor less criminal than youth in similar neighborhoods. Only the most rudimentary forms of structure existed within the gangs; membership was loose and transitory. The preeminent activity of these gangs was fighting, among themselves generally, but also with rival gangs. To be sure, many of these bands of young immigrant males represented a serious threat to the community, with a strong streak of violent territoriality reminiscent of the Middle Ages:

> The hang-out of the gang is its castle and the center of a feudal estate which it guards most jealously. Gang leaders hold sway like barons of old, watchful of invaders and ready to swoop down upon the lands of rivals and carry off booty or prisoners or to inflict punishment upon their enemies.[40]

Many of these gangs appeared to have been even more heavily armed than their predecessors. Where previously gang brawls had typically involved brickbats, brass knuckles, and clubs, by at least one account almost every 20th century gangster carried at least two pistols, some even as many as four.[41] Such weaponry was evident in a bloody battle between the Eastman and Five Point gangs in August of 1903. Taking their positions on either side of an elevated railroad structure, the two gangs opened fire, forcing the local citizenry to run for cover. After several hours, the police responded with guns blazing and the melee ended, leaving three gang members dead and several others seriously wounded. In the aftermath, local politicians were pressed to act to prevent further risk to the public, badgering leaders of the warring gangs—Monk Eastman and Paul Kelly—into a truce that apparently did reduce gang violence in the city.

There was growing concern more generally about foreign immigrants who were perceived as a threat both to the moral and political domination of White Anglo-Saxon Protestants. Immigration over the past several decades, along with rapid industrialization and urbanization, fueled the perception that among WASPs that society was careening out of control. Under the Progressive Movement that emerged during the early 20th century, many political and legal reforms were implemented to restore order, many of which focused on curtailing the vices of foreign immigrants.[42] Included among these measures were the Mann Act of 1910 (outlawing the transportation of females across state lines for the purposes of prostitution), the Harrison Tax Act of 1914 (regulating the importation, manufacture, and distribution of opiates), and the Volstead Act of 1919 (which banned the manufacture and sale of alcohol).

Of all these reforms, the Volstead Act would have the most significant effect, although not that intended by supporters. Prior to Prohibition, it is generally conceded that criminal gangs were relatively small outfits operating in seedy

◆◆ _____

> During Prohibition, many street gangs became lucrative criminal enterprises, monopolizing illegal liquor markets.

_____

neighborhoods. Leo Katcher (1985) points out that prior to Prohibition, gangsters were under the control of local politicians, offering them protection from the law in return for financial and electoral support.[43] The bootlegging industry, however, would turn these gangs into criminal empires, turning gang leaders into crime lords, no longer dependent on politicians for protection. The competition for market share also sparked a bloody period of gang violence in which Italian gangs first warred with Irish and Jewish gangs, then with each other in the pursuit of profit.

> The murder of a bootlegger became a daily event. Rumrunners and highjackers were pistol-whipped and machine gunned. They were taken for rides on the front seats of sedans, garroted from behind, and at times had their brains blown out with a bullet to the back of the head by fellow mobsters they thought were their pals. They were lined up in pairs in front of warehouse walls in lonely alleys and shot down by enemy-gang firing squads. They were slugged into unconsciousness and placed in burlap sacks with their hands, feet, and necks so roped that they would strangle themselves as they writhed. Charred bodies were found in bombed automobiles. Bootleggers and sometimes their molls were pinioned with wire and dropped alive into the East River. Others were encased in cement and tossed overboard from rum boats in the harbor.[44]

In Cook County, Chicago gang wars produced 350 to 450 murders annually during the late 1920s. At the center of the tumult was Al Capone, a notorious gang leader who as a youth had cut his teeth in New York's notorious Five Points street gang. Capone's struggle with his competitors ended with the infamous St. Valentine's Day Massacre on February 14, 1929, leaving him firmly in control of the Midwestern market and the importation of liquor from Canada. By 1930, only two Italian gangs remained standing in New York City: an older faction headed by Salvatore Maranzano (comprised primarily of Sicilians who originated from the small coastal town of Castellammare del Golfo) and a younger, but less exclusively Italian group led by Giuseppe "Joe the Boss" Masseria. Conflict between the two gangs culminated in the Castellammare War in 1931 (master-minded by Charles "Lucky" Luciano), a bloody spree that eliminated the older, less educated Sicilian bosses and left better-educated, business-oriented, and Americanized Italian gangsters in charge of organized crime. This catharsis was widely believed to lead to a national syndicate referred to as the La Costra Nostra (Mafia) by 1934 that included heads of the 24 most powerful Italian organized crime "families."[45]

In 1950, the Senate Special Committee to Investigate Organize Crime (the Kefauver Committee) was formed to assess the status and threat of organized criminal gangs. The committee reported the existence of a national criminal syndicate, one with a rigid and highly bureaucratized organizational command structure, that dominated the market for illicit substances and services, had infiltrated legitimate businesses, and was linked to the widespread corruption and bribery of public officials. The theme was revisited by the Senate Subcommittee on Investigations (the McClellan Committee) later while investigating the link between organized crime and the Teamsters Union. It is at these hearings that the testimony of Joseph Valachi was introduced, detailing the workings of the La Costra Nostra. Support for a national Italian-American crime syndicate was, however, based on fragmentary data, mostly sensationalized news stories, the public release of heavily edited and carefully selected police files and surveillance transcripts, and the testimony of a few insiders (e.g., Valachi) with questionable motives and knowledge. Research has found little evidence to support the notion of a secret national commission of gangsters. Instead, at best these gangs were only loosely organized, "patron–client" relations with syndicate bosses serving as patrons and using friends to ensure a steady flow of illicit goods and services for profit.[46]

STREET GANGS IN THE 1940s AND 1950s

Immigration restriction during the 1920s and 1930s dramatically reduced the flow of European and Asian immigrants to the United States. These restrictions exacerbated labor shortages in the booming cities of the northeast. Southern blacks, Puerto Ricans, and Mexicans rushed to fill the void. Beginning in the 1920s, waves of rural and small-town southern blacks began funneling into ghettos in New York, Detroit, Chicago, Baltimore, and Philadelphia. By the 1950s, some 6.5 million blacks had migrated to northeastern cities, more than the total number of all Italians, Irish, and Jews of previous migrations.[47] Because of their numbers, migrant blacks felt the burden of discrimination more intensely than had other nonwhite groups, such as the Japanese or Chinese.[48] Forced into the most menial ranks of industry, the earliest black migrants nonetheless were able to preserve family structures and build strong, albeit segregated, communities. Black youth were not particularly troublesome, restrained by attentive parents and strong religious beliefs. Successive waves of migration were followed by a deterioration of family structure and prosocial values.

By the early 1940s, street gangs had emerged in most black communities in the north.[49] They were hardly, however, a threat to the community; fighting, drinking, gambling, and minor rumbles were the extent of their lawbreaking. During the 1950s, black gangs became predators, the decade spawning "a generation of Black youth who seemed to thrive on callous behavior, disrespect for adults,

❧❧ _____

> In the 1940s and 1950s, street gangs became closely identified with urban blacks and Latinos.

_____

and senseless violence."[50] In addition to their crimes against their communities, black gangs warred frequently among themselves, settling disputes with zip guns, knives, bats, and brass knuckles.

The lure of good jobs also drew Puerto Ricans to the mainland. From 1941 to 1956, ships arriving in New York City harbors brought half a million migrants from Puerto Rico, most of whom settled in the Lower East Side, East Harlem, and South Bronx. The large influx of blacks and Puerto Ricans in the years following World War II reportedly sparked "the greatest era of youth gang activity in American gang history."[51] Unwilling neighbors, bands of black, Puerto Rican, Italian, and Jewish males carved out turfs to defend even at the cost of human life. Other gangs were more proactive, regularly prowling areas outside their own turf in search of trouble and excitement. Known as "bopping gangs," these bands were easily distinguished by the "rhythmic gait" and the "forward movement of the head with each step."[52]

The danger posed by such street gangs was illuminated on July 30, 1957 by the brutal gang murder of Michael Farmer, a 15-year-old polio victim, in a New York City Park. The Egyptian Kings, a largely Puerto Rican gang, had on the previous night been chased out of a local pool by the Jesters, an Irish-American gang that ostensibly controlled the area. The night of the murder, the Kings returned to Jester turf for a rumble, reserving Stitt Park as their base of operations. That same evening, less than a block from the park, Michael Farmer listened to rock 'n roll records at his home with a friend, Roger McShane. Around 10:00 P.M., Farmer decided to walk his friend home, the shortest route being through the park. Mistaken for Jesters, 18 King members confronted the boys and began their lethal assault, stabbing them with a bread knife and a machete, and bludgeoning them with baseball bats.

> I was aiming to hit him, but there were so many on him. I saw the knife go in the guy. Another guy kept hittin' him with a machete. Magician grabbed him, turned him around and stabbed him in the back . . . So I hit him with the bat. When Magician stabbed him, the guy fell. He started to stand up and I knocked him down. Then he was down on the ground, everybody was kickin' him, stompin' him, punchin' him, stabbin' him. He tried to get back up and I knocked him down again. Then another guy stabbed him again in the back with bread knife.[53]

In the southwest, Mexicans fleeing economic turmoil continued to pour into the country, the initial waves occurring in the 1920s. During the 1940s and 1950s, nearly 4 million largely unskilled, rural, and desperately poor Mexicans migrated to the United States, the vast majority settling in the interstices of cities and outlying rural areas.[54] Though they may have preferred to settle elsewhere, a lack of affordable housing and discrimination forced them into older, deteriorating neighborhoods physically distant from the surrounding community. Despite the physical condition of these neighborhoods, a sense of pride ran deep among residents.

In the absence of parks and other recreational centers, Mexican youth naturally gravitated to the street. Prior to the 1940s, however, there was little concern with bands of barrio males. Bogardus characterized it as a "boy problem."[55] These groupings were friendship groups, based on residence and shared interests. The "boy problem" became a "gang problem" as second-generation Mexican-Americans came of age and originated the *pachuco* lifestyle (or, as presently known as *cholos*): a strong sense of group as family, an antiauthoritarian attitude, bravado and machismo. Although worn by other races, the uniform of *pachucos* was the zoot suit—baggy pants; stiff, broad-shouldered jackets; long chains; and a broad-brimmed hat.[56] Though being cool was ostensibly important, barrio warfare was "endemic."[57] Substance abuse was also rampant among *pachucos*, one observer concluding that alcohol and drugs were responsible for exacerbating barrio conflicts:

> Often the gang warfare is aggravated by the use of liquor, poisonous liquor, and sometimes by the smoking of marijuana cigarettes which on occasion cost fifty cents each and which may drive their victims literally mad with hallucinations.[58]

Conflicts between *pachucos* and members of the broader community, particularly servicemen, were inevitable. Following the attack on Pearl Harbor in December 1941, Los Angeles quickly became home to one of the largest concentrations of military personnel.[59] In the mobilization for war, patriotic spirit and a disturbing xenophobia ran high, the later evidenced by Japanese internment in the early months of 1942. There was the desire to rid the country of dangerous foreign elements. In August 1942, a young Chicano was killed in a gang-related incident known as the Sleepy Lagoon case. In the following police crackdown, 22 members of gangs were arrested on charges of conspiracy to commit murder, and 17 eventually convicted on various charges. In the days and weeks that followed, newspapers and radios alerted the public to the danger of zoot suit gangs, creating an image of Chicano youth as dangerous "gangsters."[60] Tensions peaked in a series of violent confrontations between Chicanos and military personnel in 1943, known as the Zoot Suit Riots.

A new type of male group also emerged among white males during the 1940s and 1950s. Outlaw motorcycle gangs (OMGs) emerged in the years following World War II, formed largely by returning veterans who disdained the civilian lifestyle.[61]

GANGS IN THE 1960s AND 1970s

By the late 1960s, many cities believed the gang problem had been solved. Policy-makers naturally took credit for the decline, linking lower levels of gang activity to the implementation of intensive community intervention programs. During the late 1950s, several major cities attempted to resolve their gang problems by recruiting streetwise young men to work with local gangs.[62] The "street worker" model received a great deal of attention, and massive federal funding to replicate such programs in other communities. Street worker programs provided vocational training, educational assistance, and counseling to gang members. In fact, the central objective was "values transformation," in essence an attempt to inculcate middle-class norms and values into ghetto youth, similar to efforts of the charity workers and settlement house workers of the late 19th century. Gang members were generally assumed to have a psychological disturbance, making the shift toward prosocial attitudes that much more difficult.

Theorists, however, could feel even more proud. Street worker programs exemplified the proper marriage of theory, research, and public policy.[63] In the years prior to the implementation of street work programs, several criminological theories had been developed that applied to street gangs. The underlying premise of each was that gang activity was a response to the crushing burden of urban poverty. Some held that the crimes of the poor were a reaction to the chronic strain of adapting to middle class norms, values, and lifestyles.[64] Another suggested that the failure of urban youth to measure up to the middle-class measuring rod cultivated poor self-esteem and major adjustment problems. Others posited that gang members had internalized a deviant value system endemic in lower class communities, a perversion of rights and responsibilities bred by the social and economic marginalization of those residents.[65]

If there was indeed a reduction of gang activity during the period, the role of innovative gang programs would have been nominal. Much of the decline may have been due to the drug epidemic of the 1960s.[66] Poor urban males by the thousands turned from gangs to chemicals to ease the deprivations of inner city poverty. The next fix became more important than social standing or camaraderie. The civil rights movement perhaps played an even more important role in declining gang activity. The march toward equality raised racial and political

Gang theories and intervention programs were first developed during the 1960s and 1970s.

consciousness among the poor, downtrodden, urban class. Many gangs "went social," ostensibly leaving behind their criminal ways and devoting themselves to solving community problems.

Perhaps the best known example of such a metamorphosis was the Spartina Army, a Puerto Rican gang that operated in New York's Lower East Side.[67] During the years in which War on Poverty dollars were flooding into communities, the Spartican Army abruptly changed its name to the Real Great Society (RGS). RGS members sought a piece of the action, eventually receiving federal funds to operate the University of the Streets, a community education center that offered instruction in high school equivalency testing, pressing social problems, radio and television repair, and karate.

New gangs also emerged during the movement that, although also in pursuit of social justice, did so armed to the teeth.[68] The image and rhetoric of groups such as the Black Panthers, Vice Lords, Young Lords, and the Black Liberation Army during the 1960s demanded attention and fear. Concessions from local power structures were coerced by explicit threats of violence. Confrontations between militant black gangs and local law enforcement were frequent and often deadly. Shortly after the assassination of Martin Luther King, Black Panther leader Eldridge Cleaver issued an "executive order" to assassinate policemen as a retaliatory measure. A fatal shootout occurred after the assault of prominent Panther leaders Huey Newton, Eldridge Cleaver, and Bobby Seale.

Though the data do not exist to document an actual decrease in gangs during the 1960s and 1970s, it is quite clear that traditional street gangs were not identified as a major social problem by public officials or the media. Following a review of the evidence, in 1976 the National Advisory Committee on Criminal Justice Standards and Goals concluded:

> Youth gangs are not now or [sic] should not become a major crime problem in the United States . . . What gang violence does exist can fairly readily be diverted into 'constructive' channels especially through the provision of service by community agencies.[69]

Conclusion

Though gangs were "discovered" in the 1980s, this chapter's brief overview of gangs in this country prior to that decade brings much-needed perspective to the current controversy. Gangs have menaced urban streets and countrysides since at least the 19th century. The composition of those groups remains largely unchanged today: young males, radically impulsive and brutally remorseless, free from the constraints imposed by ties to the conventional social order. In combination with drugs and/or alcohol, an assortment of lethal weapons, and subcultural values that encourage crime, gangs have long represented a threat to the welfare of the general community. Indeed, given the current size and power of law enforcement, one could argue that communities in the past were actually *more vulnerable* to the gang threat. How are we to account, then, for the gang panic that has gripped the nation since the 1980s? Can it be explained, as claim-makers contend, by a sudden and unforseen increase in the threat posed by street gangs? Or could the alarm have been sounded, not because of the increased threat of such groups, but for reasons that have little to do with the safety of communities?

Notes

1. John D. Buenker. 1973. *Urban Liberalism and Progressive Reform*. New York: Scribner.
2. Herbert Asbury. 1928. *Gangs of New York: An Informed History of the Underworld*. New York: Alfred A. Knopf, p. 22.
3. Asbury, 1928, p. 29
4. James Haskins. 1974. *Street Gangs: Yesterday and Today*. New York: Hastings House Publishers.
5. (Ellis, 1966:233 in Haskins).
6. Asbury, 1928, p. 66.
7. (Taylor, 1969 cited in Blumin, 1973:44).
8. David R. Johnson. 1973. "Crime Patterns in Philadelphia, 1840–70." In A. David and M. Haller (eds.), *The People of Philadelphia: A History of Ethnic Groups and Lower-Class Life, 1790–1940*. Philadelphia: Temple University Press, p. 98.
9. Johnson, 1973.
10. Asbury, 1928, p. 112.
11. Haskins, 1974, p. 29.
12. Rodman W. Paul. 1988. *Far West and the Great Plains in Transition, 1859–1900*. New York: Harper and Row.
13. David T. Courtwright. 1996. *Violent Land: Single Men and Social Disorder from the Frontier to the Inner City*. Cambridge: Harvard University Press.
14. Richard Maxell Brown. 1994. "Violence." in C.A. Milner, C.A. Connor, and M.A. Stewart (eds.), *The Oxford History of the American West*, pp. 392–425.
15. Brown, 1994, p. 393.
16. Courtwright, 1996.
17. Roger D. McGrath. 1989. "Violence and lawlessness on the western frontier." In T. R. Gurr (ed.), *Violence in America: The History of Crime*. Newbury Park, CA: Sage.
18. Cited in Courtwright, 1996, p. 87.
19. Frank Richard Prassel. 1993. *The Great American Outlaw: A Legacy of Fact and Fiction*. Norman, OK: University of Oklahoma Press.
20. Paul Wellman. 1961. *A Dynasty of Western Outlaws*. Lincoln: University of Nebraska Press, p. 65.
21. William E. Connelley. 1956. *Quantrill and the Border Wars*. New York: Pageant Books.
22. Wellman, 1986, p. 18.
23. Wellman, 1986, p. 73.

24. Augustus Appler. 1876. *The Guerillas of the West*. Saint Louis: Eureka Press.
25. Haskins, 1974.
26. Jay Robery Nash. 1973. *Bloodletters and Badmen: A Narrative Encyclopedia of American Criminals from the Pilgrims to the Present*. New York: M. Evans and Company.
27. Nash, 1973.
28. Asbury, 1928, p. 221.
29. Nash, 1973.
30. Jacob Riis. 1971. *How the Other Half Lives: Studies among the Tenements of New York*. New York: Dover, p. 171.
31. Mark Thorton. 1991. *The Economics of Prohibition*. Salt Lake City: University of Utah Press.
32. Courtwright, 1966.
33. David Musto. 1987. *The American Disease: Origins of Narcotic Control*. New York: Oxford University Press.
34. Asbury, 1928, p. 238.
35. Haskins, 1974.
36. William Kleinknecht. 1996. *The New Ethnic Mob: The Changing Face of Organized Crime in America*. New York: The Free Press, 1996.
37. Jenna Weissman Joselit. 1983. *Our Gang: Jewish Crime and the New York Jewish Community, 1900–1940*. Bloomington, IN: Indiana University Press.
38. Daniel Fuch. Cited in Stephen Fox. 1989. *Blood and Power: Organized Crime in Twentieth Century America*. New York: William Morrow, p. 218.
39. Kleinknecht, 1996.
40. Edward Thrasher. 1927, *The Gang*. Chicago: University of Chicago Press, p. 6.
41. Haskins, 1974; Asbury, 1928.
42. Christopher Lasch. 1991. *The True and Only Heaven: Progress and Its Critics*. New York: W.W. Norton.
43. Leo Katcher. 1959. *The Big Bankroll: The Life and Times of Arnold Rothstein*. London: Gollancz.
44. Lewis Yablonsky. 1997. Gangsters: *Fifty Years of Madness, Drugs, and Death on the Streets of America*. New York : New York University Press, 1997.
45. Donald R. Cressey. 1969. *Theft of the Nation: The Structure and Operation of Organized Crime in America*. New York: Harper and Row.
46. Joseph L. Albini. 1971. *The American Mafia: Genesis of a Legend*. New York: Appleton-Century-Crofts.
47. Nicholas Lemann. 1991. *The Promised Land: The Great Black Migration and How It Changed America*. New York: A.A. Knopf.
48. Stanley Lieberson. 1980. *A Piece of the Pie: Black and White Immigrants Since 1880*. Berkeley: University of California Press.
49. Useni Eugene Perkins. 1987. *Explosion of Chicago's Black Street Gangs: 1900 to the Present*. Chicago: Third World Press; Haskins, 1974; Robison, 1946.
50. Perkins, 1987, p. 29.
51. Haskins, 1974, p. 82.
52. Haskins, 1974, p. 85.
53. Yablonsky, 1997, p. 51.
54. James Diego Vigil. 1988. *Barrio Gangs: Street Life and Identity in Southern California*. Austin, TX: University of Texas Press.
55. Emory S. Bogardus. 1943. "Gangs of Mexican-American youth." *Sociology and Social Research*. Vol. 28, p. 126.
56. Vigil, 1988.

57. Joan W. Moore. 1991. *Going Down to the Barrio: Homeboys and Homegirls in Change.* Philadelphia, PA: Temple University Press.

58. Bogardus, 1943, p. 59.

59. Mauricio Mazon. 1984. *The Zoot-Suit Riots: The Psychology of Symbolic Annihilation.* Austin, TX: University of Texas Press.

60. Alfredo Mirandi and Jose Lopez. 1992. "Chicano urban youth gangs: A critical analysis of a social problem." *Latino Studies Journal.* Vol. 3, p. 17.

61. Hunter S. Thompson. 1967. *Hell's Angels.* New York: Random House.

62. Malcolm Klein. 1995. *The American Street Gang: Its Nature, Prevalence, and Control.* New York: Oxford University Press, 1995.

63. Klein, 1996; Weiner and Horowitz, 1983.

64. Robert Merton. 1975. "Social structure and anomie." In R. Merton (ed.), *Social Theory and Social Structure.* Glencoe, IL: Free Press.

65. Walter Miller. 1958. "Lower class culture as a generating milieu of gang delinquency." *Journal of Social Issues.* Vol. 14, pp. 5–19.

66. Herbert C. Covey, Scott Menard, and Robert J. Franzere. 1997. *Juvenile Gangs.* 2nd edition. Springfield, IL: Charles C Thomas Publishers.

67. Haskins, 1974.

68. Haskins, 1974.

69. Cited in Spergel, 1995, p. 9.

chapter 3

The Police, Crime Control, and Street Gangs

◆◆◆

Law enforcement claims suggest that the gang threat today is greater than at any time in our nation's history. Street gangs are reportedly ubiquitous, present in cities large and small. Nearly one million young males (and an increasing number of females) are estimated now to fill their ranks. They are purportedly armed with machine guns and assault weapons and unconstrained by a regard for human life—their own, rival gang members', or innocent bystanders'. Street gangs are portrayed as sophisticated criminal enterprises that now dominate drug markets, particularly crack cocaine. Unlike in the past, contemporary street gangs, police contend, represent a threat not only to life and property, but to the fundamental values and order of the country itself.

Claims making by law enforcement is nothing new. In public arenas over the past several decades, police have forcefully and effectively presented the threat of crime and the need for greater investments in law enforcement. Through fervent recitations of scary statistics and beat-cop anecdotes, law enforcement bureaucrats have been able to affix the crime problem squarely in the consciousness of both the public and policymakers. They have advanced organizational interests and careers by making others afraid, and convincing them that they are capable, if sufficiently funded, of meeting the threat and restoring order.

Of course, the police are not alone in their exploitation of public fears. Politicians use a similar strategy to gain and keep public office, parroting law enforcement claims regarding the severity of the problem and attempting to distinguish themselves from their rivals by vows to "get tough on crime." While politicians have, to some extent, always capitalized on the public's fear of crime, the politicization of crime has greatly intensified over the past several decades. Today, crime is inextricably linked to the political process. The criminal justice system in general, and law enforcement in particular, has benefitted greatly from the marriage of politics and crime.

THE POLITICIZATION OF CRIME

There has always been a crime problem in the United States, but during the 1960s an explosive growth occurred in the number of crimes reported to the police. Between 1960 and 1991, the year in which reported crimes peaked, the rate of violent crime increased by nearly 500 percent; levels of property crime more than tripled. Various explanations have been proffered for the sharp increases in this social disorder: the inadequate funding of social programs, the epidemic of illicit drugs, the proliferation of guns, a demographic shift which produced a younger, more crime-prone population, structural unemployment, and soft judges, to name just a few. The simple truth is that no one knows, exactly, what happened during those years to spark and sustain those frightful levels of crime. In fact, there is continuing debate on whether or not these increases even occurred.[1]

What is clear, however, is that it was during the 1964 presidential campaign that the crime problem was dragged out of the shadows and placed center stage on the national political agenda. In his acceptance speech for the 1964 Republican presidential nomination, Barry Goldwater decried "the growing menace in our country tonight, to personal safety, to life, to limb and property, in homes, in churches, on the playgrounds and places of business, particularly in our great cities" and went on to say that "nothing prepares the way for tyranny more than the failure of public officials to keep the street safe from bullies and marauders."[2] Goldwater faulted the incumbent, Lyndon Johnson, for being soft on crime and suggested that the current lawlessness was an outgrowth of the civil rights movement, failed social experiments, and Supreme Court rulings that expanded the rights of criminal defendants, handcuffed police, and placed communities at risk. Although Goldwater's remarks resonated with many white middle-class voters, most Americans perceived him as a dangerous extremist, one likely to exacerbate rather than ameliorate domestic tensions.

Though voters ultimately rejected Goldwater, public outcries for law and order would echo throughout Johnson's presidency. Indeed, in the swirl of events that defined the late 1960s—rising crime rates, urban riots, campus unrest, the assassinations of King and Kennedy, anti-Vietnam marches—Americans came to believe that the social fabric was unraveling before their eyes, and politicians at all levels of government rushed to assuage public fears. In 1967, Johnson created the President's Commission on Law Enforcement and the Administration of Justice, its mandate a comprehensive review of the criminal justice system and the provision of critically needed reforms. Two years later, the Commission published its final report entitled *The Challenge of Crime in a Free Society*. The Commission proposed a "war on crime" analogous to Johnson's existing "war on poverty" initiative, concluding that the federal government could "make a dramatic new contribution to the national effort against crime by greatly expanding its support of agencies of Justice in the States and in the cities."[3] The report contained numerous specific recommendations, many of which were incorporated into the Omnibus Crime Control and Safe Streets Act of 1968.

That legislation signaled federal intervention into what had traditionally been held to be a local problem, one best solved by local criminal justice actors. It established the Law Enforcement Assistance Administration (LEAA), ordered the creation of state planning agencies, and, during its fourteen-year history, funneled over $7.7 billion dollars into state and local crime-control efforts. By far the largest benefactor from federal funds was law enforcement.[4] Police departments, constituting the front line in the war on crime, used this money for riot control and innovative crime-fighting equipment, fueling the growth of the police hardware industry. Federal dollars were also used for additional manpower and advanced training for officers, as well as to establish hundreds of criminal justice programs on college campuses across the country that were in return expected to provide a highly educated pool of recruits for careers in law enforcement. As had been recommended by the President's Commission, substantial government funding was also provided for university researchers to scrutinize criminal justice organizations, policies, and personnel.

The upward spiral of crime, however, continued unabated and politicians continued to make hay out of public anxieties. Nixon won a narrow victory over Humphrey in the 1968 presidential campaign, citing Uniform Crime Report data on increasing crime and labeling his opponent and the Democratic party in general as being "soft on crime."[5] He also chided the courts as having "gone too far in weakening the peace forces, as against the criminal forces, in this country."[6] Though he denied his "law and order rhetoric" was a euphemism for minority repression, he continually stressed the right to be free from criminal violence as "the forgotten civil right."[7] Working on the assumption that illicit drugs were fueling high crime rates, in 1970 Nixon declared a "war on drugs," releasing a torrent of federal money to state and local law enforcement, even providing money for more equipment, law enforcement training institutes and data-sharing techniques. Police departments were the beneficiaries of most of this revenue sharing, particularly those located in cities where minority populations were increasing most rapidly. By the time of Nixon's resignation in 1974, the number of police on American streets had increased by nearly 40 percent.[8]

Though only a minor issue in the 1976 presidential race, Ronald Reagan used the crime problem against incumbent Jimmy Carter in 1980, contending that "a murderous epidemic of drug abuse has swept through our country" and that "Mr. Carter, through his policies and his personnel, has demonstrated little interest in stopping its ravages."[9] Shortly after assuming office, Reagan introduced a seven-step plan to eradicate drugs from society, a plan which included diverting nearly $709 million dollars from his predecessor's education, treatment, and research programs to law enforcement. State and municipal law enforcement agencies created and revitalized their narcotics units, taking full advantage of the federal funds that had suddenly become available.[10]

In the 1984 election, President Reagan took credit for reported decreases in crime during his first term, specifically his support of law enforcement. His "get tough" rhetoric had much to do with the defeat of Walter Mondale, his Democratic rival who remained largely silent on the issue of crime. Shortly after Reagan's reelection, law enforcement officials began reporting an epidemic of a smokable and highly destructive form of cocaine in major urban areas across the country. The discovery of "crack" was quickly followed by major new antidrug legislation in the late 1980s that authorized $1.7 billion in new funds for drug enforcement, most of which was allotted to law enforcement.[11]

The degree to which crime had been politicized was shamefully evident in the 1988 presidential campaign. The George Bush campaign's infamous Willie Horton ads played to the worst fears of Americans: a violent crime, committed by a black stranger on a white female, let loose by a lenient criminal justice system to prey on society. These ads were believed by many to have been politically devastating to Dukakis, then governor of Maryland and thus ultimately responsible for the furlough program which released Horton, despite the fact that the furlough program actually had originated under a Republican governor. Once in office, President Bush announced a "major renewed investment in fighting violent street crime" and called on Congress to pass his proposed comprehensive crime bill which he touted as being "tough on criminals and supportive of police."[12] During the 1980s, federal, state, and local expenditures for law enforcement grew by over 400 percent; jobs in police agencies increased by 36 percent.[13]

Bush attempted to portray Bill Clinton as soft on crime in the 1992 presidential election, though by that time economic concerns had eclipsed concern about crime and drugs in the public's mind. Clinton campaigned and won largely on his promises of economic revitalization, though there were strong law and order planks in his conservative Democratic platform. As President, he linked the success of his economic initiatives to crime control, arguing that the former would "be undermined unless we can give the American people a greater sense that they are secure in their homes, on their streets, and in their schools."[14] In 1994, Congress passed the Omnibus Crime Control Act, a 30 billion dollar piece of legislation which provided funding for new prison construction, gun control, and the hiring of an additional 100,000 new police officers, a centerpiece of the Clinton campaign.

THE CRIMINAL JUSTICE EMPIRE

While politicians attempted to exploit crime to achieve the office of the Presidency, similar tactics prevailed in state and local political arenas. Over the decades the result has been a significant expansion in both the size and power of the criminal justice system. The scale of the system is mind numbing: Nearly 2 million Americans earn a living in the justice system, including over 900,000 in law enforcement, 370,000 in judiciary-related occupations, and another 600,000 in corrections. There are more than 55,000 separate public agencies in the justice system: 19,000 police departments, nearly 17,000 courts, over 8,000 prosecutorial offices, 6,000 correctional facilities, and 3,500 parole and probation departments. The cost of operating the justice system is similarly staggering, more than $100 billion a year. In the past 20 years, spending on crime control has increased at twice the rate of defense spending.[15] Of course, these figures do not include the multitude of ancillary workers and agencies, public and private, that provide technical support, contract services, and research (i.e., university and think-tank personnel who conduct government-funded studies of crime and crime control strategies).

In 1995 over 10 million criminal cases were handled by the nation's labyrinthine system of courts. Between 1984 and 1993, the number of felony cases filed in state courts alone rose by 68 percent.[16] Criminal inmate populations have, not surprisingly, skyrocketed. The average daily jail population in the United States grew from 160,863 in 1970 (shortly after the declaration of war on crime) over 700, 000 in 1999. An even more disturbing trend characterizes the growth in prison populations. In 1970, there were 196,429 inmates held in state and federal correctional facilities; by 1996, that number had grown to over 1.3 million—a nearly sevenfold increase. To accommodate such explosive and continued growth required that approximately 1,500 bed spaces and 300 new correctional officers be added each week.[17] In addition to inmates and jails and prisons, there are over 4 million offenders under the supervision of probation and parole. Together, these figures translate into a grim statistic: Today nearly 1 in 38 adults in the United States live under the direct supervision of the state.

◆◆ ───

For two decades, the criminal justice system has grown exponentially while our communities are closing libraries, freezing teacher salaries, limiting medical benefits for our senior citizens, slashing student loan programs, and de-funding Head Start and other early intervention programs.

Steven Donziger, The Real War on Crime, *1996.*[18]

The police are the "gatekeepers" for the criminal justice system and are thus to a great extent responsible for the explosive growth in expenditures for courts, public defenders, prisons, and other justice-related agencies in the past 30 years. Police made over 15 million arrests in 1995, an increase of more than 200 percent since 1971. From 1972 until 1992, total annual police expenditures (federal, state, and local) increased by over 400 percent, from $8 billion to over $32 billion.[19] The number of police employees increased from 507,877 in 1970 to 922,000 in 1996.[20]

Police powers in recent years have also expanded considerably.[21] For example, under both the Burger and Rehnquist courts, the kinds of situations in which police must obtain a judicial warrant before they take action have been slowly reduced. Today, any person riding in a car, bus, or train can be stopped and searched without a warrant, a practice held to be unconstitutional three decades ago. Defendants can also now be confronted in court with what is admitted by the prosecution to be illegally seized evidence, as long as the judge rules that the search was conducted in "good faith" by police officers. Even the legal standard that required officers to have "probable cause" before they request a warrant has been watered down: In many situations, warrants are now issued solely on the basis of the officer's "reasonable" suspicion. Federal and local asset forfeiture statutes, enacted during the 1970s, allow police to seize private property—homes, cars, cash, etc.—without anyone ever being charged, much less convicted, of any drug crime. The courts have given police the right to stop and search persons who have committed no crime, carved exceptions to the Miranda requirement, given tacit approval for deceptive interrogation practices, and eased restrictions on the electronic surveillance of citizens.

Crime Panics and Law Enforcement Growth

In *Crisis and Leviathan*,[22] Robert Higgs argues that the growth of government during the 20th century has not been smooth, but rather has racheted-up during periods of social crisis, particularly wars and depression. In times of crisis, the public looks to the state to "do something," to take actions that would end or ameliorate hardship, adversity, or danger, even at the expense of greater government intervention into their lives. After the crisis has subsided, some state interventions are axed, others scaled back, and some retained. But the government never returns to its precrisis size because the crisis has produced permanent shifts in the tolerable limits of the size and power of the state. The next crisis will provide an opportunity for yet additional growth in the size and power of the government. During World War II, for example, the government conscripted millions of Americans; imposed controls on wages, prices, and rents; rationed food, tires, gasoline and shoes; and introduced the withholding of income taxes. After the war many of the agencies and powers created to deal with the crisis were abolished, but many others at the federal, state, and local level remain until this day (e.g., federal income tax, rent controls, etc.).

The criminal justice system has reached its current proportions through a similar pattern of punctuated growth. In response to police claims of crises of various sorts—a surge in violent crime, a crack epidemic, a scourge of crimes against the elderly, a rash of child abductions, the increased incidence of multiple homicide, an upswing in the number of seemingly random killings, etc.—public fears are flamed by sensationalized media coverage, law enforcement steps forward to offer a suppressive response, and tax dollars are eventually channeled to funnel the latest front in the war on crime.[23] Police budgets and powers swell. After the crisis, there is little retrenchment because the public and elected officials have come to believe that an increased police presence is required to sustain the peace, a perception nurtured by law enforcement bureaucrats interested in maintaining funding levels.

As previously discussed, all government bureaucracies engage in political activism to protect and further organizational interests. But law enforcement arguably has been most influential in shaping public policy. Daniel Glaser (1978) writes:

> . . . the leaders of a law enforcement bureaucracy have special advantage for promulgating their views because of their ready access to the heads of executive and legislative branches of government, their ability to issue official reports and call new conferences, and their control over public information on the effectiveness of the law and the need for it.[24]

These huge increases in law enforcement expenditures over the past two decades have been necessary, police claims-makers contend, to keep pace with soaring rates of homicide and other violent crimes. To buttress that contention, police officials cite the Federal Bureau of Investigation's Uniform Crime Report (UCR) statistics showing that from 1970 to 1992, arrest rates for both violent and property crimes more than doubled.[25] UCR statistics, however, are deserving of important qualifications. First, reporting crime statistics based on arrests rather than convictions has the effect of greatly exaggerating the extent of crime in general, and violent crime in particular. As Jerome Miller points out in *Search and Destroy: African-American Males in the Criminal Justice System*, policy-makers and the public "seem not to notice that of every 100 individuals arrested for a felony, 43 were either not prosecuted or their cases were dismissed outright at the first court appearance."[26] Rather than an indication of permissive courts, Miller argues that this pattern reflects enterprising law enforcement agencies making unwarranted arrests in order to fuel the fear of crime and justify budgets requests. Moreover, UCR arrest statistics are misleading because police "routinely overcharge" arrestees. Most aggravated assaults, for example, are either dismissed or pled down to simple assault. Indeed, in approximately 68 percent of all violent crimes reported by police, there is no physical injury to the victim.

Police officials generally ignore a second and conflicting source of criminal statistics, one that has been available since the early 1970s. The National Crime Victimization Survey (NCVS), which measures both reported and unreported crimes (and thus is arguably a better indicator of the actual incidence of crime), reveals a different picture of crime trends. Although the amount of crime measured is substantially greater than that offered by the UCR, NCVS data show very little change in victimization rates from 1973 to 1990; indeed, during the 1980s—at a time when violent crime reportedly was skyrocketing—NCVS statistics actually indicate a decline in crimes against persons[27] (Figure 3–1). Some have even questioned whether UCR data itself actually shows a crime wave over the past two decades. In a comparison of UCR and NCVS data from 1979 to 1991, University of Michigan research John Bounds and Scott Boggess concluded that "[Despite] the widely held belief that there was a significant increase in the level of criminal activity during the 1980s, in general, we find neither data source depicts increasing levels of crime over this period."[28]

Local law enforcement officials are aware of the problems with official measures of crime; nonetheless, UCR statistics are presented since they offer "bigger numbers," create greater alarm, and increase the likelihood of additional resources. To preserve and advance organizational interests and careers, it is inevitable that police bureaucrats would choose numbers that put a higher premium on their services.

The Crime-Fighter Image

In addition to the selective use of numbers to command and preserve resources, law enforcement benefits from the carefully cultivated public perception that it is providing protection against street crime. Police routinely portray themselves as crime fighters, warriors capable of delivering a crushing blow to the criminal element if additional public money for personnel and hardware were simply provided. However, despite two decades of budget increases, we know that the police are unable to do much to prevent crime and protect communities. Indeed,

---

The crime problem in the United States is neither better nor worse today than it was fifty years ago, when people were not afraid to walk the streets at night or to leave their cars unlocked in their driveway.

William Chambliss. Power, Politics, & Crime, *1999.*[29]

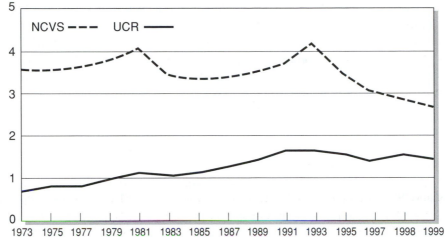

FIGURE 3–1   Two Measures of Serious Violent Crime (in millions)

most of the public would be surprised to learn that most of what police do has actually very little to do with fighting crime. What police scholar James Q. Wilson observed in the mid-1970s holds true today:

> For some time, persons who run or study police departments have recognized that the public perception is misleading. The majority of calls received by most police have little to do with crime, but a great deal to do with medical emergencies, family quarrels, auto accidents, barking dogs, minor traffic violations, and so on. And those calls that do involve serious crimes, such as burglaries, robberies and auto theft, typically occur after the event has taken place and the trail is cold; the officer who responds can often do little more than fill out a report that will contain few if any leads for further investigation. The police wish it were otherwise; most patrolmen would prefer to stop a crime in progress or catch a major felon, but only infrequently do they have the chance.[30]

Recent studies consistently show that, during a routine shift, the typical police officer will spend 75 percent or more of his or her time on routine patrol, administrative tasks, meals, and breaks. Moreover, after decades of research conducted in cities across the country, there is now a consensus among scholars that the core strategies of modern policing—preventive patrol, rapid response to crime scenes, and criminal investigations—have little effect on rates of crime or the apprehension of criminals. Nor is there is any credible evidence that increasing the number of police, a constant cry from law enforcement officials, will make a difference in how much crime occurs in a community.[31]

That police are incapable of preventing crime is, according to David Bayley, "one of the best kept secrets of modern life . . . [e]xperts know it, the police know it, but the public does not know it."[32] If the public were to learn of police impotence, law enforcement budgets would be severely jeopardized and citizens would find other, more effective means, to guard against criminal victimization. To a large degree this is already occurring. Private policing has become a $52 billion a year industry; there are now 1.5 million private police/security officers working in businesses, hospitals, public parks, apartment complexes, and some 30,000 gated communities across the country.[33] That public confidence in police is eroding is also evidenced by the growth of groups like the Guardian Angels, neighborhood watch groups, and citizen foot patrols. Still, public support for the police remains high. A national survey conducted in 1995 revealed that three-quarters of the public believes that the police provide at least some protection from crime.[34]

The inability of the police to prevent or control street crime is obscured by the manipulation of the media by law enforcement officials. By controlling the images and information relayed to the public and their elected officials, large and increasing budgets are considered responsible social policy. Frenzied, ninja-garbed narcotics officers ramming down doors of crack houses and methamphetamine labs; police cars—sirens blaring, lights flashing, motors racing—barreling down congested highways in pursuit of rapacious, gun-toting thugs; criminal investigators meticulously collecting evidence at the scene of a gruesome, high-profile homicide; patrol officers, guns drawn, towering over suspects sprawled face down on city streets—these are the images that have become staples of newspaper dailies and local newscasts. Lead stories convey warnings from law enforcement officials that crime is increasing, confirming the public's fear of crime and suggesting the urgency of greater law enforcement expenditures.

Because the media rely almost exclusively on the police for information about crime, and the public similarly relies heavily on the media (topics to be explored in detail in the following chapter), it is possible to control the public's image of both crime and the effectiveness of law enforcement. The message conveyed through the media, and by the criminal justice system itself, is that the public is under constant threat from a criminal element, a threat that erupts at uncertain times and in different forms that requires a specialized, massive, and immediate response. That threat is portrayed as emanating almost exclusively from the ranks of lower class males; their acts are portrayed as and reacted to as being the most costly, most dangerous, and most threatening to the public. The arguably greater threat posed by "suite crimes"—white-collar, corporate, or state illegalities—receives little, if any, attention.

POLICE REPORTS OF THE GANG CRISIS

In the mid-1980s, law enforcement began warning of another threat to public safety, the growing menace posed by criminal street gangs. As discussed in the previous chapter, gangs are hardly a new phenomenon in this country; bands of young, malevolent males have marred urban landscapes in the United States for nearly two hundred years. But if we are to believe law enforcement officials (and prosecutors and politicians who rely on law enforcement and the media for their information regarding street gangs), it is more than a knot of youngsters on street corners that we have to fear, more than the chance that we might suffer an assault or mugging at the hands of street urchins seeking to confirm reputations or plunder a few dollars. The threat posed by gangs is affirmed as being much more ominous. Gangs are allegedly engaged in a vast, malevolent conspiracy against the American public, a conspiracy that imperils, not only our personal safety and that of our children, but also the very moral, social, and political order that Americans have enjoyed for over 200 years.

> Presently the outlook for gangs and their violent and brutal activities is not optimistic. Unless we take pro-active steps to combat them, there is a very real danger that we may be overrun by their overwhelming menace (Sergeant Joseph Guzman, Los Angeles County Sheriff's Department, Homicide Bureau).[35]
>
> Gang violence has reached epidemic proportions and poses a serious threat to society (Sergeant Robert Jackson, Los Angeles Police Department, and Wes McBride, Los Angeles Sheriff's).[36]
>
> The greatest threat to society and young people today is gangs, and we're not immune to it in this city (Lt. Richard Ayter, Police Gang Crimes Unit, Oklahoma City).[37]
>
> Criminal street gang members are terrorizing communities throughout California, where the viciousness of the gangs [has] taken away many of the public's individual freedoms. In some parts of the state, gang members completely control the community where they live and commit their violent crimes (California Attorney General.)[38]
>
> I strongly believe that should this great nation of ours fail to come to grips with the reality of gangs, it will cause the demise of our country (Sergeant Michael Nichols, Supervisor Gang Squad, St. Louis Police Department).[39]

Claims Regarding Size of Gang Problem

These kinds of claims and prognostications are nearly always accompanied by figures purportedly measuring the magnitude of the nation's gang problem. But because there is no consensus as to what constitutes a gang or who is or is not a gang member, these figures are inevitably inaccurate and misleading. The

◆◆ _____

It's a thorny problem. . . We brought [the experts] together in '95 and '96, and
we couldn't come to an agreement on how to define gangs.

John Moore, Director of the National Youth Gang Center, 2000.[40]

_____

definitions currently employed are the outcomes of an extremely subjective
process and vary greatly across jurisdictions, agencies, and researchers, making
statements about the nature and trend in gang activity extremely difficult.[41]
Definitional problems haunt gang scholars as well, one scholar suggesting that the
number of competing definitions of a gang are "legion."[42]

Police, however, do not appear to be particularly bothered by the lack of
consistent definitions. Officers argue they know a gang, and a gang member,
when they see one: "If he walks like a duck and talks like a duck, chances are
he is a duck."[43] Operationalized, this generally means young minority males in
lower or working class neighborhoods who act, talk, and wear clothing associated
with stereotypical gang images. Though they may have their origins in gangs, such
dress, sobriquets, and gestures are clearly no longer confined to such groups. The
glamorization of the gang culture via music and movies has popularized certain
styles of clothing and mannerisms once peculiar to street gangs.[44] Consequently,
the kinds of markers that may have once been used to identify gang members are
no longer valid. Gang counts grow with each new "gang sweep" through what
police characterize as "infested areas." Each new gangbanger caught up in the
police net serves only as motivation for further hunts, attested to by an officer with
the Wood County Ohio Gang Task Force who has concluded "[G]angs are like
cockroaches . . . once you see one, you can be sure there are many more around."[45]

Given this mind set, it is difficult to interpret the findings from a 1999
survey conducted by the National Youth Gang Center (affiliated with the U.S.
Office of Juvenile Justice and Delinquency Prevention). In the survey (conducted
annually since 1995), law enforcement agencies alone were targeted, primarily
due to the prohibitive costs of including prosecution, the courts, and other justice
agencies in the study. More than 2,600 law enforcement agencies participated
in the survey. Using the following definition these agencies were asked to
provide information on the presence, number, and activity of street gangs in
their jurisdictions.

> . . . a "youth gang" is defined as: a group of youths or young adults in your juris-
> diction that you or other responsible persons in your agency or community are
> willing to identify or classify as a "gang."[46]

Again, because there is no consensus on an appropriate definition of gangs, the definition used in the survey is perhaps as good as any. Nonetheless, allowing law enforcement agencies to use their own discretion in defining groups as gangs and persons as gang members is arguably a recipe for the exaggeration and distortion. With that caveat in mind, the following are a sampling of the conclusions draw from the survey data:[47]

- Active youth gangs were present in an estimated 3,911 jurisdictions in 1999.
- In 1999, there were an estimated 26,000 gangs and 840,500 members (Figure 3–2 and Figure 3–3).
- Sixty-nine percent of all reporting jurisdictions stated that their gang problem was "getting worse" or "staying about the same." Only 31 percent felt it was "getting better."

Problems of definition also taint a survey of state prosecutors conducted by the Institute for Law and Justice (ILJ).[48] Of the 300 state prosecution offices who participated in the study, nearly two-thirds indicated that they had a "gang problem" in their jurisdiction. More than 80 percent of the larger counties (over 250,000) reported "gang activity" but gangs were also reported by prosecutors in nearly half of smaller counties as well. ILJ researchers implicitly suggest that gangs may be even more prevalent than their findings indicate, with officials in many jurisdictions denying the existence of a problem out of ignorance, public relations concerns, and the fear that public recognition "glamorizes and encourages" gangs.

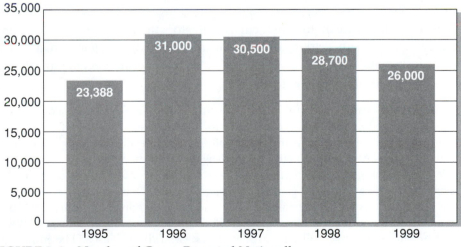

FIGURE 3–2   Number of Gangs Reported Nationally

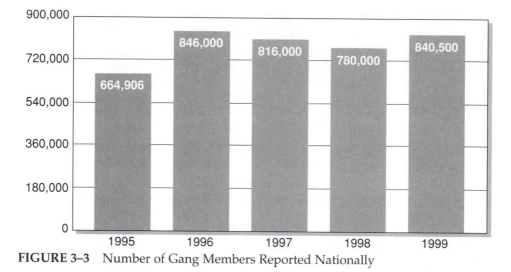

FIGURE 3–3   Number of Gang Members Reported Nationally

Indeed, any community that denies the presence of gangs is presumed to be in a state of denial.[49] Many of these communities will eventual concede a gang problem, a concession that frequently follows the police labeling of one or more high-profile crimes as "gang-related."[50] In other instances, communities become convinced only after police have pointed out evidence, ostensibly overlooked by the layperson, of gang activity: the arcane scribbling found on walls, sidewalks, fences, concrete culverts, overpasses, park benches, bus shelters, and traffic signs. The police gang expert is able to interpret this graffiti—misspelled words or letters reversed, acronyms, and cryptic signs—for unsuspecting community residents, urging them to take them as indicators that street gangs are lurking in the area. It is these markings, police instruct, with which gangs mark their "turfs," issue challenges to rival gangs, and make pronouncements of evil deeds accomplished.

> Organized graffiti is one of the first signs that street gangs are taking hold in your neighborhood and is also an excellent way to track gang growth, affiliation, and sometimes even provides membership information (Steve Nawojczyk, Advisor to the Arkansas Attorney General's Youth Gang Task Force).[51]
>
> Almost always, the first sign of gang activity is graffiti. In essence, it's the underground newspaper of gangs . . . (Memphis Police Department).[52]
>
> Graffiti is probably the most visible and common crime. Gangs use graffiti to let the community know they exist, to mark their territory, to make statements about their gang, or to issue challenges to other gangs. Graffiti is not just an idle crime (San Luis Obispo County Gang Task Force).[53]

Once a community comes around to law enforcement's definition of the situation, gangs are designated as primarily as a law enforcement problem, specialized police and prosecutorial gang units are formed, and suppression strategies are vigorously promoted and heavily funded.[54]

Claims Regarding Gang Violence

According to UCR statistics, nearly 12 million crimes were reported to police in 1999.[55] The vast majority of these victimizations (88 percent) were property crimes of larceny, motor vehicle theft, burglary, and arson. During that same year, there were over 1.4 million crimes of violence (murder, forcible rape, robbery, and aggravated assault) known by police to have occurred. Law enforcement would attribute much of this crime—particularly violent crime—to street gangs. As with "gangs," however, there is no consensus on how to define "gang-crime."[56]

The extent to which police believe gangs are responsible for crime is suggested by results from the 1994 National Institute of Justice Youth Gang Survey.[57] Law enforcement officials in all cities of 150,000 to 200,000, and a random sample of smaller municipalities (25,000 to 50,000) were contacted and asked if there was a gang problem in their jurisdiction and, if so, the extent of gang-related crime. The results from the survey were used by researchers to calculate two estimates of the extent of gang crime in 1993: a "conservative" estimate of 437,066 crimes and a more "reasonable" estimate of 580,331 crimes. Since gang-related crime is assumed to be "predominantly violent in nature,"[58] the conclusion reached was that gang members were responsible for nearly one-quarter of a million murders, rapes, robberies, and assaults in 1993.

Even more disturbing is the suggestion by police that the victims of these violent crimes are frequently innocent bystanders. Gang members reportedly spew their violence in an indiscriminate manner, and "in the process kill innocent victims."[59] Federal DEA officials warn us that "they have no respect for life and no hesitation to shoot anyone who happens to get in their way."[60] No person or place is safe from the gang threat.

> Anybody is fair game to gang violence, including men, women and children (Austin, Texas Police Department Gang Suppression Unit).[61]
>
> Gang members like to frequent the same places as most of us . . . malls, amusement parks, special events. They're showing up everywhere. When a gang attends a public event, the potential for violence and criminal activity is great. The resulting violence often claims innocent victims, which is why everyone is impacted by gang activity (Dallas Police Department).[62]

Gang members are routinely portrayed by law enforcement officials as sociopaths or antisocial personalities, outwardly quite normal but extremely egocentric, insensitive to others, and individuals who "actively seek out violent conflicts."[63] "Good kids" are reportedly drawn into the gang culture and transformed over time into brutal predators who possess " little or no conscience"[64] and demonstrate "a total disregard for human life."[65] Indeed, gang experts tell us that "in the gang culture moral restraints on violent impulses are seen as dysfunctional."[66] According to many police gang experts, violence is the dominant and uniting theme in the gang culture.

> The gang's ideal man is virtually identical to the romantic myth of the gunfighter of the Old West—a two-fisted, dangerous man who is quick to avenge any insult; he lives and dies by violence . . . (Ron Stallworth, Gang Intelligence Coordinator, State of Utah Department of Public Safety).[67]

Sergeant Wes McBride, a Los Angeles police officer who battled Los Angeles gangs for over a decade, has observed the transformation brought on by street gang membership. He reports:

> [There is] a definite increase in the deliberate intent to kill—we are not dealing with a string of deaths that happened because a gun happened to be handy. There is a social tolerance of the saturation of violence, which results in a complete lack of inhibitions about killing. Many [gang members] have no problem-solving skills. Their only answer is to kill the problem. In addition, there is an increased sense of effrontery and honor that is easily offended by any slight, leading to many shootings. We are dealing with people socialized to be sociopathic.[68]

Green Bay police detective Jim Swanson, the city's gang expert, would agree, having concluded that kids who join gangs "develop this gang mentality, and they do certain things that I don't think they would do if they didn't belong to a gang."[69]

Claims Regarding Gangs and High-Tech Weaponry

Most of those who police (as well as many gang scholars) contend that lethal violence among gangs has increased in recent years. Though other factors are involved, most believe this increase is due to the number and lethality of firearms possessed by gangsters. Where in the past gang members may have been armed with metal pipes, clubs, knives, or the occasional zip gun, those battling gangs today report that AK-57s and Uzzi assault weapons and semiautomatics like the MAC-10 have become their weapons of choice.

> The sophistication of the weapons utilized by gang members is constantly increasing . . . assault weapons like the UZI are becoming more and more common . . . these assault weapons are being used not only in gang versus gang confrontations, but also

against law enforcement officers (Sergeant Joseph Guzman, Los Angeles County Sheriff's Department).[70]

Our police officers, our children, our family members, are being gunned down by ... gang members, carrying military-style assault weapons ... The AK-47 is the gun of choice among gang members (Senator Diane Feinstein).[71]

Indeed, concern about the growing use of these high-powered weapons by gang members figured prominently in the passage of the Violent Crime Control and Law Enforcement Act enacted in September 1994. The Crime Bill included landmark legislation proposed by Senator Diane Feinstein (D-CA) which prohibited the manufacture, transfer, and possession of military-style assault weapons, the kinds of weaponry that are argued to be increasingly used by gangsters.

One crime of violence that has become synonymous with street gangs is the drive-by shooting, a crime that is, according to former FBI agent Roger Davis, increasing at an "alarming rate."[72] According to former Los Angeles District Attorney Ira Reiner, "The day of the 'rumble' is long gone; the day of the drive-by-shooting is here with a vengeance."[73] Sometimes a hit on a rival gang member who has invaded a gang's drug turf, sometimes the spontaneous act of youth high on drugs and/or alcohol, reported drive-bys are the most visible and frightening of gang crimes.

Claims Regarding Gangs and Illegal Drug Markets

The concern about street gangs has also intensified in the context of their alleged involvement in the sale and distribution of drugs, particularly crack cocaine. To some extent, street gangs have always been linked to illicit drugs, but during the 1980s gangs purportedly became major players in the illegal drug markets. In fact, law enforcement officials claim that the lure of enormous profits in the illegal drug trade has fueled the tremendous increase in gang memberships witnessed over the past decade.

Gangs have been involved with the lower levels of the drug trade for many years, but their participation skyrocketed with the arrival of "crack" cocaine. Almost overnight, a major industry was born, with outlets in every neighborhood, tens of thousands of new customers and thousands of new sales jobs. In slightly over a decade, street gangs have become highly involved in drug trafficking at all levels (Chief Steven Wiley, Violent Crimes and Major Offender Section of the FBI).[74]

As the sales force for this cocaine grew in the mid-1980s, the gangs were making a lot of money. They were recruiting members like never before. The new members were standing on every street corner, bus stop, and in every shopping center selling crack cocaine to anyone with five dollars (Mike Knox, a 15-year veteran of Houston Police Department's Westside Command Divisional Gang Unit).[75]

One such entrepreneurial gang that has attracted the attention of law enforcement and the media is the Gangster Disciples, based in Chicago. According to DEA official James Morgan, the gang is "incredibly well-disciplined and trained" with a "very sophisticated battle plan and a very sophisticated organization."[76] Modeled after Chicago's Italian Mafia, and with an estimated 50,000 members operating in 35 states, the Disciples are said to have a rigid, corporate hierarchy specifically designed to market illegal drugs. In addition to a "chairman," the Disciples have a board of directors, 15 "governors" who oversee operations in specific territories, "regents" and "coordinators" who distribute illegal drugs and manage security, "enforcers" who discipline those who would violate organizational policy, and "shorties" who actually execute retail-level drug sales. In Los Angeles, law enforcement officials are battling the Eight Trey Gangster Crips, a network of street gang members that is estimated to have distributed hundreds of kilos of crack and cocaine powder with street level sales of more than $10 million. According to federal authorities, the gang is "only one of perhaps a hundred or more in operation."[77]

> Within the past 10 years, American law enforcement agencies have encountered a number of criminal groups that engage in extensive drug trafficking, display unrestrained violence, and travel freely from one jurisdiction to another. . . . Many law enforcement officials today recognize a collage of ethnic groups that are organized for long-term criminal purposes, and that sometimes link together in powerful criminal alliances.[78]

Other authoritative sources affirm the existence of a nation-wide web of highly organized gang-bangers.

> Intelligence developed through investigations has revealed extensive interaction among individuals belonging to gangs across the nation (Steven Wiley, Chief of Violent Crime and Major Offender Section, FBI).[79]
>
> . . . many gang sects have extensive books, usually handwritten, of rules and regulations and gang history. These rules must be memorized. Often, gangs have meeting dates and read from their "Book," and discuss gang business. In a strange sort of way, these meetings resemble fraternity or civic meetings. Many gang members have told of being "violated" for not knowing certain portions of their knowledge when called upon by a gang leaders to recite it (Steve Nawojczyk, Arkansas Attorney General's Youth Gang Task Force).[80]
>
> Street gangs have long been considered loosely organized thugs, engaged in petty thefts and drugs on only a local level. Today's gangs are very different. A sophisticated gang operation today can claim as many as 30,000 members, crossing state lines to establish syndicates in dozens of other states. These criminal organizations engage in high-stakes narcotics and weapons trafficking, gambling, smuggling, robbery, and other equally serious crimes. Never before have gangs been so mobile and so dangerous, and the problem is spreading (Senator Diane Feinstein).[81]

Many persons hold the out-of-date view that gangs are, more or less, a local problem. The unfortunate truth, however, is that gangs now more resemble organized crime syndicates than small, romanticized neighborhood street toughs, like those once portrayed in *West Side Story* as the "Sharks" and the "Jets" (Senator Orrin Hatch).[82]

POLICE RESPONSE TO GANGS

In response to police claims regarding gangs and gang activity, federal, state, and local resources have been allocated to law enforcement agencies to develop specialized antigang suppression strategies. These strategies often involve the creation of organizational units targeting gang activity, gang identification and tracking systems, and multiagency law enforcement task forces. In 1997, over half of the country's largest law enforcement agencies had established gang units, engaging in a military-style campaign against street gangs that includes high-tech weaponry, armored vehicles, and helicopters.[83] Taking various forms, these specialized gang units sometimes comprise hundreds of law enforcement officers.

Working on the assumption that street gangs are criminal organizations, sophisticated gang tracking and identification systems have been developed. Gang rosters are touted as improving the surveillance, investigation, and monitoring of gang activity, particularly drug trafficking. The prototype is the Gang Reporting, Evaluation, and Tracking System (GREAT) developed by the Los Angeles County Sheriff's Department. Out of the estimated 500,000 to 750,000 gang members in the United States, the GREAT system currently contains 200,000 records.[84] Variations of the GREAT system have been implemented in Texas, Nevada, Hawaii, Colorado, Florida, and Illinois. During the early 1990s, legislation was introduced in both houses of Congress to establish a national gang roster. In 1995, a national gang database—the Violent Gang and Terrorist Organization File (VGTOF)—was designed and placed into operation by the Federal Bureau of Investigation.

There are scores of police officers across the country who are successfully marketing themselves as "gang experts." These officers, many of whom even have Web sites, crisscross the country providing seminars (for a fee, of course) to parents, neighborhood groups, churches, schools, and law enforcement officials. Through

Most large urban police departments in the U.S. now operate specialized units that often employ military-style equipment and tactics to deal with the gang threat.

their "gang awareness" seminars the community is helped in overcoming its denial of the problem, parents are told how to recognize early warning signs of gang activity in their children, schooled on weapons concealment techniques, taught the fundamentals of graffiti interpretation, and provided with lurid tales of gang crimes and practices. A national, school-based gang prevention program, the Gang Resistance Education and Training (GREAT), has been taught by police officers in elementary and middle schools since 1992. Designed to help children "learn how to resolve conflicts without violence, and understand how gangs and youth violence impact the quality of their lives," the GREAT program has now been offered to more than 1.5 million students in 47 states and the District of Columbia.[85] Over $10 million in federal funds have been allocated to the GREAT program for fiscal year 2000.

Police gang officers have formed regional associations and hold annual conferences with sessions on identification, intelligence gathering, graffiti, and other gang-related issues. These regional associations have been incorporated into a larger coalition of criminal justice professionals known as the National Alliance of Gang Investigators (NAGIA). Having concluded that "the scourge of gangs is a clear and present danger to our internal national security," the NAGIA holds regular meetings to share information, standardize training of gang officers, and create close partnerships between local, state, and federal law enforcement.[86]

Federal law enforcement agencies have become increasingly involved in fighting street gangs, a radical movement given that crime control has traditionally been defined as a local problem. Speaking to those troubled by the federalization of crime control, Senator Orrin Hatch (R-UT) contends that "in the case of criminal street gangs, which increasingly are moving interstate to commit crimes, it is very proper for the federal government to step in and play an important role."[87] As evidence of its commitment, the FBI has reassigned 300 agents, formerly assigned to foreign counterintelligence, to investigating urban street gangs.[88] Other federal agencies have stepped forward to form partnerships with local law enforcement efforts, including the Drug Enforcement Administration (DEA), the Bureau of Alcohol, Tobacco, and Firearms (ATF), and the Immigration and Naturalization Service (INS).

The political activity of law enforcement has been critical to the passage of a spate of local, state and federal legislation enacted over the past decade designed to control, prosecute, and punish gang members. Several states have declared gangs to be "a clear and present danger" to public safety (e.g., California Penal Code 186.21).[89] Specialized gang prosecution units have now been implemented in about a third of all large jurisdictions, staffed with attorneys familiar with local gang culture, activities, and rivalries.

Conclusion

The politicization of crime over the past several decades, and aggressive lobbying by law enforcement bureaucrats, has resulted in dramatic increases in the size and power of law enforcement. Claims-making by law enforcement necessarily entails a focus on particular individuals within the community: drug dealers, prostitutes, violent street criminals, serial killers, satanists. Obviously, these claims are not without substance. Organizational and career interests aside, the police are also motivated by a genuine desire to protect their communities. The problem, however, is the exaggeration and distortion that accompanies such claims, the deflection of public attention from more severe threats (e.g., white collar crime, domestic violence, etc.), and the imprudent use of limited resources.

Street gangs exist, as they have for generations, and no doubt commit serious crimes against persons, property, and the public order. But do law enforcement reports of the scale and scope of the gang problem today reflect the objective risks posed by such groups? Or has the gang problem been "hyped" by police in pursuit of organizational interests and career advancement? To what extent have the media been appropriated by law enforcement officials in pursuit of these goals?

Notes

1. See, for example, Jerome G. Miller. 1996. *Search and Destroy: African-American Males in the Criminal Justice System.* New York: Cambridge University Press; Victor Kappeler, Mark Blumberg, and Gary Potter. 1996. *The Mythology of Crime and Criminal Justice.* Second edition. Prospect Heights, IL: Waveland Press.
2. *The New York Times*, July 17, 1964.
3. President's Commission on Law Enforcement and Administration of Justice. 1967. *The Challenge of Crime in a Free Society.* Washington, D.C.: U.S. Government Printing Office, p. 283.
4. Samuel Walker. 1980. *Popular Justice: A History of American Criminal Justice.* New York: Oxford University Press.
5. David Burnham. 1996. *Above the Law: Secret Deals, Political Fixes, and Other Misadventures of the U.S. Department of Justice.* New York : Scribner.
6. "Nixon Comments on Law and Order," *The New York Times*, September 5, 1968.
7. Thomas E. Cronin, Tania Z. Cronin, and Michael E. Milakovich. 1981. *U.S.* v. *Crime in the Streets.* Bloomington, IN: University Press, p. 64.
8. Pamela Irving Jackson. 1989. *Minority Group Threat, Crime, and Policing: Social Context and Social Control.* New York: Praeger.
9. Ronald Reagan. 1980. Republican Platform Text, *Congressional Quarterly Almanac.* Vol. 36, pp. 58B–66B.
10. Kappeler, et al., 1996.
11. Nancy E. Marion. 1994. *A History of Federal Crime Control Initiatives, 1960–1993.* Westport, CT: Praeger.

12. George Bush. 1982. Address before a Joint Session of Congress on the State of the Union. *Public Papers of the President*. January 28, pp. 156–163.

13. Steven R. Donziger. 1995. *The Real War on Crime: The Report of the National Criminal Justice Commission*. New York: HarperPerennial.

14. Bill Clinton. 1995. *Weekly Compilation of Presidential Documents*, April 18. Vol. 30(15), p. 775.

15. Donziger, 1996.

16. Joseph J. Senna and Larry J. Siegel. 1996. *Introduction to Criminal Justice*. Seventh edition. Minneapolis: West Publishing Company, p. 393.

17. Harry E. Allen and Clifford E. Simonsen. 1998. *Corrections in America*. Upper Saddle River, NJ: Prentice Hall, p. 218.

18. Donziger, 1996, p. xv, p. xvi.

19. Kathleen Maquire, Ann Pastore, and Timothy Flanagan. 1994. *Sourcebook of Criminal Justice Statistics*. Bureau of Justice Statistics. Washington, D.C.: GPO.

20. Kathleen Maquire, Ann Pastore, and Timothy Flanagan. 1997. *Sourcebook of Criminal Justice Statistics*. Bureau of Justice Statistics. Washington, D.C.: GPO.

21. *Florida* v. *Bostwick*, 111 S. Ct. 2382 (1991); *United States* v. *Leon*, 468 U.S. 897 (1984); 21 U.S.C. §881(a); Steven B. Duke and Albert Gross. 1993. *America's Longest Drug War*. New York: G. P. Putnam; David W. Rasmussen. 1994. *The Economic Anatomy of a Drug War*. Lanham Way, MD: Rowman & Littlefield; *Terry* v. *Ohio*, 392 U.S. 1, 88 S. Ct. 1868, 20 L.E. 2d 889 (1968); Jerome H. Skolnick and James F. Fyfe. 1993. *Above the Law*. New York: The Free Press.

22. Robert Higgs. 1987. *Crisis and Leviathan: Critical Episodes in the Growth of American Government*. New York: Oxford University Press.

23. Harry G. Levine and Craig Reinarman. 1988. "The politics of America's latest drug scare." In R. Curry (ed.), *Freedom at Risk: Secrecy, Censorship, and Repression in the 1980s*. Philadelphia: Temple University Press, pp. 251–58; Mark Fishman. 1978. "Crime waves as ideology.' *Social Problems*. Vol. 25, pp. 531–43; Phillip Jenkins. 1994. *Using Murder: The Social Construction of Serial Murder*. New York: Aldine De Gruyter; Donziger, 1996.

24. Daniel Glaser. 1978. *Crime in Our Changing Society*. New York: Holt, Rinehart, and Winston, p. 22.

25. Federal Bureau of Investigation. *Crime in the United States, 1992. Uniform Crime Reports*, 1992. Washington, D.C.: Government Printing Office.

26. Jerome Miller. 1996. *Search and Destroy: African-American Males in the Criminal Justice System*. New York: Cambridge Press, p. 27.

27. Michael Rand, James P. Lynch, and David Cantor. 1997. *Criminal Victimization, 1973–1995*. U.S. Department of Justice. Bureau of Justice Statistics. Washington, D.C.: GPO; *Uniform Crime Reports, 1999*. Federal Bureau of Investigation. GPO: Washington, D.C.

28. John Bounds and Scott Boggess. 1993. *Comparison Study of UCR, NCS, and Imprisonment Rates*. National Bureau of Economic Research. University of Michigan. Ann Arbor.

29. William Chambliss. *Power, Politics, and Crime*. 1999. Boulder, CO: Westview Press, p. 2.

30. James Q. Wilson. 1984. *Thinking About Crime*. New York: Vintage Books, p. 61.

31. David H. Bayley. 1994. *Police for the Future*. New York: Oxford University Press; Malcom K. Sparrow, Mark H. Moore, and David M. Kennedy. 1990. *Beyond 911: A New Era for Policing*. New York: Basic Books; George Kelling and Catherine M. Coles. 1996. *Fixing Broken Windows: Restoring Order and Reducing Crime in Our Communities*. New York : Martin Kessler Books.

32. Bayley, 1994, p. 3.

33. Gayle M.B. Hanson. 1997. "Private policing is secure industry," *Insight on the News*, Vol. 13, p. 19.

34. Greg Shaw, Robert Shapiro, Samuel Lock, and Lawrence Jacobs. 1997. "The polls—trends: crime, the police, and civil liberties." *Public Opinion Quarterly*, Vol. 62, pp. 405–406.
35. Joseph Guzman, Sergeant. 1997. Los Angeles County Sheriff's Department. Homicide Bureau. *Hispanic Gangs*. Mimeographed copy, p. 17.
36. Robert Jackson and Wes McBride. 1995. *Understanding Street Gangs*. Costa Mesa, CA: Custom Publishers.
37. Richard Ayter. 1997. Lieutenant, Police Gang Crimes Unit, Oklahoma City, Oklahoma cited in Diane Feinstein, *The Federal Gang Violence Act*, p. 5.
38. California Attorney General. 1993. *GANGS 2000: A Call to Action*. The Attorney General's Report on the Impact of Criminal Street Gangs on Crime and Violence. California Department of Justice, Division of Law Enforcement, Bureau of Investigation, p. 1.
39. Michael Nichols. 1994. Sergeant and Supervisor Gang Squad, St. Louis Police Department. Prepared statement at Hearing Before the Subcommittee on Juvenile Justice of the Committee on the Judiciary, United States Senate. 103rd Congress. *The Gang Problem in American: Formulating an Effective Federal Response*. February 9, p. 20.
40. John Moore. 2000. Cited in "The Youth Gang Epidemic That Was—or Wasn't," *Youth Today*. Vol. 9(8), p. 48.
41. Scott Decker and K. Kempf-Leonard. 1995. "Constructing Gangs: The Social Definition of Youth Activities." In M. Klein, C. Maxon, and J. Miller (eds.), *The Modern Gang Reader*. Los Angeles: Roxbury Publishing, pp. 112–137; Malcolm Klein and Cheryl Maxson. 1989. "Street gang violence." In M. Wolfgang and N. Weiner (eds.), *Violent Crime, Violent Criminals*. Beverly Hills, CA: Sage, pp. 198–234.
42. Albert Cohen. 1990. "Forward and overview." In R. Huff (ed.), *Gangs in America*. Beverly Hills, CA: Sage, p. 9.
43. Malcolm Klein. 1995. *The American Street Gang: Its Nature, Prevalence and Control*. New York: Oxford University Press, p. 89.
44. Klein, 1995.
45. Wood County Gang Task Force and Youth Violence Prevention. 1998. Wood County Prosecuting Attorney's Office. Bowling Green, Ohio. p. 1.
46. U.S. Department of Justice. 2000. Highlights of the 1999 National Youth Gang Survey. OJJDP Fact Sheet. Office of Juvenile Justice and Delinquency Prevention.
47. U.S. Department of Justice. 2000.
48. Institute for Law and Justice. 1993. *Gang Prosecution in the United States*. Mimeographed copy. September. Alexandria, VA.
49. C. Ronald Huff. 1990. *Gangs in America* (ed.). Second edition. Thousand Oaks: Sage Publications, 1996.
50. Klein, 1995.
51. Steve Nawojczyk. 1997. *Street Gang Dynamics*. Advisor to the Arkansas Attorney General's Youth Gang Task Force. The Nawojczyk Group, p. 4 .
52. Memphis Police Department. 1998. *Gang Awareness*. Organized Crime Unit. p. 1.
53. San Luis Obispo County Gang Task Force. 1997. *Street Gangs: A Guide to Community Awareness*, p. 3.
54. Huff, 1990.
55. Federal Bureau of Investigation. 1999. *Crime in the United States, 1999. Uniform Crime Reports*, 1992. Washington, D.C.: Government Printing Office.
56. See Klein, 1995; Irving Spergel. 1995. *The Youth Gang Problem*. New York: Oxford University Press.

57. G. David Curry, Richard A. Ball, and Scott H. Decker. 1996. "Estimating the national scope of gang crime from law enforcement data." *Research in Brief.* U.S. Department of Justice. National Institute of Justice, Office of Justice Programs. Washington, D.C., August.

58 G. David Curry and Scott Decker. 1995. "The Impact of Gang Membership on Participation in Crime and Delinquency." A review of the literature prepared for Abt, Associates and the National Institute of Justice. Mimeographed copy. July, p. 1.

59. Guzman, 1995, p. 14.

60. U.S. Department of Justice. 1998. Drug Enforcement Administration. *Briefing Book: Crime, Violence, and Demographics.* Washington, D.C.: Government Printing Office, p. 1.

61. Austin, Texas Police Department. 1998. Gang Suppression Unit. *Basic Gang Facts* p. 1.

62. Dallas Police Department. 1998. *A Parent's Guide to "Gangland."* Web page. Dallas, Texas, p. 1.

63. San Luis Obispo County Gang Task Force, 1998, p. 3.

64. Guzman, 1995, p. 14.

65. California Attorney General, 1993, p. 1.

66. Norman Randloph, Alan McEvoy, and Edsel Erickson. 1998. *Youth Gangs: Guidelines for Educators and Community Leaders.* Holmes Beach, FL: Learning Publications, p. 3.

67. Ron Stallworth. 1994. Gang Intelligence Coordinator, State of Utah Department of Public Safety. Testimony before U.S. Senate Judiciary Committee, February 23.

68. Wes McBride, Sergeant. 1992. Cited in Ira Reiner. 1992. District Attorney, City of Los Angeles. *Gangs, Crime and Violence in Los Angeles: Findings and Proposals from the District Attorney's Office.* National Youth Gang Information Center, NYGIC Document D0049, p. 86.

69. Green Bay Press–Gazette (WI). March 7, 1999. "City gangs getting younger, rougher."

70. Guzman, 1995, p. 7.

71. Diane Feinstein. 1995. Senator, United State Senate. Floor speech in support of assault weapons ban legislation, December 11, 1995, p. 2, p. 3.

72. Roger H. Davis. 1995. "Cruising for trouble: gang-related drive-by shootings." *The FBI Law Enforcement Bulletin.* Vol. 64, p.16.

73. Ira Reiner. 1992. District Attorney, City of Los Angeles. *Gangs, Crime and Violence in Los Angeles: Findings and Proposals from the District Attorney's Office.* National Youth Gang Information Center, NYGIC Document D0049, p. 56.

74. Steven Wiley. 1997. Chief of Violent Crimes and Major Offender Section, FBI. Testimony before the Senate Committee on the Judiciary, April 23, p.1, p. 2.

75. Mike Knox. 1995. *Gangsta in the House: Understanding Gang Culture.* Troy, MI: Momentum Books, p. 59.

76. James Morgan. 1996. Special Agent, Drug Enforcement Agency, cited in Ann S. Tyson "How Nation's largest gang runs its drug enterprise." *Christian Science Monitor*, July 15, p. 1.

77. Jordan Bonfante. 1995. "Entrepreneurs of Crack." *Time.* Vol. 145 (8), p. 22, February 27.

78. United States General Accounting Office. 1991. *Nontraditional Organized Crime: Law Enforcement Officials' Perspectives on Five Criminal Groups.* Report to the Chairman, Permanent Subcomittee on Investigations, Committee on Governmental Affairs, United States Senate, p. 2.

79. Wiley, 1997, p. 2.

80. Nawojczyk, 1997, p. 6.

81. Feinstein, 1997, p. 1.

82. Orrin Hatch. 1997. United States Senator. Prepared statement before the U.S. Senate hearing on Gangs: a National Crisis. April 23, p. 1.

83. Spergel, 1995; Klein, 1995.

84. U.S. Department of Justice, Bureau of Justice Assistance. 1997. *Urban Street Gang Enforcement.* Washington, D.C.: U.S. Government Printing Office.

85. Gang Resistance Education and Training Program (GREAT). 1999. The Bureau of Alcohol, Tobacco and Firearms. Washington, D.C. Web site.

86. The National Alliance of Gang Investigators Associations. 1999. *About NAGIA*. Web Site, p. 1.

87. Hatch, 1997, p. 2.

88. William Sessions. 1992. "FBI reassigns 300 agents to violent crimes." *The Police Chief.* Vol. 59(10), p. 1.

89. See, for example, California Penal Code 186.21;West Supp. 1993.

chapter 4

Crime, Gangs, and the News Media

Our conceptions of crime and justice are generally not based on our personal experience. Crime, particularly violent crime, is a relatively rare phenomenon. Few Americans have contact with the justice system beyond the occasional traffic citation. Consequently, the public relies heavily on the media for information about the prevalence of crime, images of criminals, and the effectiveness of the police, the courts, and prisons.[1] Research has clearly and consistently shown, however, that the news media are more likely to misinform than inform, presenting consumers with a seriously distorted picture of the crime problem and the criminal justice system.

Even fewer Americans have direct experience with street gangs. Nonetheless, perhaps most have firm conceptions of *gang-bangers* and a crude sense of the danger posed by such persons. Such perceptions are the product of intense and sustained media coverage, particularly over the past several years. Images of swaggering young minority males in $200 sneakers, thick gold chains, pagers, and semiautomatic weapons have become media icons for urban crime.

This chapter examines media coverage of street gangs in the context of crime news more generally. The media have come under severe criticism for the manner in which they collect, process, and present stories of crime. Critics rail against the amount of space and time given to atypical, violent crime stories relative to other, often more pressing, public issues and problems (e.g., education, health care, etc.). Public fears are fanned, critics contend, simply to sell newspapers and attract viewers. Perhaps even more disturbing is the media's dependence on law enforcement for information about crime. Crime stories are based almost exclusively on police reports and quotations. As a result, law enforcement officials have become the primary definers of crime in society. This reliance on the police extends to information regarding gangs as well, meaning that the public's perception of the gangs is based largely on police claims regarding the extent and nature of the problem. As primary definers of crime and gangs, the police have been able to steer criminal justice policy in directions that serve organizational, rather than public, interests.

EXTENT AND NATURE OF CRIME NEWS

Prevalence of Crime News

It should come as no surprise to learn that crime is one of the principal components of news reporting in the United States. Within newspapers, crime news accounts for as much as one-quarter of all news reported, one of the top five overall categories.[2] Though generally appearing in the most important sections (front pages, at the top, etc.), it is not unusual for crime news to appear throughout a newspaper—even the obituary pages.[3] Coverage by local television stations follows closely, with approximately 20 percent of air time committed to crime news.[4]

In a recent and comprehensive effort to document the prevalence of crime news, on March 11, 1998 the Rocky Mountain Media Watch (RMMW) taped and analyzed 102 local television newscasts from 52 U.S. metropolitan areas.[5] The findings revealed that, on average, less than one-half (41.3 percent) of the broadcast was actually devoted to news. Among the 26 news topics, crime stories (most often of murders) were dominant, representing 26.9 percent of all news stories. Four stations in large markets, the group argued, were devoting so much time to crime and violence that they were failing to report on issues important to the community, such as education, local elections, and AIDS. RMMW was so disturbed by its findings that it petitioned the Federal Communications Commission to deny these stations' requests for license renewal.

Not only is there a great deal of it, crime news is also read and remembered by a greater proportion of consumers than any other type of news. In a study of Chicago newspaper readers, Doris Graber questioned respondents on selected crime (e.g., individual crimes, drug crimes, gun control, etc.) and noncrime topics (e.g., education, Congress, state government, foreign affairs, etc.).[6] Not only was the recall rate for crime stories higher, respondents also reported a higher degree of involvement with crime stories, demonstrated by readers having more reactions to crime than noncrime stories and that they were more likely to relate crime news to previous or current experiences. Watching, listening, and reading about crime is so popular that it has been described as a daily ritual for Americans.[7]

Coverage of crime in the mass media, therefore, is not only selective but is a distortion of the everyday world of crime.

Richard Quinney. The Social Reality of Crime, *1970.[8]*

Distortions in Crime Reporting

These consumption patterns would be less troublesome if the information provided by the media accurately depicted the crime problem. Unfortunately, accumulated research over the past several decades has firmly documented the lack of correspondence between the media's coverage of criminal events and the reality of crime. Distortions are evident in many ways. The media, for instance, give us the impression that crime rates are continually increasing, frequently depicting crime as a "spreading cancer" or a "battle" at risk of being lost without an immediate and overwhelming show of force.[9] As evidence of this inclination, in 1998 the Center for Media and Public Affairs reported that, though national homicide rates had fallen by 20 percent since 1990, the number of murder stories on network newscasts actually rose by 600 percent.[10] To be fair, on occasion the media do report declines in crime, but they appear to do so reluctantly and almost always find a way to qualify the positive trends.

> **"Ominous Trends Undercut Dip in City's Crime Figures"**
> (*Boston Globe,* August 15, 1994)

> **"Crime Statistics: The Whole Truth?" Law Enforcement:** Statistics provide only a limited picture of general crime trends, experts say.
> (*Orange County Register,* December 4, 1994)

> **"America's Silent Victims: How Much Crime is There?"**
> (*Indianapolis Star,* August 21, 1994)

> **"Rise in Teen Population Might Mean More Crime"**
> (*Christian Science Monitor,* January 9, 1996)

> **"Good News on Crime Rates May be Lull Before the Storm"**
> (*Daily Herald,* December 30, 1997)

Even when coverage of declining crime rates is not qualified , it is more than negated by the prevalence and nature of crime news. According to media critic David Krajicek, the occasional report of a positive crime news story represents little more than " a dinghy bobbing in a rolling sea of information about crime."[11]

The media also lead us to believe that violent crime is much more common than it actually is. As a rule, the least frequent crimes are reported most often.[12] One study of newspaper coverage found that one in four crime stories was about murder, yet murder represented only 0.2 percent of all reported crimes in the city.[13] A study of Chicago newspapers by Sanford Sherizen revealed that though larceny/theft was 117 times more prevalent than murder, homicides received ten times the coverage.[14] He also found that while 9 percent of index crimes known to police were robberies, nearly one-quarter of crimes news stories concerned robberies. In New Orleans, researchers Joseph Sheley and Cindy Ashkins noted that 45 percent of crimes reported in a local newspaper involved murder and robbery (80 percent in local television newscasts), though these offenses represented less than 13 percent of that city's total crime count.[15] In one large newspaper in New York City, one-half of all crime stories pertained to robberies but robberies were only 14 percent of all crimes reported to the police.[16]

The focus on violent crimes is not reserved to newspapers and television broadcasts. Popular weekly news magazines provide similarly distorted views. For example, among articles on crime appearing in *Time* magazine in the post-World War II period, nearly three-quarters have dealt with crimes of violence.[17]

Because violent crimes dominate news coverage, the portrait of criminal offenders conveyed is also a distortion. Indeed, crime today has become synonymous with the acts of the *predator criminal*, the dark, menacing figure who springs from the shadows to rape, rob, and murder.[18] Though such offenders do not represent the common criminal, contemporary mass media have raised the phantom of the predator criminal from a relatively minor character to a common, ever-present one. As with other icons, the predator criminal represent a largely unquestioned set of beliefs about the world, a constructed reality in which perceptions are often more powerful than reality itself, and where the mass media have the ability to shape the real world to fit the image presented by the media. As Surette notes, predator crime has become "a metaphor for a world gone berserk, for life out of control."[19]

Historically, the image of the predator criminal has long dominated both the news and entertainment media. By the 1850s, the image of the criminal presented by the media had shifted from earlier, romantic portrayals to more negative images. Over the course of the 20th century, portraits of the predator criminal have become more animalistic, less rational, their crimes more brutal, senseless, and sensational, and their victims more random, vulnerable, and innocent. Criminals are depicted as "exemplifying evil . . . Driven by innate, immorality, greed, or madness, or—more recently—the effects of illegal drugs or the criminogenic 'peer pressure' inherent in youth gang subcultures."[20] Today, the prevailing criminal predator icon has become closely associated with young, black, urban males.[21] In recent years a new twist has been added to the criminal predator stereotype, that of the "super predator." This term was coined by political scientist John DiIulio to refer to an emerging generation of more than a quarter of a million ruthless sociopaths. The icon and prediction were presented to a national audience in early 1995 in a conservative weekly magazine. Within months they were picked up by media outlets across the country. Though the concept, and DiIulio's prediction, has been denounced as hype by many criminologists (even DiIulio has since recanted), the super predator icon has been firmly established in the minds of the American

◆◆

> By the year 2010, there will be approximately 270,000 more juvenile super-predators on the streets than there were in 1990.
>
> *John DiIulio, "The Coming of the Super-Predators," 1995.*[22]

public and according to Vince Schiraldi, executive director of the Center on Juvenile and Criminal Justice, has left its fingerprint on national criminal justice policy.[23]

Victims are also a point of distortion, with the media's messages suggesting that the elderly and whites are the most frequent victims of predatory crimes.[24] From national victimization surveys, we know such groups do not represent the typical victims of violent crime. Persons between the ages of 12 and 19, for example, are 20 times more likely than those ages 65 and older to be victims of violent crimes.[25] Blacks are twice as likely as whites to be victims of robbery and nearly seven times as likely to be homicide victims. One out of every 21 black men can expect to be murdered—a death rate double that of American servicemen in World War II.[26]

Perhaps more important for perpetuating the criminal predator stereotype, the news media fosters the impression that all are equally likely to become the next victim. Henry Brownstein's study of crime news in New York City during the late 1980s clearly illustrates this particular form of distortion. In the numerous stories on crack cocaine published between 1986 and 1990, intense print media coverage of a small number of events developed a theme suggesting that drug violence was spreading and becoming more random in selection of victims. The media, according to Brownstein, "encouraged a belief in the growing vulner-ability of white, middle-class people" in large part simply to sell more papers.[27] To be sure, street crime did increase during those years, but according to Brownstein the number of innocent bystanders who were victims of violence remained quite small. Moreover, the violence continued to be directed not at whites, but at poor, inner city minority members. This kind of distortion is also reported by Robert Elias after conducting a content analysis of crime stories in *Time, Newsweek,* and *U.S. News and World Report* magazines from 1956 to 1991.[28] Elias found that these magazines, through selective coverage, fostered the concept of one-on-one offenses committed by strangers, even though most crime involves people who know one another.

Aside from random violence, national crime statistics indicate that the probability of victimization by a stranger is extremely small. Strangers were responsible for less than 2 out of every 10 violent crimes in 1998 (Table 4–1).[29] The probability of being murdered by a stranger that year was 1 in 100,000.

TABLE 4–1   **Crimes of Violence Committed by Strangers, 1998**

Crime	Rate per 1,000 U.S. Residents
All crimes of violence	18.2
Murder and nonnegligent murder	.01
Rape/sexual assault	.4
Robbery	2.8
Assault	4.9
Aggravated assault	4.5
Simple assault	10.4

MEDIA COVERAGE OF THE CRIMINAL JUSTICE SYSTEM

According to career journalists Wallace Westfeldt and Tom Wicker, the press once served a vital function in our democratic system, closely monitoring and reporting the activities of those institutions charged with enforcing our system of criminal law. Based on their observations of the press's coverage of the justice system over the past several decades, Westfeldt and Wicker conclude that the criminal justice system today "operates mostly unobserved and unchecked by a lethargic press devoted more nearly to profit than to public service" (p. xii).[30]

Compared to crime events, the news media provide relatively little coverage of the criminal justice system. That reporting is also highly selective, distorted, and uncritical. Most stories deal with the initial stages of the system (discovery of the crime and arrest); post-arrest procedures are apparently deemed less newsworthy.[31] These police-related stories generally emphasize the crime-fighting role of police and suggest that the police are more effective in controlling crime than the hard numbers indicate.[32] For example, while the FBI's Uniform Crime Reports reveals that arrests occur for only one in every five serious crimes, 90 percent or more of media-covered crimes are solved.[33] Furthermore, criticism of the police by journalists is rare; problems, when reported, are portrayed as isolated rather than systemic.[34]

In the judicial system, arraignments, trials, and sentencing hearings receive the most coverage. Since the Supreme Court approved cameras in the courtroom (*Chandler* v. *Florida*, 1981), television coverage of courtroom activities, particularly trials, has increased dramatically.[35] Nonetheless, court coverage is often biased, uninformed, and incomplete. Reporters portray court activities as morality plays, underreport civil rights violations, and give large headlines to front-page coverage of cases in which a suspect was freed because of "technicalities." In hearings and trials, bits of testimony are selected based on what the reporter believes is more interesting. Critics contend this kind of coverage results from reporters simply not knowing how the system works, their impatience with legal jargon and procedures, and complexities of courtroom arguments and decisions. Supportive of this criticism, most court stories presented are major felonies that occur in courts of general jurisdiction; appellate decisions, because of their complexity, are thus rarely covered.

The correctional system receives virtually no coverage, except occasionally to highlight some particular problem or policy.[36] Escapes, riots, and parole decisions are deemed newsworthy because they can be used to fuel public fears and stimulate media consumption. The lack of attention to corrections in comparison to policing can be explained by two factors:

1. The press (perhaps accurately) assumes that the public is no longer interested in lawbreakers once they are behind bars.
2. Correctional stories are difficult to produce because of limited access and a lack of systematic links to correctional officials.

In short, there is little systematic coverage of the criminal justice system. Media reports provide the public with little valid information about the operation and effectiveness of the justice system. Ray Surette is certainly correct in concluding that

> Learning about the criminal justice system from the news media is analogous to learning geology from volcanic eruptions. You will surely be impressed and entertained, but the information you receive will not accurately reflect the common daily reality, whether you're looking at volcanoes or the criminal justice system.[37]

MEDIA COVERAGE OF GANGS

The public's primary source of information about gangs, and a major actor in the gang phenomenon itself, is the media.[38] Coverage of gangs has exploded during recent years. A search of major U.S. newspapers and magazines from 1983 to 1999 (Figure 4–1) reveals that media coverage of gangs increased by nearly 2500 percent.[39]

While the extent to which this kind of national coverage accurately reflected an increased gang threat cannot be determined, the findings from a study of gang news in Hawaii raise serious doubts. Paul Perrone and Meda Chesney-Lind conducted a content analysis of the *Honolulu Star Bulletin* for 1987 through 1996. While there was no evidence of a dramatic increase in gang membership or gang activity, over those 10 years the coverage of gangs in the newspaper increased by 4000 percent![40]

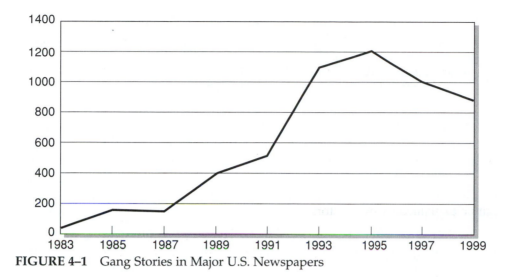

FIGURE 4–1   Gang Stories in Major U.S. Newspapers

As with crime in general, the media's coverage of gangs is distorted in a number of ways. Little accurate or useful information is thus actually provided to the public about the extent and nature of the gang problem in this country. Noted gang researcher Walter Miller opines:

> A prime source of misconception about gangs is the mass media. Almost everyone except those whose professional activities bring them in direct and continuing contact with gangs depends on information from media coverage. What the media choose to report about gangs, the kinds of gangs they select for attention, and even whether they choose to report on gangs at all, are determined by considerations only indirectly related to the actual situation. Most of what the average observer "knows" about gangs stems from a series of editorial decisions oriented primarily to the question "What is newsworthy?" rather than "What is accurate?"[41]

One popular misconception comes from media reports linking the growth of gangs to the migration of big-city gangs to mid-size and small cities. Such a conclusion is not supported by the research: Most gangs emerge from indigenous groupings within communities.[42] Neither do gangs, as the media frequently reports, dominate crack cocaine markets.[43] Gang members do sell crack, and other drugs as well, but use is far more common than sales and even involvement in sales is low.

Perhaps the greatest distortion concerns gang violence. Gang scholar Malcolm Klein examined newspaper coverage of street gangs in Los Angeles and found that most stories focused on violent offenses: shootings, stabbings, and beatings. Arrest statistics, however, indicated that gang members were far more likely to be charged with property crimes, drug offenses, and truancy.[44]

◆◆ _____

. . . media accounts are not to be trusted as a true picture of gang behavior.

John Hagedorn, People and Folks, *1988.*[45]

Critical of his own newspaper's focus on gang violence, *Los Angeles Times* reporter David Freed notes that in 1991 the paper carried 411 gang shootings involving 615 victims; incidents involving another 8,000 crime victims received no mention in the press.[46] John Hagedorn similarly found little correspondence between the Milwaukee Sentinel's coverage of local gangs and his own in-depth research of gangs and gang activity in that city.[47]

Like crime stories generally, media reports of gang crime are highly inflammatory and sensationalized. Stories on even minor confrontations involving gangs typically include references to "urban terrorism," "war," "hoodlum bands," and "gang war battles."

> If many American ghettos now resemble Beirut, *urban terrorists* like Hagan are largely responsible, acting as roving gangs peddling drugs and violence and terror. Despite the fratricide among gangs, most of their victims are innocent bystanders. . . . Hungry for customers, a growing number of gangs are going national, with black gangs like Los Angeles' Crips and Chicago's Disciples establishing franchises in cities from Seattle to Shreveport. (*LA Times*, August 24, 1987)
>
> Whole sections of urban America are being written off as *anarchic badlands*, places were cops fear to go . . . (*U.S. News and World Report*, April 10, 1980)

In the war between gangs, the news media suggest no one is safe, that anyone could become the next causality. One national newspaper reports that "[e]veryone is potential fodder to be a victim."[48] Naive media consumers are even instructed on how to reduce their risks of confrontation with a *gangsta* with a fragile ego and a hair trigger.

> Keep your eyes to yourself. Read your paperback. Read your magazine. Do not make eye contact. They are children so wary of any "dis" they might "smoke" you for staring. (*Mother Jones*, January–February 1994).

Metaphors are used frequently depicting gangs as a "terminal disease " and the tone of reporting generally encourages a fatalistic attitude toward the gang problem.

> Gangs are growing like a cancer. (*U.S. News and World Report*, April 8, 1991)
>
> The time has come to talk of gangstas. Actually, the time is long past. We should've talked of gangstas 10 or 15 years ago when Southern California killers made mass murder a drive-through convenience. Should've broached the discussion when the boys

in the 'hood started turning on one another with savage ferocity and the graveyards began to fill with children not yet old enough to shave. . . . But we didn't speak up . . . And now here we sit, in the grip of gangstas . . . (*Miami Herald*, September 19, 1993)

Modern gangs are well organized, and most of their members are more concerned with being ostracized than with the eventuality of bleeding to death on the street. . . . If there are solutions to the gang plague, they will not be easy to effect. (*Arizona Republic*, April 18, 1993)

UNDERSTANDING MEDIA COVERAGE OF CRIME AND GANGS

How can we account for the manner in which the media cover crime and gangs? Various explanations have been offered. Under the *market model*, the media are simply giving their customers what they are interested in reading or viewing.[49] The primary goal of the news media is, of course, profit; and market research shows that people are interested in reading and watching crime news.[50] Thus the media are simply providing objective, albeit stylized, information on the kinds of crime stories that will attract consumers, and thus advertisers. The most compelling evidence against the market model is the lack of correspondence between events as reported by the media and accounts offered by informed outside experts such as Stanley Cohen and Jock Young:

> The media's portrayals here are often very mythological—depicting worlds with well-structured delinquent gangs, an all-embracing Mafia, crazed dope fiends, drug pushers who corrupt their innocent victims, women who deliberately invite rapists, muggers who hold law-abiding communities in terror, police who spend most of their time on the streets investigating crime . . . These are all characterizations which criminological research has consistently contradicted.[51]

Nonetheless, it may be true that media coverage of crime is a reflection of the public's apparent fascination with gore and pathos.[52] Some have suggested that the attraction to violent crime stories is part of a complex psychological process known as "downward comparison" in which individuals feel better by comparing themselves to others worse off.[53] Author Jack Katz believes the public is attracted to crime news because it speaks to the "existential dilemmas" or moral questions each one of us confront in our lives on a daily basis.[54] According to Katz, stories of vicious and audacious crimes are used by readers and viewers to maintain their own moral boundaries, to reinforce daily "their moral sensibilities through shock and impulses of outrage."[55]

A second explanation for the prevalence and nature of crime news is the *dominant ideology model*, based on Antonio Gramsci's Marxist concept of hegemony.[56] Gramsci argued that capitalist societies are ordered and maintained through a combination of coercion and consent. Though coercion is a necessary element of order, social life functions more smoothly when the masses consent. Because the dominant or ruling class has the greatest investment in the status quo, it uses its control over the intellectual means of production—televison, newspapers, magazines, etc.—to cultivate and maintain a world view consistent with its interests. Important news is disregarded, reality distorted, and public opinion shaped to manage and mitigate the conflicts inherent in a class-based society. Images of crime and gangs are constructed to deflect attention from the crimes committed by the powerful against the masses.

The Production of Crime News: The Role of Law Enforcement

Like the market model, the dominant ideology model has been criticized for being simplistic and inadequate. Both ignore the organizational realities of news production.[57] A more convincing explanation for the media's coverage of crime points to the process through which crime stories are collected and the criteria used to determine newsworthiness. Each day the media are confronted with a large number of potential crime stories, simply because (nonviolent) crime is consistently available and abundant.[58] To make the production of crime news more manageable, the media routinize the task by placing themselves in positions where there is *easy access to credible crime news stories*. Obviously, there is a number of potential sources of crime information. Reporters could, for example, interview the offender, victim, and any witnesses involved in a particular crime. Statements from those directly involved, however, might be judged by readers or viewers as biased and lacking credibility. There is also a wide array of knowledge sources available— official documents, texts, surveys, and trend statistics, for example. Such sources are, however, rarely consulted simply because of the pressure to meet deadlines.

Instead, journalists limit their news-gathering to press releases and interview quotations from source organizations, primarily the police.[59] By relying on police, crime news becomes easy news and also offers journalists protections from claims of bias. In every city across the country, police supply news organizations with a steady stream of crime incidents ("crime blotters"). In smaller towns, information regarding all crimes may be supplied; in large urban areas, police usually provide only a summary of a subset of crime events. Moreover, most cities have full-time reporters at police stations and are frequently provided with the written reports of crimes submitted by investigative officers.

In the past, the police adopted essentially a reactive approach to the media, either defending their actions when questioned or criticized and supplying information on crime or the organization. Over the past several decades the police have become much more proactive, selectively disclosing information to the media on a regular basis in an effort to cultivate a positive image of their organization to the public.[60] One clear indication of this more active approach has been the creation of the public information officer (PIO). Prior to this organizational role, interaction with the media was generally ad hoc and idiosyncratic.[61] The PIO represents a new, formal link between the police and the media and provides a consistent and carefully filtered account of law enforcement policies and activities. In a sense, the real reporter is the PIO, often writing news releases that are cited in whole or part, but always contributing substantially to the crime news story.[62] Information from PIOs is cited as fact; reporters rarely attempt to substantiate that information through further investigation.

The police are willing to invest substantial resources in their relationships with the media because of the benefits that can be obtained. They recognize that the news media are, in a very real sense, a part of the police apparatus and can be put to good use.[63] To that end, the media are often provided space (newsroom facilities), placed on organizational charts, and included in police operational manuals. Media scholar Sanford Sherizen observed the benefits of the press to police over two decades ago:

> For the police, either as a department or for individual officers, crime reporters provide relationships with benefits. The police have a vested interest in crime news appearing in newspapers and other media. Their position as authorities on crime is reinforced as their views and opinions about crime develop from news reports on crime. As crimes become more publicly known, the almost instinctive response of the public is to seek out more police. Thus, the more crimes which become known, the more aid the police may be able to gain in seeking increases in departmental budgets. Further, crime news results in a strengthening of the police view of the causes and solutions to the crime problem.[64]

Crime reporters are generally "cubs"—young, green, and not yet qualified for the more prestigious beats.[65] With no training, cubs are placed on police beats, often working out of stations and essentially becoming subunits within the police organization. Over time, these young reporters become socialized into the police culture to the point where they come to share the same understanding of and attitudes toward crime as the police.[66]

Due to the dependence of the news media, the police are allowed to shape public images of crime and crime control. Reporters simply serve as conduits for police views of crime while at the same time presenting their reports as unbiased, thus making "objective what is truly an official interpretation of reality."[67] By simply rewriting police releases as crime news items, by failing to think critically about the processes and events observed, and by failing to ask pertinent questions, the police become the primary definers of crime and crime control to the public.

◆◆▶ _____

> The police are the primary definers of crime . . . they delineate the phenomenon
> they subsequently control.
>
> *Renee Goldsmith Kasinsky, "Patrolling the Facts: Media, Cops, and Crime,"*
> *1994.*[68]

_____

The bottom line is that the public learns little about crime from the news media. Since police are, in essence, the gatekeepers, selecting which crimes to pass along to reporters and which to withhold, and thus an unrepresentative view of crime is presented.[69] Moreover, only police perspectives on crime are generally presented, omitting or marginalizing competing ideologies.

Determining What Is Newsworthy

The media do, however, retain considerable autonomy in terms of what, and *how*, to print or broadcast. A number of general criteria of newsworthiness have been identified and an event is most likely to be selected as news if one or more of these elements are present. Though there is no "secret crime-reporting manual . . . the rules do exist, and every crime reporter in the United States learns them."[70]

Above all, a story must be simple and unambiguous so that it can easily be followed by an audience. This standard perhaps explains why there is so little coverage of white-collar crime. Events are more likely to be selected if they are *novel, unexpected*, and/or *dramatic*. In journalism, "ordinary crime is not news." Thus the news media tend to report only "exception, unusual, and violent crimes."[71] Crimes involving wealthy or prominent people—either as victims or perpetrators—will get more attention than crimes involving the poor and obscure. Victims in high-status occupations also get attention: bankers, doctors, lawyers, stockbrokers. Crimes against secretaries, clerks, and cooks are less likely to be reported.[72]

Also more likely to appear in the morning paper or evening broadcast are crimes involving multiple victims, and random acts of violence and victimization that are particularly cruel. Location is important. Gunfire in a public park will receive considerably more attention than stray bullets fired from the back yard of a crack house. Events are also more likely to be included as news if they can be situated in some broader concept or "theme."[73] A crime incident is rarely reported unless the journalist sees it as related to a past or emerging trend in criminal activity.

CRIME NEWS, ATTITUDES, AND PUBLIC POLICY

Given the nature of crime news, one would expect to find very strong relationships between exposure to crime news and perceptions of crime and fear of victimization. The findings, however, are equivocal. Numerous studies report inconsistent findings regarding media consumption and the individual's perception of crime rates, the relative seriousness of crime compared to other social problems, and fear of crime.[74] The lack of consistent findings is due largely to differences in the manner in which key concepts in these studies have been operationalized. As an example, in some research, exposure to crime news has been measured by extensive content analysis of multiple newspapers coupled with a series of questions regarding readership patterns. In other studies, exposure is measured by a single question regarding how frequently one "comes across" crime news stories in the newspaper.[75] What is clear is that the use of more detailed operationalizations leads to much stronger relationships between media, perceptions of crime, and fear.

More sophisticated methodologies also allow the researcher to specify mediating variables in the relationships. Linda Heath, for example, performed a content analysis of newspapers in 26 cities that varied in terms of the sensationalism of crime (bizzare or violent), the extent to which crime was presented as random, and location of the crime. She then conducted telephone interviews with residents of those cities regarding their readership and perceptions of crime. Her findings were intriguing. Reports of local crimes that were sensational or random were associated with higher levels of fear; reports of nonlocal random or sensational crime were correlated with lower levels of fear. Heath concluded that

> The more newspapers print articles about criminals in other places running amok, picking victims at random, and trampling social norms, the more secure readers feel in their own environments. In essence, readers like the grass to be browner on the other side of the fence, and the browner the better. Far from frightening, reports of grisly, bizarre crimes in other cities are reassuring. Readers are still exposed to some reports of crime that occur locally, but the severity and outrageousness of such crimes appear to be judged in comparison with crimes from other places. When crimes are occurring on the local turf, however, the tables are turned . . . Readers do not appreciate criminals choosing their victims at random (or, at least, media accounts that make it appear so). Reports of crime that lack rhyme or reason are frightening. If the victim apparently did nothing to precipitate the crime, then the reader can do nothing to avoid the crime. If, on the other hand, the victim took some action that made him or her more vulnerable to the victimization, then the reader can avoid that action and presumably remain safe . . . The unexpected, the quirky, the heinous crimes that are reported in newspapers increase fear of crime among readers in that crime locality, even if the reporting style itself is nonsensational.[76]

In short, newspaper reporting of crime appears to affect the reader's fear of crime differently depending how that news is presented; more specifically, newspaper coverage of crime in other cities makes people feel safe by comparison.

The Media and Agenda-Setting

Studies have, however, consistently demonstrated an *agenda-setting* influence on the public by the media.[77] Agenda-setting refers to the process involving the transmission, from news sources to the person, information that gives certain cues as to the importance of particular social issues.[78] Simply put, the more a person reads the newspaper or watches television newscasts, the more his or her judgments about the importance of issues correspond to the value attributed to those issues by the media. Though the agenda-setting effect of the media is strong, it is not simple or direct, the impact contingent on such factors as age, sex, socioeconomic status, attentiveness, and personal experience. We get some sense of how great the media's influence is from a study of public opinion shifts by Benjamin Page and his colleagues. These researchers found that even a single commentary by a news professional—an anchor person, field reporter, or special correspondent—in support of a particular policy position was followed by a 4 percentage point change in public opinion![79]

The Media and Public Perceptions of the Gang Problem

Findings from two studies suggest that the media shape the public's perception of the gang problem. In a survey of residents in a small city in Wisconsin, Susan Takata and Richard Zevitz (1990) found that adults were more likely than youth to describe the threat of gangs as "very serious, " a pattern ascribed to the fact that adults were more likely to have relied on news reporting for their information about gangs in the city.[80]

A second survey of adults in Indianapolis by Douglas Pryor and Edmund McGarrell more clearly demonstrates the impact of the media on assessments of the gang problem.[81] While most survey respondents did not view gangs as a serious problem in their neighborhood, those who had watched a gang story on a television newscast were more likely to perceive gangs as "quite" serious in other parts of the city. Pryor and McGarrell concluded:

> For most individuals, youth gang crime is seen as a serious, escalating, and dangerous problem, but one that is a problem "over there"—that is, in other parts of the city. We suggest that this reflects the tendency for perceptions of youth gang crime in "other areas" to be shaped by stereotypes and media presentations.[82]

The Media and Criminal Justice Policy

The media can influence criminal justice policy in three ways.[83]

1. The media can spark reform by focusing attention on specific issues. This is relatively easy to do, given the media's tendency to exploit and sensationalize high-profile events. By focusing on an issue and providing substantial and sustained coverage, the interest of both the public and elected officials will be elevated and maintained. Amplification of the issue will also result from the tendency of news organizations to share topics.

2. The media can largely determine what policy alternatives are seriously considered, publicizing those deemed by the media as most viable and ignoring or minimizing others.

3. The news media are a tool used by policy entrepreneurs to further or sustain their own interests. Highly publicized events constitute opportunities for preferred policy solutions.

Evidence of the influence of the news media on criminal justice policy is mounting. For example, a study of prosecutors in Indiana revealed that the strongest predictors of whether formal charges were filed in pornography cases was the prosecutor's perception of public and press opinion toward this type of offense.[84] Another study of prosecutorial decisions, in Wisconsin, found that the greater the extent of coverage of a homicide, the less likely prosecutors were to plea bargain. The length of the story was a more important predictor than legal factors that are also known to influence charging practices: the victim–offender relationship, the prior record of defendant, and the seriousness of initial charge (first degree vs. manslaughter).[85]

Nor is the influence of the media simply felt by prosecutors. One study has shown that variations in the day-to-day coverage of crime was a solid predictor of legislative activity during the post-World War II era.[86] Research has also linked media coverage of high-profile crimes involving weapons (the assassinations of Kennedy and King, the shooting of George Wallace, etc.) to increased Congressional hearings on gun-control policy.[87]

The Media and Gang Policy

Little research has been conducted examining the impact of the media on policy-makers' perceptions of the gang problem. It is generally believed, however, that public officials hold distorted views of gangs.[88] This conclusion is supported by at least one study.[89] To assess perceptions of gangs and gang activity among officials, Scott Decker and Kimberly Kempf-Leonard surveyed members of the St. Louis Schools Anti-Drug/Anti-Gang Task Force, a group of 90 individuals formed to respond to gang activity in local schools. Task Force members were queried regarding their knowledge of local gangs, the extent of gang activity in the area, and the source of their information on gangs. Responses were compared to a sample of incarcerated juvenile offenders and members of the local police department.

The study revealed that Task Force members' primary source of information about gangs was the media. Not surprisingly, Task Force members' knowledge of local gangs was inaccurate and incomplete. Decker and Kempf-Leonard concluded:

> Members of the Task Force had the least direct knowledge of gangs and gang activity. Their primary source of knowledge about gangs was the media, a source they thought did not accurately portray gangs. The Task Force was the group least likely to identify gang names correctly, and [was] also the group most likely to identify juvenile nuisance activities as gang-related. Of the groups studied, the Task Force was clearly the least informed and most dependent upon secondhand information in their understanding of gangs.[90]

Conclusion

Crime stories are a staple of news reporting, but the image of crime and gangs presented by the media is grossly distorted. This distortion is due, in part, by media judgments regarding what is newsworthy—in short, what will sell. Distorted images of crime and gangs also are the result of the media's reliance on the police for information. Enjoying a near-monopoly on crime information, police officials supply the media accounts of crime and police practices that place law enforcement in a favorable light and further organizational interests.

It seems reasonable to conclude that the police have utilized the media to promote their claims regarding street gangs. By presenting police accounts of gang activity as objective and unbiased, the media fosters a distorted image of gangs in the mind of the public. By manipulating the media, the police are also able to increase organizational resources and powers.

Notes

1. Richard V. Ericson, Patricia M. Baranek, and Janet B.L. Chan. 1989. *Negotiating Control: A Study of News Sources*. Toronto: University of Toronto Press; Doris Graber. 1980. *Crime News and the Public*. New York: Praeger; Steven Chermak. 1998. "Police, courts, and corrections in the media," In F. Bailey and D. Hale (eds.), *Popular Culture, Crime and Justice*. Belmont, CA: West/Wadsworth Press, pp. 87–99.

2. R. Jerin and C. Fields. 1995. "Murder and mayhem in USA Today: A quantitative analysis of the national reporting of states' news." In G. Barak (ed.), *Media, Process, and the Social Construction of Crime*. New York: Garland, pp. 187–202; Ericson, Baranek, and Chan. 1989; J. Dominick. 1978. "Crime and law enforcement in the mass media." In C. Winick (ed.), *Deviance and the Mass Media*. Thousand Oaks, CA: Sage Publications, pp. 105–128.

3. Sanford Sherizen. 1978. "Social creation of crime news: All the news fitted to print." In C. Winick (ed.), *Deviance and the Mass Media*. Beverly Hills, CA: Sage Publications, pp. 203–224.

4. Graber, 1980.

5. Cited in Wallace Westfeldt and Tom Wicker. 1998. *Indictment: The News Media and the Criminal Justice System*. Nashville, TN: The First Amendment Center.

6. Graber, 1980.

7. Jack Katz. 1987. "What makes crime 'news'?" *Media, Culture, and Society*. Vol. 9, pp. 47–75.

8. Richard Quinney. 1970. *The Social Reality of Crime*. Boston: Little Brown & Company.

9. S. Gorelick. 1989. "Join our war: The construction of ideology in a newspaper crimefighting campaign." *Crime and Delinquency*. Vol. 35, pp. 421–436.

10. Westfeldt and Wicker, 1998.

11. David J. Krajicek. 1998. *Scooped: Media Miss Real Story on Crime While Chasing Sex, Sleaze and Celebrities*. New York: Columbia University Press, p. 12.

12. M.A. Bortner. 1984. "Media images and public attitudes toward crime and justice." In R. Surette (ed.), *Justice and the Media: Issues and Research*. Springfield, IL: Charles C Thomas, pp. 15–30.

13. Graber, 1980.

14. Sherizen, 1978.

15. Joseph Sheley and Cindy Ashkins. 1981. "Crime, crime news, and crime views." *Public Opinion Quarterly*. Vol. 45, pp. 492–506.

16. Gorelick, 1989.

17. Melissa Hickman Barlow, David E. Barlow, and Thomas G. Chiricos. 1995. "Mobilizing support for social control in a declining economy: Exploring ideologies within crime news." *Crime and Delinquency*. Vol. 41(2), pp. 191–204.

18. Ray Surette. 1994. "Predator criminals as media icons." In G. Barak (ed.), *Media, Process, and the Social Construction of Crime*. New York: Garland Publishing, pp. 131–158.

19. Surette, 1994, p. 147.

20. Clinton R. Sanders and Eleanor Lyon. 1995. "Repetitive retribution: Media images and the social construction of criminal justice." In J. Ferrell and C. Sanders (eds.), *Cultural Criminology*. Boston: Northeastern University, p. 42.

21. Greg Barak. 1994. "Between the waves: Mass-mediated themes of crime and justice." *Social Justice*. Vol. 21(3), pp. 133–147.

22. John DiIulio. 1995. "The coming of the super-predators." *The Weekly Standard*. Vol. 1, pp. 23–28, November 27.

23. David J. Krajicek. 1999. "Super-predators: The making of a myth." *Youth Today*. April, p. 1, pp. 50–51.

24. David Chermak. 1998. *Victims in the News: Crime and the American News Media*. Boulder, CO: Westview Press.

25. Kathleen Maguire, Ann Pastore, and Timothy Flanagan. 2000. *Sourcebook of Criminal Justice Statistics*. http: www.albany.edu/sourcebook.

26. Adam Walinsky. 1995. "The crisis of public order." *Atlantic Monthly*. July.

27. Henry Brownstein. 1995. "The media and the construction of random drug violence." In J. Ferrell and C. Sanders (eds.), *Cultural Criminology*. Boston: Northeastern University, pp. 45–65.

28. Robert Elias. 1994. "Official stories: Media coverage of American crime policy." *The Humanist.* Vol. 54, pp. 3–8.

29. Maguire, Pastore, and Flansgan, 2000.

30. Westfeldt and Wicker, 1998, p. xii.

31. Chermak, 1994; Sherizan, 1978.

32. Vincent Sacco. 1995. "Media constructions of crime." AAPSS, vol, pp. 141–154.; H. L. Marsh. 1988. *Crime and the Press: Does Newspaper Crime Coverage Support Myths About Crime and Law Enforcement?* Dissertation: Sam Houston State University. Huntsville, TX. Ann Arbor, MI: University Microfilms International.

33. Ray Surette. 1998. *Media, Crime, and Criminal Justice: Images and Realities.* Second edition. Belmont, CA: Wadsworth.

34. Chermak, 1994; Graber, 1980.

35. Chermak, 1998.

36. Chermak, 1998.

37. Surette, 1998, p. 80.

38. M. Jankowski. 1991. Islands in the Street: Gangs and American Urban Society. Berkeley: University of California Press.

39. Randall Shelden, Sharon Tracy, and William Brown. *2001. Youth Gangs in American Society.* Belmont, CA: Wadworth.

40. Paul Perrone and Meda Chesney-Lind. 1997. "Representations of gangs and delinquency: Wild in the streets?" *Social Justice.* Vol. 24(4), pp. 96–117.

41. Walter Miller. 1974. "American youth gangs: Past and present." In A.S. Blumstein (ed.), *Current Perspectives on Criminal Behavior.* New York: Knopf, p. 212.

42. Malcolm W. Klein. 1995. *The American Street Gang: Its Nature, Prevalence, and Control.* New York: Oxford University Press; John M. Hagedorn. 1988. *People and Folks: Gangs, Crime and the Underclass in a Rustbelt City.* Chicago: Lake View Press; James Diego Vigil. 1988. *Barrio Gangs: Street Life and Identity in Southern California.* Austin: University of Texas Press; Ruth Horowitz. 1990. "Sociological perspectives on gangs: Conflicting definitions and concepts." In C. R. Huff (ed.), *Gangs in America.* Newbury Park, CA: Sage Publications, pp. 37–54.

43. Jeffrey Fagan. 1989. "The social organization of drug use and drug dealing among urban gangs." *Criminology.* Vol. 27(4), pp. 633–669; Klein, 1995.

44. Malcolm Klein. 1971. Street Gangs and Street Workers. Englewood Cliffs, NJ: Prentice-Hall.

45. Hagedorn, 1988, p. 24.

46. David Freed in Klein, 1995.

47. Hagedorn, 1988.

48. *USA Today.* 1989. "Just Another Night in Gangland." Dec. 8, p. 6a.

49. Stanley Cohen and Jock Young. 1981. *The Manufacture of News: Social Problems, Deviance, and the Mass Media.* Beverly Hills, CA: Sage Publications.

50. Sanders and Lyon, 1995; Westfeldt and Wicker, 1998; Chermak, 1994; Krajicek, 1998.

51. Cohen and Young, 1981, p. 21.

52. Herbert Gans. 1979. *Deciding What's News.* New York: Pantheon.

53. Surette, 1998.

54. Katz, 1987.

55. Katz, 1987, p. 67.

56. Antonio Gramsci. 1971. Selections from Prison Notebooks. New York: International Publishers.

57. Cohen and Young, 1981; Ericson, Baranek, and Chan, 1987.

58. Jeremy Turnstall. 1971. *Journalists at Work.* London: Constable.

59. Ericson et al., 1987, 1989.
60. Renee Goldsmith Kasinsky. 1994. "Patrolling the facts: Media, cops, and crime." In G. Barak (ed.), *Media, Process, and the Social Construction of Crime*. New York: Garland, pp. 203–234.
61. Surette, 1998.
62. Ericson et al., 1989.
63. Ericson et al., 1989; Kasinsky, 1994.
64. Sherizen, 1978, p. 212.
65. Krajicek, 1998.
66. Ericson et al., 1989; Surette, 1998.
67. Sherizen, 1978, p. 209.
68. Kasinsky, 1994, p. 207.
69. Ericson et al., 1987: Surette, 1998; Sacco, 1995.
70. Krajicek, 1998, p.101.
71. Chermak, 1994, p. 99.
72. Krajicek, 1998.
73. Mark Fishman. 1978. "Crime waves as ideology." *Social Problems*. Vol. 25(5), pp. 531–543.
74. Graber, 1980; I. Gomme. 1986. "Fear of crime mounting among Canadians: A multivariate analysis," *Journal of Criminal Justice*. Vol. 14, pp. 249–258; M. Gordon and L. Heath. 1981. "The news business, crime, and fear." In D. Lewis (ed.), *Reactions to Crime*. Thousand Oaks, CA: Sage, pp. 227–250; Vincent Sacco. 1982. "The effects of mass media on perception of crime." *Pacific Sociological Review*. Vol. 25, pp. 475–493; Vincent Sacco and R. Silverman. 1982. "Crime prevention through the mass media: Prospects and problems." *Journal of Criminal Justice*. Vol. 10, pp. 257–269. W. Skogan and M. Maxfield. 1981. *Coping with Crime*. Thousand Oaks, CA: Sage.; P. Williams and J. Dickerson. 1993. "Fear of crime: Read all about it?" *British Journal of Criminology*. Vol. 33, pp. 33–56.
75. Linda Heath and Kevin Gilbert. 1996. "Mass media and fear of crime." *American Behavioral Scientist*. Vol. 39, pp. 379–386.
76. Linda Heath. 1984. "Impact of newspaper crime reports on fear of crime: Multimethodological investigation." *Journal of Personality and Social Psychology*. Vol. 47 (2), pp. 263–276.
77. Surette, 1998.
78. Dominic L. Lasorsa and Wayne Wanta. 1990. "Effects of personal, inter-personal and media experiences on issue saliences." *Journalism Quarterly*. Vol. 67(4), pp. 804–813.
79. Benjamin Page, Robert Shapiro, and Glenn Dempsey. 1987. "What moves public opinion." *American Political Science Review*. Vol. 81 (1), pp. 23–43.
80. Susan R. Takata and Richard G. Zevitz. 1990. "Divergent perceptions of group delinquency in a midwestern community: Racine's gang problem." *Youth and Society*. Vol. 21 (3), pp. 282–305.
81. Douglas W. Pryor and Edmund F. McGarrell. 1993. "Public perceptions of youth gang crime: An exploratory analysis." *Youth and Society*. Vol. 24(4), pp. 399–418.
82. Pryor and McGarrell, 1993, p. 415.
83. Steven M. Chermak and Alexander Weiss. 1997. "The effects of the media on federal criminal justice policy." *Criminal Justice Policy Review*. Vol. 8(4), pp. 323–342.
84. David Pritchard, Jon Paul Dilts, and Dan Berkowitz. 1987. "Prosecutors' use of external agendas in prosecuting pornography cases." *Journalism Quarterly*. Vol. 64, pp. 392–398.
85. David Pritchard. 1986. Homicide and bargained justice: The agenda-setting effect of crime news on prosecutors. *Public Opinion Quarterly*. Vol. 50, pp. 143–159.

86. A. Heinz. 1985. "The political context for the changing content of criminal law." In E. Fairchild and V. Webb (eds.) *The Politics of Crime and Criminal Justice*. Thousand Oaks, CA: Sage Publications, pp. 77–95.

87. Chermak and Weiss, 1997.

88. Ruth Horowitz. 1990. "Sociological perspectives of gangs: Conflicting definitions and concepts." In R. Huff (ed.), *Gangs in America*. Beverly Hills, CA: Sage, pp. 37–54.

89. Scott Decker and Kimberly Kempf-Leonard. 1991. "Constructing gangs: The social definition of youth activities." *Criminal Justice Policy Review*, Vol. 5, pp. 271–291.

90. Decker and Kempf-Leonard, 1991, p. 284.

chapter 5

Gangs and the Sociological Perspective

◆◆◆

The increased attention directed toward street gangs over the past decade can also be explained by the resurgence of interest in the phenomenon by criminologists. Because of the deindustrialization of urban America, and the resulting social isolation of inner city residents, most criminologists now believe gangs have become institutionalized in impoverished communities, representing alternative opportunity structures and agents of socialization that aggressively compete with families and schools for the hearts and minds of urban youth. More now than in the past, criminologists thus tend to view gangs as a major cause of crime. Because they are an important source of crime information for policy-makers, the media, and the public, the criminologist's perspective has proven important in shaping the social reality of street gangs today.

Contemporary scholarly discussions of gangs are framed almost exclusively by sociological concepts and principles. Indeed, most of the theory and research related to crime in general, and street gangs in particular, has been produced by criminologists working within the sociological perspective. Accordingly, variables such as social disorganization, structural unemployment, economic inequality, and group processes are used to account for the prevalence and patterns of crime and gangs. Few criminologists give anything more than passing attention to the psychological or biological approaches to crime, and one rarely hears references to either perspective in discussions of the contemporary street gang problem.

The psychological perspective locates the cause of crime in the human personality, holding that it is possible to distinguish criminals from noncriminals by measurable traits such as hyperactivity, impulsivity, short attention span, and temperament. These personality traits are generally the result of poor parenting and/or a turbulent family life and begin to manifest themselves early in the child's development.

Biological perspectives, on the other hand, locate the causes of crime even earlier; some unfortunate individuals are predisposed at birth to criminal behavior as the result of genetic, biochemical, and hormonal abnormalities. What the psychological and biological perspectives share is the assumption that crime is primarily the activity of pathological individuals, unfortunate victims of dysfunctional family processes or the vicissitudes of nature. The damage, in either instance, occurs early in the life of the individual.

The sociological approach locates the roots of crime considerably later in life and outside the home in experiences with peer groups and social institutions. It is the dominance of "sociological criminology" that accounts for much of the current attention, concern, and resources directed to street gangs. The implications of the perspective are clear: since group processes—gangs—cause crime, any understanding of or solution to the crime problem must begin with the dynamics that occur within those groups.

This chapter provides a description of and explanation for the ascendancy of the sociological perspective in criminology. The first objective of this chapter is to present a broad overview of two major schools of criminological theory: social disorganization and cultural deviance. Our treatment of theories is not intended to be exhaustive; the reader will not find, for example, a discussion of radical criminology, the feminist perspective, or labeling theory. We have confined ourselves to those theories which are most often applied to the study of street gangs. The two schools that are discussed differ on a number of dimensions; perhaps the sharpest contrast is the role each ascribes to subcultures in the production of crime. In one set of theories, gang subcultures are, at best, of marginal significance; in the other, their role is critical.

A second objective of this chapter is to show how profound changes in the urban landscape over the past two decades have influenced the theoretical debate surrounding gangs, impressed empirical research, and ultimately distorted the reality of the gang problem in this country.

THE ASCENDANCY OF SOCIOLOGICAL CRIMINOLOGY

We begin with a reminder that sociology's dominance in criminology is of relatively recent origin. Throughout the late 19th and early 20th century, most criminologists considered themselves biological determinists.[1] That orientation was primarily the result of the revolutionary work of Charles Darwin. In *On the Origin of the Species* (1859) and *The Descent of Man* (1871), Darwin presented evidence suggesting that humans were not divinely created, but rather evolved into their present form through a process of natural selection. Neither did humans act out of their own volition; as with other animals, human behavior was influenced, if not determined, by biological antecedents and instinctual behavior. By the early 1880s, the principles of evolutionary biology had become the foundation of a new field of study in European criminology known as criminal anthropology.[2] Several scholars, most notably Cesare Lombroso, Charles Goring, and Enrico Ferri, sought to identify the inherited physical and biological degeneracies that caused some individuals to commit crime.

During the early 20th century, efforts to distinguish criminals from noncriminals shifted from a focus on physical characteristics to identifying differences in intelligence, a shift brought about by introduction of the intelligence test to social science.[3] In 1905, Alfred Binet, a French psychologist, developed a test to identify problem learners among school children. Soon thereafter American social scientists began using Americanized versions of the IQ test on a large scale, and not for the purposes for which Binet had intended. By the second decade of the 20th century, such tests had revealed that a large proportion of delinquents, criminals, and prisoners were not, in fact, very smart. Low intelligence, or "feeblemindedness," was inherited and linked to crime, poverty, and licentiousness.

The general acceptance of the inheritability of feeblemindedness, and its link to crime and other individual pathologies, prompted demands from the public that measures be taken to mitigate this threat. Thus was born the eugenics movement, and state-sanctioned efforts to prevent criminals and other undesirables from reproducing. Tens of thousands of Americans—almost always poor immigrants—were sterilized, castrated, and confined during the first three decades of this century.[4] Ironically, shortly after the *Buck* v. *Bell* (1927) decision affirming the constitutionality of forced sterilization, the eugenics movement—and the biological perspective of crime—fell into disrepute. The was due in part to the extremes to which eugenics was being practiced in Nazi Germany. Certainly, the Great Depression also played a role. With millions of formerly middle-class Americans standing in soup lines and sleeping in lean-tos, the link between intelligence and poverty no longer seemed tenable. The increasing political power of racial and ethnic groups who had borne the brunt of eugenics policies, also contributed to the decline of biological explanations and solutions for crime.[5]

By the 1940s, sociology had replaced biology as the preeminent perspective in the field of criminology. Why sociology and not psychology? After all, psychology is defined as the study of human behavior, and crime is human behavior. And it was not as if psychologists had rejected crime as appropriate subject of study. Many labored hard and long to account for the onset of delinquency by pointing to psychological disturbances that originated in early childhood, including unresolved conflicts and unconscious motivations,[6] personality deficits,[7] and psychopathy.[8] According to Michael Gottfredson and Travis Hirschi,[9] psychology's lack of influence in criminology was largely due to its treatment of major concepts such as aggression. In psychology, aggression is equated with criminality, though crime involves not only overt acts of force (e.g., robbery) but also acts of stealth and passivity (e.g., shoplifting or embezzlement).

Psychology's influence was further weakened by its "multiple factor" approach: A psychological disturbance would manifest itself in criminal behavior only in combination with social or biological factors. Such a qualified approach precluded psychology from claiming dominance in the field of criminology. But sociology could. It rejected the notion that humans were motivated by self-interest, arguing instead that humans were naturally social and, since all behavior is social, crime must have social, not psychological, causes. In short, "sociology possessed a conceptual scheme that explicitly denied the claims of all other disciplines potentially interested in crime."[10]

There is at least some empirical support for the "crime as social behavior" argument. It is well established that a disproportionate share of all delinquency—but not adult crime—is committed by young males in the company of their peers. According to the 1997 Uniform Crime Report, persons under age 21 represented nearly one-third of all arrests for violent crime and half of all property crimes.[11] This age–crime relationship has been remarkably stable over the 20th century.[12]

Moreover, since the turn of the century criminologists have documented group offending patterns among youth. During the 1920s, for example, Clifford Shaw and Henry McKay found that 82 percent of Chicago youth committed their offenses in groups.[13] More recently, Maynard Erickson and Gary Jensen's self-report survey of delinquency among high school youth in four Arizona communities revealed that over two-thirds of all property crimes and half of all violent crimes occurred in groups.[14] In New York, Paul Strasburg discovered that 69 percent of all violent juvenile crime was group related.[15] Self-reports studies of California prison inmates also reveal that offenders aged 18 to 20 were much more likely to have committed their crimes in a group than those aged 21 and over.[16] Victimization surveys, in which victims report whether their assailants acted alone or in a group, also indicate that younger offenders are more likely to have been a part of a group when the crime occurred.[17] This group nature of youth crime has provided strong support for sociology's claim to the field of criminology.

Before moving on, it is important to consider one further explanation for the ascendancy of sociological criminology. In their controversial 1985 book, *Crime and Human Nature*,[18] James Q. Wilson and Richard Herrnstein contend that sociology has been widely embraced by criminologists because it is, more often than not, consistent with their liberal political ideology. The authors suggest that during the 1950s and 1960s, a newer cohort of criminologists emerged, critical of the American society and possessed by "reformist impulses" which led them to "explain social problems by reference to those factors that are, or appear to be, susceptible to planned change."[19] Certainly, ideology can not be ignored as one of the factors affecting the criminologist's choice of theories, concepts, questions, and methods.[20]

Regardless of how it may have achieved preeminence, over the past several decades the sociological perspective has strongly influenced how scholars, public officials, and the general public define and respond to street gangs. That influence emanates from the many sociological theories of crime which ascribe both theoretical and causal significance to peer groups, although differing on the specific mechanisms accounting for the relationship. It is to a review of those theories that we now turn.

SOCIOLOGICAL THEORIES OF CRIME

There are two major theoretical approaches to understanding crime.[21] One locates the cause of crime in social disorganization, the other in culturally deviant sub-cultures. Social disorganization models assume that human nature is endowed with strong impulses and appetites that, if overly frustrated or not sufficiently constrained, will lead to criminal deviance. Individuals are fully equipped and capable of inventing illegal means to satisfy their needs; deviant subcultures or street gangs are neither a necessary nor sufficient element.

The assumptions of the cultural deviance models are quite different. Under these models, no universal set of human needs or "human nature" is recognized, a position allegedly affirmed by the cultural variability of humans evidenced throughout the world. Rather, man's nature is plastic and malleable, his thoughts and actions the product of complete socialization into the groups in which he is embedded. Individuals are thus incapable of committing illegal acts unless those acts are approved of or condoned by the group. And in modern societies characterized by a multitude of subcultures, some will inevitably contain norms and values that conflict with criminal law. According to cultural deviance theorists, all individuals are conformists—even criminals; only subcultures can be considered deviant. Consequently, in cultural deviance models, deviant subcultures or street gangs are a principal cause of criminal behavior.

Though the acceptance of both models in criminology has ebbed and flowed over the past several decades, most contemporary gang scholars subcribe to what can be described as a mixed model. They assume that social disorganization, particularly at the level witnessed in central cities across the country, makes youth more vulnerable to crime and creates the conditions in which gangs will most likely emerge. However, in communities where gang subcultures do emerge, over time gangs become *institutionalized* and contribute to levels of crime over and above that which would inevitably occur in socially disordered neighborhoods. The gang becomes, in many instances, the predominant agent of socialization in the community, capable of converting innocent youth into violence-prone gangbangers.

Social Disorganization Models

The social disorganization models were first developed at the University of Chicago early in the 20th century.[22] Chicago, like many northeastern cities, had been transformed by rapid urbanization, mass immigration, and industrialization. Population growth had been phenomenal. Many of those who settled in Chicago—European immigrants, blacks fleeing the rural South, displaced farm workers—had little but the clothes on their backs when they arrived. Life in the city was probably not what most had imagined: 16-hour days in smoke-filled factories, dismally low wages, and life in crowded, deteriorated, inner-city tenements. Within only a few years, many of these slums became cesspools of crime and vice. It became common parlance among native Chicagoans to attribute slum conditions to the moral and biological inferiority of its most recent inhabitants.

The faculty at the "Chicago School" rejected the racial and ethnic explanations for the pathologies of the inner city. They argued instead that inner city problems were the result of changes in the physical and social environment of the city itself, changes that had weakened the ability of families and community institutions to adequately socialize, supervise, and control residents. The product of these changes was "social disorganization," a term coined by W.I. Thomas and Florian Znaniecki to explain the breakdown of community among second-generation Polish immigrants to Chicago.[23] Thomas and Znaniecki defined social disorganization as the "decrease of the influence of existing social rules of behavior on individual members of the group."[24] A formal elaboration of the concept was, however, left to other scholars.

Frederick Thrasher's Theory of Gang Formation   Greatly influenced by Thomas and Znaniecki, Frederick Thrasher used their concept of social disorganization to account for the formation of street gangs in south Chicago during the 1920s.[25] His work remains a major influence on gang research today. For Thrasher, a gang was "an interstitial group, originally formed spontaneously, and then integrated through conflict."[26] Using this definition, he was able to identify over 1,300 youth gangs in the area that varied tremendously in terms of size, types of leadership, organizational structure, and activities. These gangs were endemic to the "slums of the city where an inordinately large number of children are crowded into a limited area."[27]

Social disorganization models hold that human nature is endowed with strong impulses and appetites that, if frustrated or not sufficiently constrained, will lead to criminal behavior.

Thrasher concluded that the primary cause of both crime and gang formation is "the failure of normally directing and controlling institutions to function effectively."[28] In disorganized communities, institutions fail to adequately socialize or address the basic needs of youth. Gangs were viewed as a response to the lack of order in the lives of slum youth, a replacement structure designed to bring structure to their lives while providing for particular needs of adolescent males.

> . . . the spontaneous effort of boys to create a society for themselves where none adequate to their needs exists. What boys get out of such associations that they do not get otherwise under the conditions that adult society imposes is the thrill and zest of participation in common interests, more especially in corporate action, in hunting, capture, conflict, flight and escape. Conflict with other gangs and the world about them furnishes the occasion for many of their exciting activities.[29]

Thrasher's gangs began as "play groups" of boys with similar interests and pursuits. Many did not evolve beyond this diffuse stage; others simply dissolved. There were some groups, however, that became tightly integrated as a result of conflict with other groups over scarce resources in the slum and/or with authorities in the community.

> If conditions are favorable to its continued existence, the gang tends to undergo a sort of natural evolution from a diffuse and loosely organized group into the solidified unit that represents the mature gang . . . which may take several forms. It sometimes becomes a specialized delinquent type such as a criminal gang . . . [30]

Thrasher's account of gang formation relied almost exclusively on weak controls as the basic cause of both delinquency and gang formation. Unlike later theorists, he did not propose a strong causal relationship between gang membership and delinquency. Moreover, he never used the term subculture to refer to the gang's moral code and did not believe that delinquency was the result of socialization into an autonomous gang subculture. Rather, those who joined gangs were already hooligans; the street gangs he observed did not recruit and corrupt "good boys." At best, gangs were facilitators of delinquency, one possible—but not necessary— link in the chain. For Thrasher, the gang "facilitates demoralization by giving added prestige to already existing patterns of unwholesome conduct and by assimilating its members to modes of thinking, feeling and acting which would not be so emphasized without group influence . . .".[31]

Robert Merton's Anomie (Strain) Theory   In Thrasher's theory, crime is the result of the *weakened controls* over youth produced by social disorganization. In Robert Merton's anomie theory, all crime is the product of the *strain* which occurs when there is a discrepancy between aspirations and expectations regarding their fulfillment.[32] This idea was first developed by Emile Durkheim in *The Division of Labor in Society* (1893).[33]

Durkheim was convinced that the motivation for crime lies in the appetites and impulses inherent in human nature itself, what he often described as "the incorrigible wickedness of men."[34] In simple, primitive, *mechanical solidarity* communities, these desires and ambitions are constrained through integration into kinship networks and by a powerful, rigid "collective consciousness" or moral consensus based on religion. Those same drives exist in modern man as well, although the mechanisms of control are quite different. In modern, complex societies the collective conscious is considerably less influential, in part because of the plurality of religious belief systems. Also weakened is the power and authority of the family over the individual. However, the regulation of individual passions is still achieved through integration into the social structure, but that integration is now produced by a high degree of division of labor and the resulting functional interdependence among members.

Durkheim conceded that these two types of societies—mechanical and organic—exist only as ideal types, but suggested that all societies were moving from organic to mechanical structures, though the progression is not always smooth. Under rapid change, "greed is aroused" and there is suddenly the "thirst for novelties, unfamiliar pleasures, and nameless sensations . . ."[35] He referred to this state of normlessness as "anomie," and under such conditions he predicted crime, as well as other pathologies, would increase.

In *Social Theory and Social Structure* (1957), Merton modified Durkheim's concept by viewing anomie as a condition that occurs when there is a discrepancy between "culturally defined goals" and the "institutionalized means" for obtaining them. Unlike Durkheim, Merton argued that human appetites and desires are not natural, but are culturally induced. In American society, Merton saw the primary cultural goal as the acquisition of wealth; avarice was assumed to be a characteristic of societies, not a feature of human nature. From the family, the school, the media and other sources, individuals learn to equate happiness and "self-actualization" with material success. Cultures also specify the legitimate means to acquire socially approved goals. An integral part of American culture is the idea that through the application of middle class values—hard work, education, thrift, and deferred gratification—all have an equal chance to achieve the American Dream. Although not all are expected to become Donald Trumps, all are expected to try. Those who do not give it their all are looked upon as lazy or unambitious.

Because the legitimate means for obtaining material success are not evenly distributed across social classes, a strain is created which produces various coping strategies, or "modes of adaptation."

> . . . these situations exhibit two salient features. First, incentives for success are provided by the established values of the culture *and* second, the avenues available for moving toward this goal are largely limited by the class structure to those of deviant behavior. It is this combination of the cultural emphasis and the social structure

which produces intense pressure for deviation. Recourse to legitimate channels for "getting in the money" is limited by a class structure which is not fully open to men of good capacity.[36]

For Merton, the mode of adaptation most closely associated with crime was *innovation*. The innovator continues to chase material success, but rejects or replaces socially approved means with theft, prostitution, drug selling, and other crimes. Absent in Merton's theory is any discussion of the role of subcultures in the production of crime. Frustrated needs, real or imagined, were considered sufficient to motivate criminal behavior.

Neither Thrasher nor Merton attributed causal significance to criminal or gang subcultures. According to both theorists, human beings are completely capable of conceiving and implementing illegal strategies to satisfy their needs.

Cultural Deviance Theories

Cultural deviance theories of crime propose that crime is the product of conflicting subcultures endemic to complex, highly differentiated societies. Some of these subcultures will contain norms and values that conflict with those codified in criminal law. Those socialized into these subcultures will conform to the norms of the group and, in so doing, will inevitably come into conflict with the norms and standards of behavior of other subcultures. The concept of deviance in these theories has meaning only as it is ascribed by other groups, particularly those that can wield sufficient political power such that their norms are written into law and enforced by the state. Indeed, in cultural deviance theories there are no criminals or delinquents.

> In cultural deviance models there is no such thing as deviance in the ordinary sense of that word. If conformity is defined as obedience to the norms of one's culture and deviance as violation of those norms, then human beings apparently lack the capacity for deviance. Except for the idiot and the insane, who cannot know what they are about, the universal experience of man is conformity to the norms of the groups into which they have been socialized and to which they owe allegiance. People never violate the norms of their own groups, only the norms of other groups. What appears to be deviance is simply a label applied by an outgroup to the conforming behavior endorsed in one's own culture.[37]

Cultural deviance models reject or minimize innate human impulses or appetites, instead proposing that crime is the product of conformity to deviant subcultural norms and values.

Edwin Sutherland's Differential Association Theory   Perhaps the best example of this line of thinking is Edwin Sutherland's differential association theory, contained in his 1924 text, *Principles of Criminology*.[38] According to the theory, a youth becomes delinquent as a result of an excess of contacts with persons and groups that advocate criminal behavior, the impact of those contacts varying by their "frequency, duration, priority, and intensity." Two elements are at the core of differential association theory: the *content* of what is learned, which includes not only the techniques for committing crimes but also the motives, values, and "definitions favorable to law violation"; and the *process* by which this learning takes place, most often in intimate social groups.[39]

For Sutherland, the role of criminal subculture is critical: Unless there are those to instruct the adolescent in the motivations and techniques of delinquency, no lawbreaking will occur.

> the person who is not already trained in crime does not invent criminal behavior, just as a person does not make mechanical inventions unless he has had training in mechanics . . . When persons become criminal, they do so because of contact with criminal patterns and also because of isolation from anticriminal patterns.[40]

Sutherland also discussed the social conditions under which differential association was most likely to occur. He rejected the term social disorganization to describe those conditions that produced competing values, replacing it with *differential social organization*. Under social disorganization, individuals are isolated from the mainstream culture and develop a distinct and knowingly deviant set of norms and values that help them cope with the psychological and physical realities of poverty and social immobility. Differential social organization, on the other hand, suggests that society is composed of a variety of groups, each with its own views about appropriate values and standards of behavior.

Walter Miller's Focal Concern Theory   The notion that delinquency is actually conformity to the values and norms of a criminal subculture is also a theme in Walter B. Miller's focal concern theory. The central premise of his theory is that "the motivation for 'delinquent behavior' engaged in by members of lower class corner groups involves a positive effort to achieve states, conditions, or qualities valued within the actor's most significant milieu."[41] According to Miller, there is a separate, identifiable culture existing in lower class communities that contains an interrelated system of attitudes, practices, behaviors, and values. This culture has "a long established, distinctively patterned tradition with an integrity of its own," having evolved over generations to fit the realities of the slum.[42] The characteristics of street gangs—their norms, values, and behaviors—do not *originate* in the street gangs; these groups simply *reinforce and amplify* a set of values or *focal concerns* endemic to lower class culture.

The theory describes six such focal concerns:

1. Getting into and out of *trouble*, Miller notes, is a major concern in poor communities. In these communities, people are evaluated on the basis of or potential for fighting, drinking, and sexual conduct. Status is often conferred upon those considered trouble-makers.

2. Physical *toughness*, as demonstrated by the ability to subdue an opponent, is also highly valued. Miller contended that this fixation on toughness is directly related to the absence of a father, or any other significant male role model, in the home. Lacking appropriate role models, poor male youth internalize cultural messages regarding masculinity that generally include traits of aggression, stoicism, and misogynism.

3. Another critical concern in lower class culture is *smartness*, or maintaining a street-savvy image that allows one to outfox, manipulate, and con others. Smartness is valued because it allows an individual to obtain scarce resources and personal status without exerting much physical effort.

4. The search for *excitement* is another focal concern, driven by the need to bring stimulation and excitement into an otherwise drab and monotonous environment.

5. Lower class residents also have adopted the view that their lives are subject to forces beyond their control, thus accepting the notion of destiny or *fate*. As a consequence of this belief, it makes little sense to defer gratification by attending school, earning good grades, or staying out of trouble.

6. A final focal concern is *autonomy*, which refers to a desire for personal independence and, thus, a deep hostility toward authority figures.

Like Sutherland, Miller suggests that gang members who violate the law are not deviants, but conformists. All adolescents, but especially those who are poor, desperately seek attachment and status among peers. To meet those universal needs, lower class youth adhere to the norms and values of their cultural milieu, but in so doing place themselves in conflict with those of conventional society.

Mixed Models

Shaw and McKay's Cultural Transmission Theory   Contemporaries of Frederick Thrasher, Clifford Shaw and Henry McKay[43] examined broader patterns of crime in early 20th century Chicago. Working under the assumptions of social disorganization theory, the two researchers attempted to determine if crime rates would conform to the prediction of the model: higher rates of delinquency in the transitional, unstable neighborhoods located in the inter-city (the "zone of transition") over time and regardless of their racial or ethnic composition . In conducting their study, they examined official records for all males age 16 to 18 processed into the Cook County Juvenile Court for delinquency charges during three time periods: 1900–1906, 1917–1923, and 1927–1933. For each period, and regardless of ethnic or racial composition, the highest rates of delinquency were observed in the areas adjacent to the central business and industrial areas, corresponding to Robert Park and Ernest Burgess's "zone of transition." These communities were also the most socially disorganized, distinguished by low economic status, high ethnic hetero-geneity, deteriorating housing, and rapid population turnover.

Shaw and McKay interpreted their findings in the context of social disor-ganization theory, arguing that the dynamics of transitional neighborhoods had produced a breakdown of institutional, community-based controls over youth.

> The successive changes in the composition of population, the disintegration of the alien cultures, the diffusion of divergent cultural standards, and the gradual industri-alization of the area have resulted in a dissolution of the neighborhood culture and organization. The continuity of conventional neighborhood traditions and institutions is broken. Thus, the effectiveness of the neighborhood as a unit of control and as a medium for the transmission of the moral standards of society is greatly diminished.[44]

In an attempt to learn more about why youth become delinquent, they con-ducted a series of interviews and compiled their autobiographies in a format called life histories. In a series of publications, they describe how in socially disorganized neighborhoods, unsupervised, undirected youth found the company of their peers on the street, formed "play groups," and began to engage in minor acts of delinquency.

> The boy who grows up in this area has little access to the cultural heritages of con-ventional society. For the most part, the organization of his behavior takes place through his participation in the spontaneous play groups and organized gangs with which he had contact outside the home . . . this is an especially favorable habitat for the development of boys' gangs and organized criminal groups.[45]

In a joining of social disorganization and cultural deviance models, Shaw and McKay argue that over several generations these gangs become *fixed institutions* in the community that constitute rival cultures and alternative opportunity structures for neighborhood youth. Indeed, due to the concentration of delinquency, age-graded integration, and the presence of adult organized crime gangs in the area, the strength of the gang culture soon exceeds that of the disordered community. When this point is reached, Shaw and McKay argue that boys no longer become delinquent because of weakened controls; no youth are invulnerable to being recruited and socialized into the criminal gang culture. At this stage in their evolution, gangs become a *cause* of crime.

. . . boys in these areas have contact not only with other delinquents who are their contemporaries but also with older offenders, who in turn had contact with delinquents preceding them, and so on back to the earliest history of the neighborhood. This contact means that the traditions of delinquency can be and are transmitted down through successive generations of boys, in much the same way that language and other social forms are transmitted.[46]

Albert Cohen's Theory of Delinquent Subcultures   A mixture of strain and cultural deviance theory emerged during the 1950s with the publication of Albert Cohen's *Delinquent Boys: The Culture of the Gang*.[47] According to Cohen, while lower class males internalize middle-class values, inadequate parenting has not instilled in them the skills and attitudes necessary to actually succeed in middle class institutions, particularly the school. Frustrated by the experience, these youth seek the company of those who have had similar experiences. Among certain groupings of *strained* youth, norms emerge in opposition to middle class values and, collectively, they engage in irrational, malicious, nonutilitarian acts of delinquency. This gang subculture thus provides lower class youth the means and justification for striking back at the middle class that has rejected them.

While acknowledging that not all delinquents are gang members, Cohen is convinced that "for most delinquents delinquency would not be available as a response [to strain] were it not socially legitimized and given a kind of respectability, albeit by a restricted community of fellow-adventurers."[48] Moreover the innovative delinquent norms and behaviors associated with the gang subculture can not be ascribed to any one member of the group, but instead are products that emerge out of social interaction among strained adolescents. According to Cohen,

> We may think of this process as one of mutual conversion. The important thing to remember is that we do not first convert ourselves and then others. The acceptability of an idea to oneself depends upon its acceptability to others. Converting the other is part of the process of converting oneself.[49]

Current Gang Theory: A Mixed Bag   Most of the current thinking on street gangs is grounded in some combination of social disorganization and cultural deviance models. In particular, over the past decade a near consensus regarding the causal chain has emerged among gang scholars: social disorganization → gang subculture socialization → crime. This is not to say that all those who study gangs believe that in the absence of these subcultures there would be no crime. Still, from their work it is clear that most believe that gangs have become institutionalized in recent years, having evolved into permanent fixtures in many impoverished communities, with an influence over the very young that frequently transcends that of traditional agencies of socialization (families, schools, churches, etc.). In

◆◆

> Most contemporary gang theories are a combination of social disorganization
> and cultural deviance theories. That is, gang subcultures emerge in communities
> where structural economic change has weakened traditional social institutions.

accounting for the institutionalization, scholars emphasize the role of adult gang
members. Where in previous generations such persons "matured out" of gangs and
assumed new roles as employees, husbands, and fathers, social scientists argue
that dramatic social and economic dislocations in urban America since the 1970s
have all but removed these options for many inner city males. Without jobs or
families, continued life in the gang too frequently becomes their only option. This
line of thinking has been greatly influenced by what many recognize as the transformation of urban landscapes and the rise of the urban underclass.

THE EMERGENCE OF THE URBAN UNDERCLASS

The deteriorating conditions of inner city America were painfully exposed to the
nation in the mid-1960s with *The Negro Family: The Case for National Action
(1965)*[50] by Daniel Patrick Moynihan (then an assistant secretary of labor).
Moynihan described a subpopulation of the poor, an "increasingly disorganized
and disadvantaged lower-class" which he insisted was caught up in a "tangle of
pathology." The book generated a tremendous uproar, particularly from liberals and
civil rights groups who impugned his motives and accused him of being a racist. So
negative was the reaction to Moynihan's portrayal of urban blacks that, for many
years, others were deterred from commenting on the issue. By the 1970s, ghetto conditions had deteriorated to the extent that denial was increasingly difficult, though
liberals continued to summarily dismiss the notion of an "underclass" of poor.[51]

By the late 1980s, even the most ardent of critics had conceded, in large part
due to the work of a prominent black sociologist, William Julius Wilson. Wilson's
contribution to the debate was his historical explanation for the emergence of an
urban underclass. In *The Truly Disadvantaged* (1987),[52] Wilson argued that large-
scale changes in the urban environment during the second half of the 20th century
had created a new class of inner city poor, distinct and significantly more troubled
than those of the past.

> Today's ghetto neighborhoods are populated almost exclusively by the most disad-
> vantaged segments of the black urban community, that heterogenous grouping of
> families who are outside the mainstream of the American occupational system.
> Included in this group are individuals who lack training and skills and either experience

long-term unemployment or are not members of the labor force, individuals who are engaged in street crime and other forms of aberrant behavior, and families that experience long-term spells of poverty and/or welfare dependency. These are the populations to which I refer when I speak of the *underclass* . . . [they are] collectively different from those that lived in their neighborhoods in earlier years.[53]

What makes the underclass of today different, according to Wilson, is the concentration of poverty and related social pathologies present in inner city neighborhoods and isolation from mainstream American norms, values, and opportunities. Though we would refer the reader to his text for greater detail, Wilson's theory goes something like this.

During the first half of the 20th century, massive waves of southern blacks were lured into northeastern cities by labor shortages associated with World War I. Rigid segregation laws forced all blacks—professionals, laborers, education, uneducated—to live in the same neighborhoods. These neighborhoods were well ordered, vibrant communities. Middle class role models abounded and there was an abundance of entry-level jobs at decent wages that offered others the opportunity for economic mobility.

During the 1960s and 1970s, however, there was a transformation in the American economy: Core manufacturing industries either moved to the suburbs or were replaced by lower paying service industries. This deindustrialization effectively pulled up the economic rope on which previous cohorts of inner city blacks had climbed their way out of poverty. In 1964, fair housing laws were enacted, ending *de jure* segregation and leading to an exodus of middle class blacks to the suburbs. With limited job opportunities and few middle class role models, those left behind in the inner city began a downward spiral into pathology. Young males drifted into illegal labor markets and fathered children with women who regarded their partners as not "marriageable" (economically stable). Children raised in these welfare-dependent, female-headed households—surrounded by neighbors acting irresponsibly, selling drugs or engaging in other illegal activities—began engaging in deviant behaviors themselves. With each successive generation, the American underclass becomes more entrenched.

The Urban Underclass and Contemporary Gang Research

Wilson's version of social disorganization theory has been employed to explain delinquency in general, not simply gang delinquency.[54] Though in his original work Wilson made no mention of gangs, his underclass theory is currently the most popular and influential explanation for the evolution of street gangs, particularly in African-American inner city communities.[55]

◆◆▶ _____

> The street gang is viewed by most gang scholars as a rational adaptation to the ghetto, a cultural institution through which the "truly disadvantaged" can hope to secure for themselves some measure of order, status, and prosperity.

John Hagedorn   Hagedorn's rich ethnographic study *People and Folks* (1988)[56] is based on interviews with 47 gang members, founding members of Milwaukee's 19 largest gangs. He draws extensively on underclass theory to explain the emergence and "institutionalization" of street gangs in Milwaukee during the 1980s. Beginning in the 1970s, the city's ethnic working class (Germans and Poles) moved to the suburbs, leaving the central city to growing numbers of young poor blacks and Hispanics. A sharp decline in the core manufacturing industries in Milwaukee effectively snatched up the "industrial ladder" on which previous ethnic groups had climbed to the middle class. Urban minorities were forced into low-wage, often part-time, jobs in secondary labor markets, welfare, and illegal activities. Suburban flight and deindustrialization also negatively impacted social institutions in the inner city (in particular, public schools), diminishing their ability to socialize and provide for the needs of minority youth. Within this environmental context, Hagedorn contends, gangs emerged and secured a foothold in inner city Milwaukee neighborhoods.

> With Wilson, we believe that a minority underclass is becoming entrenched in our nation's cities. This underclass is the result of the changing structure of the U.S. economy accompanied by a weakening of *institutions* within some minority communities. Gangs have become *institutionalized* (italics added) within some minority ghettos as one means for juveniles and young adults to cope with present conditions.[57]

Hagedorn suggests that street gangs have already become "permanent institutions" in some communities, offering what traditional social institutions could no longer provide. Indeed, for Hagedorn it is the continued participation of these young adults in street gangs that is largely responsible for the strength and persistence of gang subcultures. Active gang membership into the 20s and even 30s, he further contends, is a result of the loss of "good jobs" in Milwaukee, a trend that has " altered the maturing out process" and has "contributed to the institutionalization of gangs as a means for young adults to cope with economic distress and social isolation."[58]

Joan Moore   Underclass theory also provides the framework for Joan Moore's extensive research with Mexican-American gangs in East Los Angeles. Her most recent book, *Going Down to the Barrio* (1991) details the dramatic increases in Mexican immigration during the 1970s and 1980s.[59] During these years individuals and families, like previous waves of Mexican immigrants, settled in the poorest barrios within East Los Angeles, areas vacated by the upwardly mobile, middle- and working-class Hispanics. Coinciding with increased immigration, however, was a decline of better paying, "good jobs" in the manufacturing sector and an expansion in low-wage jobs in the service economy. According to Moore, these two trends created "a stratum of men and women who simply cycle around and around with little if any chance to climb out of the realities of their decayed and defeated neighborhoods."[60]

For Moore, the gangs that emerged during the 1980s were markedly different from the barrio gangs of previous generations: more violent, drug dependent, and alienated from the community. They were also older, a pattern she attributes to the transformation of the urban economy and the inability of young Chicano males to find meaningful employment. Absent good jobs, adult gang members, or *veteranos*, became powerful agents of socialization for youth in the barrio and solidified the gang as an institution in the community.

> It [*the presence of veteranos*] also has had an effect on the youngsters in the gang because it enhances the importance of the street socialization that takes place there. It also makes the gang seem even more like an accepting family, now with "older brothers" readily available. Gang veteranos are no longer remote figures—they are right there, and some even get involved in the affairs of the younger cliques. Street socialization—*quasi-institutionalized* in the gang—becomes more competitive with conventional socialization, especially in the family and school.[61]

From in-depth interviews with more than 150 male and female gang members in East Los Angeles, Moore discovered that youth from both conventional and underclass families were continuously recruited into the gang by older members. By socializing young people into the gang culture, she concludes, street gangs play a significant role in perpetuation of the underclass.

Felix Padilla   Felix Padilla's study of gangs in Chicago includes similar themes and findings. His 1992 book, *The Gang as an American Enterprise*,[62] is based on field work with the "Diamonds," a Puerto Rican drug-dealing gang located in a neighborhood known by residents as Suburbia. As in East Los Angeles, large-scale Latino immigration coupled with a loss of good-paying manufacturing jobs significantly diminished role models and opportunities for earning a traditional living. An "ethnic enterprise," Padilla argued that the Diamond's drug dealing was directly "linked to a lack of job opportunities and openings for Latino young-sters within the conventional culture . . ."[63] The gang is portrayed as a "counter-organization" that provides members with alternative, albeit illegal, means of achieving broader cultural goals of material success. Padilla also speaks to the persistent and prominent role of this gang-as-institution in Suburbia:

. . . the short-lived histories of members of the Diamonds have unfolded within a social environment wherein the youth gang has persistently played a central role. Thus, young people from the neighborhood have grown up witnessing and learning the specific elements of the gang culture. There youngsters have been altogether familiar with the workings of the gang for a very long time . . . [64]

Socialization into the gang foments a rejection of middle class values, particularly the value of education and legitimate employment. Like other gang researchers, Padilla found that older males—some 30 years old or more—were still actively involved in the gang and wielded tremendous influence over younger members. Suburbia youth were "systematically socialized by older and influential gang members . . .",[65] inculcating into the novice the norms, values, and traditions of the Diamonds. Older gang members, known as "mainheads" or "chiefs," also oversaw street-level drug operations and taught new recruits the specific skills required for drug dealing. According to Padilla, many of the older members of the Diamonds talked of "going legit" and leaving the drug business, but few did because of what was perceived as a lack of opportunities in the conventional job market. Fearful of spending a life time working in low-paying, "dead end" jobs, older Diamonds choose to remain active in the gang well into adulthood.

Carl Taylor   The emergence and nature of street gangs in Detroit have also been accounted for by underclass dynamics. In *Dangerous Society* (1990),[66] Carl Taylor links the rise of the underclass in Detroit, and the institutionalization of street gangs in the central city, to the decline of the auto industry during the 1970s. Prior to that period, Padilla reports that inner city black communities were vibrant, ordered, and occupied by families from across the economic spectrum. The poorest blacks were surrounded by positive role models and had ample opportunities to climb the economic ladder themselves through entry-level, low-skill, but relatively high-paying jobs in auto plants. The exodus of manufacturing and the black middle class from Detroit's inner city left behind a group of African Americans that "has given up all hopes and desires of achieving success by legitimate means" and has given rise to a black market drug economy.[67]

From this underclass emerged street gangs, some of which evolved into what Taylor refers to as "corporate gang structures" that control illegal drug markets in urban Detroit. In these highly structured, organized, older gangs, middle-class norms are rejected and replaced with those that condone and encourage violence, exploitation, sexual promiscuity, and irresponsibility. With their huge drug profits, they purchase flashy cars, gold necklaces, and expensive clothing and parade ghetto streets crowded with demoralized youth. For these youth, older gang members are most seductive role models, appearing to have everything that is missing in their own lives—money, glamor, and thrills.

> Corporate gangs deliver a one–two punch to inner city youth. First, the image of corporate members is stating "This is it, this is the *organization to belong to* . . ." Secondly, the impression has visible hard-core evidence that crime pays, and pays well.[68]

For Taylor, the deprivation of the inner city is too great, the lure of the gang too strong, and the young are easily drawn into the gang subculture.

James Vigil   Vigil's *Barrio Gangs* (1988) is based on three years of fieldwork compiling the life histories of 67 Chicano gang members in Los Angeles.[69] Like other gang scholars, Vigil uses a similar set of social and economic dynamics to account for the emergence of Chicano gangs within the working class barrios of Southern California. Vigil describes how Mexican immigrants were forced to live in deteriorating neighborhoods and argues that good jobs for adult males were a rarity. Nonetheless, there were sufficient opportunities that many were able to achieve a decent lifestyle; those who immigrated later, in the wake of deindustrialization, were not as fortunate and became hopelessly mired in poverty. Among this smaller underclass, economic pressures often disrupted family life, leaving children unsupervised outside the home and in the company of peers. Torn between cultures, a *cholo* subculture emerged among second-generation immigrants reflecting deviant street norms, values, and goals. According to Vigil, by the third generation this subculture had become institutionalized.

> Once rooted, the gang subculture has developed a life of its own to recruit new members by normal street enculturation and socialization as well as by threats and intimidation. The syncretized nature of the subculture provides cholorized, troubled youth with the opportunity to reconcile conflicts and ambiguities by adopting a set of norms and values that, at least to them, lessen confusion.[70]

The youngest learn the cholo ways from their peers, but especially from *veteranos*, who provide "models for new normative behavior, values, and attitudes."[71] Though most mature out of the gang by adulthood, Vigil reports that a small group of older gang members continues to be active in gangs well into their 20s and 30s. These are Chicano males, he suggests, that have been unable to adapt to American culture as a result of persistent racism, poor schooling, and chronic unemployment. The influence of these older males within the gang subculture, along a number of dimensions, is substantial.

Conclusion

Underclass dynamics—the flow of immigrants to urban centers, the radical restructuring of the American economy, the resulting concentration of poverty, social isolation, and pathology—are themes present in the work of those cited, and many other contemporary gang scholars.[72] All would agree that the plight of the underclass today is fundamentally different from that faced by previous generations of urban poor. Where once industrial cities offered their poor the hope of a better life through low-skill, entry-level jobs, among the underclass today there resonates a deep and pervasive sense of hopelessness. For some observers, this attitude is a rational response to the employment opportunities available in central city labor markets: Low-paying, dead-end jobs can hardly be expected to inspire optimism and diligence.

Many scholars contend that street gangs also represent a rational response to urban poverty. Gangs are portrayed as cultural adaptations to the ghetto, alternative institutions through which the "truly disadvantaged" can hope to secure some measure of order, status, and prosperity for themselves. Isolated from legitimate opportunity structures and routine interactions with mainstream society, vulnerable inner city youth are pushed or pulled into the gang. Once in, they are converted from mischievous children to gangbangers who ultimately come to reject middle class norms and values, even losing the ability to distinguish between right from wrong.

This conversion is reportedly facilitated by the adult members who serve as managers, mentors, and disciplinarians in the gang. Often they direct the gang's drug operations, securing venture capital for wholesale purchases and overseeing street-level sales.

From gang scholars, we also learn that the aging of street gangs populations is a recent trend. These adult gang members reportedly have a strong work ethic and a desire to "go legit"—and would, in fact, make the transition into conventional life if there were simply more good jobs (i.e., low-skill, good-paying) available.

Rarely stated but routinely implied, these same scholars suggest that the fundamental issue behind the current gang problem is unemployment. Society has failed to provide requisite training and jobs to those most in need: young minority males. Because of our indifference to this population, street gangs have become fixed, powerful institutions in urban centers throughout the country. These gangs, it is claimed, are corrupting our youth, threatening our property and our lives, and jeopardizing the American way of life. As such, many criminologists claim gangs are deserving of all the attention and resources that the nation can muster.

Notes

1. George B. Vold and Thomas J. Bernard. 1986. *Theoretical Criminology*. Third edition. New York: Oxford University Press; Randy Martin, Robert J. Mutchnick, and W. Timothy Austin. *Criminological Thought: Pioneers Past and Present*. New York: Macmillan Publishing, 1990.
2. Vold and Bernard, 1986.
3. Stephen Jay Gould. 1981. *The Mismeasure of Man*. New York: Norton; R.C. Lewontin, Steven Rose, and Leon Kamin. 1984. *Not in Our Genes: Biology, Ideology, and Human Nature*. New York: Pantheon Books.

4. Carl N. Degler. 1991. *In Search of Human Nature: The Decline and Revival of Darwinism in American Social Thought*. New York: Oxford University Press.

5. Degler, 1991; Piers Beirne. 1993. *Inventing Criminology*. New York: SUNY Press, 1993.

6. August Aichorn. 1935. *Wayward Youth*. New York: Viking Press; David Abrahamsen. 1944. *Crime and the Human Mind*. New York: Columbia University Press.

7. Shelden Glueck and Eleanor Glueck. 1950. *Unraveling Juvenile Delinquency*. Cambridge: Harvard University Press; G.W. Allport. 1937. *Personality: A Psychological Interpretation*. New York: Holt.

8. Arthur Fink. 1938. *Causes of Crime*. New York: A.S. Barnes; Harvey Cleckley. 1964. *The Mask of Sanity*. St. Louis: Mosby.

9. Michael Gottfredson and Travis Hirschi. 1990. *A General Theory of Crime*. Stanford University Press.

10. Gottfredson and Hirschi, 1990, p. 70.

11. Federal Bureau of Investigation. *Crime in the United States, 1997. Uniform Crime Reports, 1992*. Washington, D.C.: Government Printing Office.

12. Chester Britt. 1990. "Constancy and Change in the U.S.: Age Distribution of Crime, 1953–1987." Paper presented at the annual meeting of the American Society of Criminology, Baltimore, MD, November.

13. Clifford Shaw and Henry McKay. 1931. *Social Factors in Delinquency*. Washington, D.C.: Government Printing Office.

14. Maynard Erickson and Gary Jensen. 1977. "Delinquency is still group behavior!: Toward revitalizing the group premise in the sociology of deviance." *Journal of Criminal Law and Criminology*. Vol. 68, pp. 262–273.

15. Paul Strasburg. 1978. *Violent Delinquents*. New York: Monarch Press.

16. Peter Greenwood, Joan Petersilia, and Fran Zimring. 1980. *Age, Crime, and Sanctions: The Transition from Juvenile to Adult Court*. Report R-2642-NIJ. Santa Monica, CA: Rand.

17. Michael McDermott and Michael Hindelang. 1981. *Juvenile Criminal Behavior in the United States: Its Trends and Implications*. Washington, D.C.: Office of Juvenile Justice and Delinquency Prevention.

18. James Q. Wilson and Richard J. Herrnstein. 1985. *Crime and Human Nature*. New York: Simon and Schuster.

19. Wilson and Herrnstein, 1985, p. 215.

20. Hedy Bookin-Weiner and Ruth Horowitz. 1983. "The end of the youth gang: Fad or fact?" *Criminology*. Vol. 21, pp. 585–602.

21. The classification presented is based on Ruth Rosner Korhhauser's 1978 *Social Sources of Delinquency: An Appraisal of Analytic Models*. Chicago: University of Chicago Press.

22. J. Robert Lilly, Francis T. Cullen, and Richard A. Ball. 1995. *Criminological Theory: Context and Consequences*. Thousand Oaks, CA: Sage Publications; Frank P. Williams III and Marilyn D. McShane. 1994. *Criminological Theory*. Second edition. Englewood Cliffs, NJ: Prentice-Hall.

23. W.I. Thomas and Florian Znaniecki. 1920. *The Polish Peasant in Europe and the United States*. Volume 4. Boston: R.G. Badger.

24. Thomas and Znaniecki, 1920, p. 1228.

25. Frederic Thrasher. 1936. *The Gang*. Chicago: University of Chicago Press, 1936. (First published 1927.)

26. Thrasher, 1936, p. 57.

27. Thrasher, 1936, p. 21.

28. Thrasher, 1936, p. 22.

29. Thrasher, 1936, pp. 32–33.

30. Thrasher, 1936, p. 58.

31. Thrasher, 1936, p. 382.

32. Robert Merton. 1968. *Social Theory and Social Structure*. New York: The Free Press.

33. Emile Durkheim. 1984. *The Division of Labor in Society*. New York: The Free Press (First published 1893.)

34. Emile Durkheim. 1982. *The Rules of Sociological Method and Selected Texts on Sociology and Its Method*. Steven Lukes, ed. London: MacMillan, p. 98. (First published 1895.)

35. Emile Durkheim. 1951. *Suicide: A Study in Sociology*. New York: The Free Press, p. 256.

36. Robert Merton. 1985. "Social structure and anomie." In S. Traub and C. Little (eds.), *Theories of Deviance*. Third edition. Itasca, IL: F.E. Peacock, p. 119.

37. Kornhauser, 1978, p. 29.

38. Edwin Sutherland. 1924. *Principles of Criminology*. Philadelphia, PA: Lippincott.

39. Vold and Bernard, 1986.

40. Edwin Sutherland and Donald Cressey. 1985. "The theory of differential association." In S. Traub and C. Little (eds.), *Theories of Deviance*. Third edition. Itasca, IL: F.E. Peacock, pp. 179–180.

41. Miller, 1970.

42. Miller, 1970.

43. Clifford Shaw and Henry McKay. 1942. *Juvenile Delinquency and Urban Areas*. Chicago: University of Chicago Press.

44. Clifford Shaw. 1951. *The Natural History of a Delinquent Career*. Philadelphia, PA: Albert Saifer, p. 15.

45. Shaw, 1951, p. 15.

46. Shaw and McKay, 1942, p. 168.

47. Albert Cohen. 1955. *Delinquent Boys: The Culture of the Gang*. New York: The Free Press.

48. Cohen 1955, p. 135.

49. Cohen, 1955, p. 61.

50. Daniel Patrick Moynihan. 1965. *The Negro Family: The Case for National Action*. Washington, D.C.: Department of Labor.

51. William Kelso. 1994. *Poverty and the Underclass: Changing Perceptions of the Poor in America*. New York: New York University Press.

52. William Julius Wilson. 1987. The Truly Disadvantaged: The Inner City, the Underclass, and Public Policy. Chicago: University of Chicago Press.

53. Wilson, 1987, p. 7–8.

54. See for examples, Robert Bursik. 1988. "Social disorganization and theories of crime and delinquency: Problems and prospects." *Criminology*. Vol. 26, pp. 519–551; J.M. Byrne and R. Sampson (eds.), *The Social Ecology of Crime*. New York: Springer-Verlag; R. Sampson and W. Groves. 1989. "Community structure and crime: Testing social disorganization theory." *American Journal of Sociology*. Vol. 94, pp. 774–802.

55. Irving Spergel. 1995. *The Youth Gang Problem*. New York: Oxford University Press.

56. John M. Hagedorn. 1988. *People and Folks: Gangs, Crime and the Underclass in a Rustbelt City*. Chicago: Lake View Press.

57. Hagedorn, 1988, p. 165.

58. Hagedorn, 1988, p. 111.

59. Joan W. Moore. 1991. *Going Down to the Barrio: Homeboys and Homegirls in Change*. Philadelphia: Temple University Press.

60. Moore, 1991, p. 5–6.

61. Moore, 1991, p. 134.

62. Felix Padilla. 1992. *The Gang as an American Enterprise*. New Brunswick, NJ: Rutgers University Press.
63. Padilla. 1992, p. 186.
64. Padilla. 1992, p. 62.
65. Padilla. 1992, p. 167.
66. Carl Taylor. 1990. *Dangerous Society*. East Lansing, MI: Michigan State University Press.
67. Taylor, 1990, p. 93.
68. Taylor, 1990, p. 61.
69. James Diego Vigil. 1988. *Barrio Gangs: Street Life and Identity in Southern California*. Austin, TX: University of Texas Press.
70. Vigil, 1988, p. 124.
71. James Diego Vigil. 1990. "Cholo and gangs: Culture change and street youth in Los Angeles." In R. Huff (ed.), *Gangs in America*. Newbury Park, CA: Sage, p. 128.
72. G. David Curry and Irving Spergel. 1988. "Gang homicide, delinquency, and community." *Criminology*. Vol. 26, pp. 381–405; Spergel, 1995; Klein, 1995; Short, 1990.

SECTION II

The Gang Panic in Nevada

During the late 1980s, a gang panic swept across Nevada's two largest cities, Las Vegas and Reno. The panic, which would continue for several years, was sparked by several high profile, violent crimes committed by minority males who allegedly had gang affiliations. Local media coverage of gangs intensified, the nature of which suggested to the public that their communities were being overrun by invading armies of drug-dealing, trigger-happy sociopaths. Exploitive and sensationalized, these press accounts of gangs were based almost exclusively on news releases and interviews provided by local law enforcement officials. Reporters never challenged or evaluated the manner in which police presented the threat, allowing the police to shape public images of gangs and also to advance specific policy alternatives. Police claims-making could also be heard in political arenas before anxious bodies of lawmakers. Gangs were presented by police spokesmen as a clear, present, and growing threat, one that could only be curbed by additional police resources and a more general expansion of the criminal justice system. Lawmakers accepted those claims and admonitions, providing additional funding to create or beef up police gang units and passing some of the toughest antigang legislation in the country.

This section provides a narrative of the "discovery" and evolution of the gang problem in both the cities, and the state as a whole. We also do what others during these years did not—examine the basis of law enforcement claims. In general, we found that those claims were inaccurate and misleading. One could argue, of course, that our assertions regarding the actual threat posed by gangs during these years are also "claims." To some extent this characterization is irrefutable; all that can be known about the world is, after all, a social construction. This should not preclude efforts to measure discrepancies between claims and empirically derived (albeit imperfect) knowledge about social conditions, including street gangs. In this section, we also deal with the legislation and practices that followed the discovery of the gang problem in Nevada. Given the distorted image of gangs that served as the basis for the response by state and local government, it is not surprising that the policy outcomes have proven useless.

chapter   6

The Gang Panic in Las Vegas

When most people think of Las Vegas, images of casinos, neon lights, and showgirls with long legs generally come to mind But beyond the glitter there is a city that, in many ways, is much like any other. There are families, neighborhoods, voluntary associations, churches, schools, businesses and also all the ills attendant to a large urban area: traffic congestion, pollution, crime, poverty, and so on. Las Vegas is also a city straining to keep pace with the tremendous growth that it has experienced over the past decade. The construction of billion-dollar casinos and family-oriented theme parks has not only attracted millions of tourists, but waves of job seekers and retirees. Between 1983 and 1998, the population of greater Las Vegas (Clark County) more than doubled, to 1.2 million residents.[1] Much of that growth was due to the migration of Hispanics and African-Americans to the city. It was during these boom years that the city learned it had a festering gang problem, a cancerous growth that quickly grew to be seen as a threat to the lives and livelihoods of local residents and the continued prosperity of the city itself

EVOLUTION OF THE GANG
PROBLEM IN LAS VEGAS

According to law enforcement officials, there have been street gangs in Las Vegas since at least the 1960s.[2] Most were formed by transplanted youth gang members from Southern California, their families lured by the jobs created as the resort city boomed. These gangs, however, were few, not particularly troublesome, and confined largely to public housing projects and minority communities in the Westside and in North Las Vegas. An incident in the late 1970s reveals the level of police concern regarding gangs at that time. In 1979, an officer on routine patrol stopped a black male in Gerson Park (a public housing project in the Westside), curious as to the meaning of the letters CRIPS running across the shoulders of the pedestrian's jacket.[3] Surprised by the question, the teen explained that he had been a member of the Crips gang in Los Angeles, but he and his mother had recently moved to Las Vegas to escape gang violence. Only later did police realize that this teen's story was not an isolated case. In the weeks that followed, a group emerged in the housing project calling themselves the Gerson Park Kingsmen, the first Crips gang sect known to have developed in the city.

The emergence of a gang can often have a ripple effect: When a gang forms in one neighborhood, those in another must organize for protection. The result is often a violent clash, such as that which occurred early in January 1983 in Las Vegas. In celebration of what would have been Martin Luther King's 54th birthday, thousands of Las Vegans assembled in West Las Vegas to watch a parade of high school bands, clowns, and drill teams. Late in the afternoon, a fight between two neighborhood gangs broke out at Nucleus Plaza, a local shopping center. Police reinforcements responded quickly, but retreated when confronted by an angry mob hurling threats and rocks. The fight spilled over to a nearby housing project; shots were fired, killing one and wounding three others. A fifth person sustained serious head injuries from a blow from a blunt object. Three days later, yet another person was shot in Westside in what police called a "related incident." Retaliatory violence among gangs continued throughout the remainder of the year.

Reports of gang activity increased in 1983, punctuated by two brutal slayings that received considerable media attention. In May, Timothy Weaver Bradley, a fifteen-year-old black male and alleged Piru gangster, gunned down Ronald Lee Holmes, reported to be a member of the rival Cqs gang, during a party held in a North Las Vegas home. Bradley fired the weapon, a .357 magnum stolen just 12 hours earlier from his employer, when an older brother of the victim pulled a gun on Eleverino "Googa" Williams, a fellow Piru member, and ordered him to leave the party. District Attorney Mike O'Callaghan confessed it would be a "complicated" case to prosecute given that the 200 persons in attendance at the raucous gathering had "not seen anything." Nonetheless, the prosecutor elected to pursue the death penalty for Bradley because his state of mind at the time was, he argued, "outrageously, wantonly violent, horrible and inhuman," his conduct "evil, corrupt, and perverted."[4]

A second incident occurred in December when the body of 16-year-old Esteban Aragonez was found at 2 A.M. lying in an intersection in North Las Vegas. Described by the media as a "perceptive, sensitive boy who wrote mellifluous prose and poetry," police knew Aragonez as a member of the 28th Street Barrios, a Hispanic gang known for its deadly rivalries with all other gangs in the Las Vegas area. Apparently, Aragonez and his friends had a run-in with members of the Lil Locos at a party over some trivial issue. Unarmed, Aragonez attempted to run away, but was stabbed repeatedly in the back, collapsing to the pavement and then hit by a car. In a story carried by local newspapers, Aragonez's mother vehemently protested police portrayals of her son as a violent gangster, contending that the police had been too quick to classify the friends of her son as gang members and his death as gang related.

LAW ENFORCEMENT RESPONDS

Efforts by law enforcement to deal with local gangs began in 1981, but a specialized unit within the Las Vegas Metropolitan Police Department (LVMPD) was not created until 1983. Prior to that, officers might be assigned to certain places or public functions with very general directives to look out for gang activity and possible trouble. LVMPD also used ad hoc community interaction programs—typically, basketball games pitting local youth against police officers—in the Westside to develop rapport and gather information about gang activities in the area. Because of increased gang activity, a Gang Diversion Unit (GDU) was formalized in 1983, with the objectives of gathering intelligence and diverting at-risk youth from gangs. However, enthusiasm and funding for the unit quickly waned and the program was dissolved, its duties dispersed among patrol officers in the Westside area.

In the wake of the two high-profile killings, in 1985 the Gang Diversion Unit was resurrected and two officers from the West Area Command Station were assigned to gang duty. The unit's function remained primarily intelligence gathering: officers made no arrests, arranged no drug busts, and answered no dispatches. They simply drove through neighborhoods where gangs were believed to be active, which were nearly always black or Hispanic, cultivated relationships with informants, and learned to interpret gang hand signs, understand gang argot, and decipher graffiti.[5] Officers also engaged in what they referred to as "slamming," a practice of selective enforcement where persons living in known gang areas were stopped, frisked, and asked for information regarding gang identities or activities. Procedures were developed for identifying and recording information on gang members and their associates. Gang turfs were mapped and activities monitored.

After several months of intelligence gathering, GDU officers began discussing the extent and nature of the gang problem in Las Vegas. The first official count of gangs appeared in late 1985: 15 gangs with some 1,000 members.[6] The city learned that area gangs were heavily involved in residential and commercial burglaries, larceny, vandalism—even devil worship. Gang-related homicides and drive-bys were claimed to be on the rise, the result of turf battles among rival gangs. But GDU officers also portrayed Las Vegas gangs as "less sophisticated" than those that plagued the streets of Los Angeles or Chicago. Street gangs, GDU officers reported, lacked the leadership and organization that would allow them to comandeer the city's drug market, as gangs reportedly have in other urban areas.

The potential for a Los Angeles–Las Vegas drug connection was recognized, but seen as undeveloped and not of major concern to police officials in either city. Still the GDU was only a pilot project, its officers argued that the increasing gang presence in the city demanded the continued funding of their unit.

THE COMMUNITY MOBILIZES IN RESPONSE TO REPORTS OF THE GANG THREAT

By late 1985, street gangs were reported to be causing major havoc in the Westside area, allegedly holding its 30,000 residents hostage in their own community.[7] Responding to a recent shooting spree in which a newspaper carrier was killed and six innocent bystanders wounded, elected black officials and law enforcement spokesmen began a series of impromptu meetings with Westside residents during the summer of 1985. At one meeting, more than 300 residents turned out to hear black spokesmen decry gang violence in the community, urging increased cooperation with law enforcement as a means of combating the plague of street gangs. Pausing for the occasional "Amen," a Las Vegas Commissioner told a worried audience that "we can no longer afford to condone being victimized by gangs," and promised to work with local police and service agencies to find "remedies, diversions, and some immediate community actions that can be employed collectively to reclaim our community from criminal elements."[8] One GDU officer speaking at the meeting consoled listeners by adding there was still time to avert disaster, but that "it would be only a matter of time when that won't be true and Las Vegas will be facing a serious gang problem such as the one that currently exists in Los Angeles.[9] In the following years, Las Vegas law enforcement officials would frequently remind the public and policy makers of the severity of the gang problem in Los Angeles, warning that a similar state of affairs could only be prevented in the city by a well funded gang unit.

The need for decisive action was affirmed by black leaders in the community, though of a different type than conceived by police officials. A prominent black spokesman, juvenile probation officer, and future state drug czar, for example, characterized the gang problem in Las Vegas in the mid-1980s as a time bomb, likely to explode if city officials continued in their state of denial. He predicted

---

Police resources were mobilized in Los Angeles, Detroit, Cleveland, and other cities during the late 1980s in response to reported gang assaults against college students, members of prominent community families, and police officers.[10]

that, unless more minority youth were offered meaningful recreational and employment opportunities, "violent demonstrations of territorial control" by area gangs would increase and much of the city would soon be in chaos.[11] Concerned about the plight of young blacks and Hispanics in the city, social workers, teachers, and community activist groups spoke out about the growing gang threat and the critical need for the large-scale infusion of funds into decaying neighborhoods throughout the city where gangs were reportedly flourishing.[12]

Concern over a growing gang problem was also being increasingly expressed by local businesses, particularly those located near areas marred by gang violence. During that same summer of 1985, business leaders reacted angrily to a Clark County School Board decision regarding the creation of a ninth grade center. The plan, a response to crowded junior high schools, entailed funneling students to a single school located near a business district in West Las Vegas. Such a move would have increased the minority population of that center by nearly half and, according to police officials, thrown eight rival gangs together in one place. Business leaders were understandably upset with the plan, given that it would almost certainly increase the flow of young minority males in their stores, possibly shoplifting and almost certainly frightening customers. One spokesman for area businessmen argued that these gang members would "be walking to and from school right through our business district" and that the increase in gang activity would cause "irreparable damage" to area businesses.[13]

Early in 1986, the Gang Diversion Unit abruptly announced there were now 28 gangs in the city, many of which were heavily into drug sales.[14] Law enforcement spokespersons characterized area gangs as "organized crime" engaged in "narcotics capitalism." Gang members were reportedly pulling in $1,000 a day selling crack cocaine.[15] In response to these pronouncements, a community-action group comprised of some 60 public agencies and private businesses was formed: Citizens Interested in Today's Youth (CITY). The purpose of CITY, which met weekly, was to learn about the gang phenomenon and to develop an appropriate community-wide response. GDU officers were often in attendance to provide information about gang culture and activities, at one meeting announcing that "hard core" L.A. gang members were in the process of building sophisticated drug trafficking organizations in Las Vegas, aggressively recruiting disadvantaged school kids in the area by offering them the opportunity to make $1,000 or more a day selling crack on the streets.[16] CITY was informed that, in addition to drug trafficking, street gangs were increasingly involved in burglary, vandalism, animal abuse, and satanism. To combat the growing menace of gangs, officers suggested that CITY work to create more employment and recreational opportunities for low income youth, providing an alternative to the streets.

By late 1987, the strategy of combating gangs through jobs and gyms seemed hopelessly naive. Conflicting law enforcement reports now placed the number of gang members at anywhere from a low of 2,400 to 4,000 or more. More disturbing than the increased number was the apparent movement of gang activity from the traditionally troubled neighborhoods to recreation centers, theaters, and public schools across the city. In February 1988, a gunfight broke out at a skating rink on Family Night.[17] A crowd of nearly 300 parents and children found themselves in the crossfire between two rival black gangs, the West Coast Bloods and the Gerson Park Kingsmen. In July, two unrelated gang shootings near casinos on the Las Vegas Strip sent terrorized tourists scrambling for cover.[18] At a local high school dance in September 1988, several dozen gang members in attendance suddenly brandished weapons, fired, and then fled into the night.[19] That same month a Little League game held at a public park was interrupted by gunfire in what law enforcement described as clash between rival gangs. Players and parents dropped to the ground to avoid a spray of bullets from semiautomatic weapons.[20] In the midst of this chaos, police announced that gangs were responsible for 90 percent of the drug trafficking in Las Vegas.[21]

According to law enforcement reports, increased gang activity was linked to the influx of Southern California gang members to Las Vegas in search of new drug markets.[22] As these gang members moved into the city, police claimed, conflicts with local gangs over drug markets were spilling over into public areas throughout the community. Police contended that no neighborhoods—not even those in the "best" parts of town—were safe from the gang threat. Los Angeles gangs, in particular, were portrayed by Las Vegas police officials as responsible for the increased flow of illegal drugs and violence in the city. Despite the fact that L.A. gang members were rarely identified or arrested in Las Vegas, according to one GDU officer ". . . we know they are there."[23] No evidence of an L.A. gang presence in the city was taken by law enforcement as evidence of their stealth and sophistication of these criminal organizations.

INCREASED MEDIA ATTENTION AND PUBLIC CONCERN

Media coverage of the gang problem rose dramatically during the late 1980s (Figure 6–1). In 1983, only 4 stories on gangs appeared in local newspapers; at its peak in 1989, the number of gang-related stories had reached 164. Local papers

Coverage of youth gangs in major U.S. newspapers and magazines increased by more than 1,000 percent between 1983 and 1989.[24]

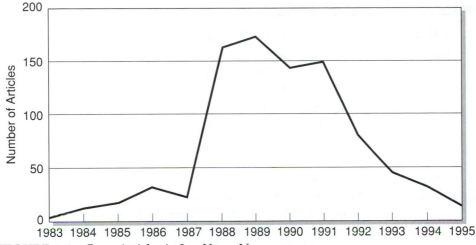

FIGURE 6–1   Gang Articles in Las Vegas Newspapers

continued to carry well over 100 stories a year through 1991. Though many of these were part of the extensive coverage of the events described above, most were simply conventional accounts of run-of-the-mill crimes having been committed in the city. Some reference to gangs inevitably appeared in the headline, accompanied by a statement from police that the suspect was "believed" to be a gang member or the offense was "believed to be" gang related.

Also common were the "in-depth" pieces, often offered as part of a series, on gang culture. Readers were introduced to gang values, norms, and even provided with a "typical day" in the lives of local gang members (see below).[25] Almost without exception, the focus of these articles was black and Hispanic gangs, a pattern a prominent black judge believed was damaging given that it only "intensified the public's existing fear and prejudice toward minority youth."[26]

Media coverage undoubtedly affected public concern about gangs, sentiments tapped by an omnibus telephone survey of Las Vegans conducted in 1989.[27] Results from the poll revealed that 77% of residents were "very concerned" about gangs in the community, up from 67% percent from 1987. Moreover, 89% of those polled believed that the gang problem was worsening and perhaps out of control. These concerns were voiced regularly in the local media beginning in 1988, typically in the wake of some high-profile act of gang violence. For example, following the gang shooting at the high school dance, students and parents alike voiced their concerns:[28]

> I realize they can hit anywhere, but I'm not going to let her go to the dances. Chances are it might happen again. It's just not worth it.
>
> We always thought it would happen on the other side of town. We never thought it could happen here.

A DAY IN THE LIFE OF A GANG MEMBER

Early Afternoon:	First, they put on their colors (red for "Bloods," blue for "Crips"). They begin the day by hanging out with "homeboys" (partners) usually by sitting on a wall within their "turf" (neighborhood).
Mid-Afternoon:	Members separate to buy and sell drugs, usually rock cocaine. To avoid being spotted by police, members rarely travel in large groups for this function.
Late Afternoon:	Members regroup, sometimes to split profits and share drugs. Many sellers are users. Even though a particular member may make $600 to $2,000 a day selling drugs, much of the money is reinvested in the purchase of more drugs for personal use and sales.
Early Evening:	Older members don't usually allow younger members to travel with them during the evening hours for fear that if the police catch them, the younger ones will get scared and tell authorities about the gang's activities. So the gangs are split into subgroups by age difference. Older members often commit crimes such as burglaries and robberies either individually or in groups to raise money for drug purchases.
After Dark:	Gangs cruise the city looking for their favorite targets, rival gang members walking alone. Drive-by shootings usually occur at this time.
Mid-Evening:	Beer-drinking as a group is a popular way to prepare for partying, which takes up the bulk of the night's activities.
Late Night, Early A.M.	Gang members party during this time, either at places where they are invited or crash. Friday night post-high school football game parties have become popular targets as of late.

If I could afford it, I'd send him to a private school. It's a difficult situation for a parent. You don't want to keep him locked in at home, but you don't want him to get hurt either. I'm really concerned.

For many residents, the random and irrational nature of gang violence made the world seem a dangerous, unpredictable place. The paranoia of some residents was expressed in comments of the President of the Clark County Classroom Teachers Association during a public hearing:

> Public surveys conducted in the late 1980s revealed public perceptions of gang
> were heavily influenced by the media.   A majority of adults believed gangs to
> be highly structured and organized, much more than they actually are.[29]

We are dealing with an organized group of individuals. They are one up on us. We do not know *where they are* or *who they are*.[30]

Gangs became a recognized menace in the community, the equivalent of domestic terrorists, changing the mood and manner in which the community governed itself. Gangs were particularly salient in the planning and administration of the school district. In a hearing held to redraw attendance zones for local high schools (due to the opening of several new facilities), one angry school board official commented on how gangbangers had perverted their normal decision-making procedures:

We are giving them too much power. We are giving them [gangs] representation on the school board. They're not even here and they're getting a big consideration. None of us can do our jobs and just redraw the lines.[31]

Across the city of Las Vegas, community meetings were held to discuss the response to gangs, providing a forum for residents to share their anger, frustration, and solutions.[32]

I see violent crime. I see drug trafficking. I see a host of unemployed young adults. Enough is enough. I'm not going to be held prison in my house anymore.
. . . the gangs doing nothing but a whole lot of the devil's work.
They are anti-American, anti-law, anti-everything! They're enemies to our country. We shouldn't have them here.

The first of what was to be a series of "gang experts" from public and private agencies in California arrived in the late 1980s. The California-based Save Every Youngster Youth Enterprise Society (SEYYES), for example, offered—for a price— to train local school teachers on how to identify early warning signs of gang membership, how to dissuade kids from joining gangs, and how to deal with the presence of active gangs in the schools. Several months later, another gang expert from Los Angeles's Community Youth Gang Services promoted such services to Las Vegas parents, teachers, and politicians. Seminars for youth workers with the Las Vegas Juvenile Court Services were provided by a speaker from the Soledad Enrichment Youth Program, another L.A.-based agency with purported gang expertise. In 1991, the mayor of Las Vegas announced that $57,000 in private and public funds were being awarded to former football great Jim Brown's Amer-I-Can program. Taught by ex-gang members, Brown's Amer-I-Can curriculum offered gang members a 15-step program in personal responsibility, money management, and anger control. After only four weeks in operation, Brown claimed the city's gang problem had been "greatly reduced" and began lobbying for additional funds to expand the program to Nevada prisons (local law enforcement officials questioned Brown's claim, stating there was no evidence that the gang problem had diminished).

THE WAR ON GANGS INTENSIFIES

Claims surrounding the gang threat paid off for law enforcement. Early in 1988, local government officials in Las Vegas approved funding for an additional 16 officers for the Gang Diversion Unit. The increased size of the unit was accompanied by a radical shift in strategy, from one that emphasized intelligence-gathering and selective enforcement to a more hard-line stance promising deterrence and punishment. More proactive strategies were called for, according to one high-ranking police official, because gangs had become "the most serious problem we have faced in the last two to three decades."[33] Other law enforcement officials promised that gang-infested neighborhoods were going to be targeted and aggressive sweeps conducted that would "rid Las Vegas of hoodlum gangs" once and for all. On the assumption that gangbangers followed local news, GDU officers issued warnings in newspapers that gangs should "cease activities, leave town, or go to the penitentiary."[34]

In the weeks that followed, press reports trumpeting the success of the new GDU tactics appeared in local papers. According to media accounts, in its first month GDU had orchestrated the arrest of nearly 300 gang members, leading to the confiscation of 25 handguns and over $10,000 worth of crack cocaine.[35] The locally infamous Los Angeles connection came under attack as police officials promised to end the influence of L.A. Bloods and Crips in the Las Vegas drug market. Stake-outs at the local airport led to the arrest of twenty suspected Los Angeles gang members and the seizure of $50,000 in drug money.[36] Reporters, cameras rolling, frequently accompanied police on drug sweeps of areas purportedly controlled by gangs, raiding crack houses and arresting "high-level" gang leaders. In only a few months, law enforcement officials, while not declaring victory, proclaimed that the tide had turned, that gangbangers were retreating in the face of superior forces. According to the head of GDU,

> It's having an effect . . . the neighbors aren't afraid to come out of their homes and have cookouts anymore. It's safe to come out again. . . . If the Sheriff hadn't expanded the Unit last month, we could have been looking at a big problem a year or two from now.[37]

Claims of success increased the receptiveness of local officials to law enforcement requests for even more funding to fight the war on gangs. Funds were provided in late 1988 to expand the GDU from 16 to 30 officers. It was also during this period that the unit was renamed the Special Enforcement Detail (SED).

THE GANG PANIC ON HIGH SCHOOL CAMPUSES

Talk of victory would have indeed been premature, particularly given reports of an outbreak of gang violence on high school campuses in Spring 1989. Two high school teens, on their walk back to campus after lunch break, were fatally wounded by bullets fired from a passing vehicle occupied, police claimed, by gang members.[38] A rash of minor altercations, almost always categorized as gang-related, then erupted on campuses across the city. Law enforcement officials offered explanations for the disruptions, claiming that gangs were moving from the street to the campus in order to recruit new members and expand drug distribution networks. School officials agreed, reporting that by the late 1980s gangs had become more numerous and disruptive on campuses across the city.[39] In response, LVMPD stepped up patrols; undercover police officers wandered on and near campuses. Fearing further outbreaks of school violence, school district officials began to pressure local government for more money to hire additional school police and petitioned that school police be authorized to carry weapons on campus.[40] Calm eventually returned to the high school campus, with only few and very minor interruptions reported that year.

The alarm was sounded once again following the shooting death of a student on the first day of the 1990 school year. By all accounts, the tragedy started as a minor altercation between two students in the cafeteria.[41] A melee ensued when hundreds of students took sides, shoving, punching, and throwing chairs, forcing a terror-stricken faculty to flee the building. Two shots rang out, students scattered, and a 16-year-old male slumped to the floor from fatal wounds. The gunman, a 15-year-old Hispanic male, was arrested and charged with murder, his act characterized by police as a "gang-related slaying," an accusation never substantiated despite repeated challenges from the attorney assigned to represent the teen.

Despite this apparent outbreak, by 1992 the Special Enforcement Detail was asserting that it now had control over the gang problem.[42] Hundreds of gang members were reported to have been imprisoned, many with their sentences

◆◆ ───

The percentage of students reporting the presence of street gangs at school nearly doubled between 1989 and 1995.[43]

◆◆

By 1997, 53 percent of all state and local law enforcement agencies had established specialized gang units.[44]

---

doubled under the new gang legislation (these laws will be discussed in Chapter 8). Newspaper coverage plummeted. The problem of gangs had been addressed but even if it had not, more dramatic issues—deepening state budget deficits, a battle between a university president and a basketball coach, the federal government's plan to store radioactive waste only 90 miles from the city—now dominated media coverage. The gang panic had apparently run its course.

INSTITUTIONALIZATION OF THE GANG PANIC

When we began our study in 1995, the fervor about street gangs in Las Vegas had considerably abated. Newspaper coverage of gangs, as noted earlier, declined sharply after 1991. In fact, there were fewer gang stories in 1995 than in 1985, when the city first learned it had a gang problem. The attention of criminal justice officials, politicians, and the public had shifted to other issues. Still, the gang panic produced a deep and lasting impression on institutional structures, most notably local law enforcement.

By the mid-1990s, the ranks of the Las Vegas police gang unit had grown to 37 full-time officers. According to the GIS policy and procedure manual, the unit's objectives are to "suppress street gang criminal activity through lawful arrests and prosecution, and to deter street gang criminal activity through the lawful collection, analyzation, and dissemination of intelligence information."[45] GIS is comprised of four subunits delineated by function: (1) an intelligence unit; (2) an investigation unit; (3) a Task Force unit; and (4) an enforcement unit. Officers in the intelligence unit are responsible for gathering information in order that new or emerging trends in gang activity be identified. The investigative unit, on the other hand, is charged with tracking down suspects in gang-related crimes, following leads provided by physical evidence at the scene of the crime and information obtained from informants, witnesses, and victims. The Task Force unit is part of a cooperative effort with the Southern Nevada Gang Task Force, a consortium of federal, state, and local agencies (the Drug Enforcement Agency, Nevada Division of Investigation, Henderson Police Department) that attempt to use narcotic enforcement as a means to prosecute and remove violent gang members from the community.

The primary tasks of the enforcement unit (there are two teams) are gang suppression, achieved by patrolling gang-infested areas and responding quickly to reported gang incidents. After each afternoon briefing, enforcement officers pair up and form a parade of two or three unmarked patrol cars, in the course of a shift moving through perhaps 8–10 housing projects or low-income neighborhoods scattered throughout the city. The selection and order of sites to be patrolled is sometimes guided by information obtained during briefings: a report of a drive-by that occurred the previous night, a rumor of an impending intergang battle, notice of a neighborhood party likely to attract gang members. More often, enforcement officers randomly patrol low-income neighborhoods in much the same manner as traditional patrol officers.

On several occasions, we were allowed to ride along with enforcement officers during their shifts. Perhaps because of the presence of gang officers, there was little activity on the streets in the neighborhoods selected for patrol. When one or more youths were spotted, particularly if they were male, GIS officers would quickly pull their cars to the curb. The young males would be stopped and repeatedly questioned as to whether they were gang members or had knowledge of gang activity in the area. In the process, field interview (FI) cards were completed that recorded the individual's name, visible tattoos, known monikers, and other information. Next, the youth would be told to stand against a block wall or other structure and a photograph would be taken. The entire procedure was conducted with a lack of formality; most who were stopped and questioned offered little protest or resistance. Of course, if GIS officers witnessed what they believed to be a crime in progress—for example, a drug sale—an arrest was promptly made, regardless of whether the participants were gang members. The arrest was justified, according to GIS officers, because it provided them contact with residents and thus an opportunity to gather additional gang intelligence.

A limited number of higher ranking officers in GIS are charged with screening all FI cards and arrest reports, completing Subject Identification Cards only for persons judged to meet the criteria for a gang membership (Table 6–1).[46]

For those individuals so designated, the cards and photographs are placed in a file that can be subsequently accessed only by officers in the GIS intelligence unit. GIS intelligence officers are also responsible for maintaining the gang file. Departmental policy stipulates that the gang file be reviewed every two years. If there has been no information in that period to suggest continued gang membership or activity by an individual, that file is designated inactive. These inactive files are maintained for an additional two years. Unless there is information regarding gang activity, after that period the individual's file is to be purged and destroyed. There are two exceptions to the purge rule: (1) gang members that have pending felony cases against them and (2) gang members who are incarcerated.

TABLE 6–1   Gang Intelligence Section Criteria for Gang Member and Gang Associate

Gang Member: An individual who has been positively identified as being a member of a particular gang. Examples of positive identification are:

1. self admittance to a law enforcement officer;
2. gang-related tattoos;
3. participation in gang-related criminal activity; or
4. any other circumstance when an officer can articulate obvious gang membership.

Gang Member Associate: A person who admits to criminal street gang association and either:

1. resides, or frequents, a particular street gang's area and adopts their style of dress, use of hand signs or symbols;
2. is identified as an associate by a parent, guardian, or corroborated statement of an informant;
3. is identified as an associate by physical evidence such as photograph other documentation; or
4. has been arrested more than once in the company of identified gang members for offenses consistent with criminal street gang activity.

GIS OFFICERS REPORTS ON THE NUMBER OF GANGS AND GANG MEMBERS

According to GIS records in 1996, there were 146 active gangs in the Las Vegas area, with 6,959 known gang members or associates currently in the gang file.[47] If peripheral gang members—"wannabees"—were to be included in that count (though no actual numbers are available), the estimates reportedly would double.

Throughout the years of the panic, police estimates of gang membership were frequently reported by the media (Figure 6–2). A year after the first gang count appeared in 1985, police claimed the number of gang members had doubled to 2,000; by 1987, the figure had doubled once again. Las Vegas residents must have been both frightened and confused by the extent of the gang problem as pronounced by law enforcement. For example, after two years of consecutive and substantial increases in the gang population, in 1988 the number of gang members apparently fell by nearly half to 2,400 (this is the only count that appeared in local papers during the entire year). Over the next several years, law enforcement claims regarding the number of area gang members were anything but consistent, though the reports clearly suggested

In 1996 law enforcement agencies reported there were more than 31,000 gangs in the U.S. with 846,000 members.[48]

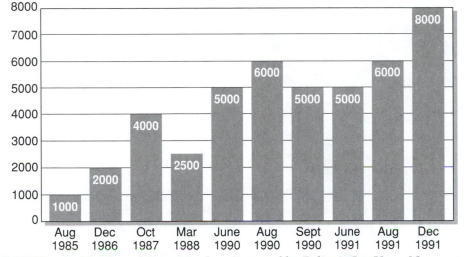

FIGURE 6–2   Number of Gang Members Reported by Police in Las Vegas Newspapers

the gang problem was worsening. Indeed, from the first official count provided by Las Vegas police in 1985 until 1991 (no counts appeared in local media from 1992 through 1995), police counts of gang members increased by a whopping 800 percent.

GIS records indicate that roughly three-fourths of the individuals in the gang file are adults, suggesting that, at least in Las Vegas, the term "youth gang" is a misnomer (Figure 6–3). The vast majority of those labeled as gang members/associates are, not surprisingly given GIS patrol patterns, minorities (Figure 6–4). Blacks and Hispanics comprise all but a small portion of the total gang population, although GIS officers report an increasing number of Asian gang members. White gangs and mixed-race gangs are fewer, and are said to be less criminally active.

GIS officers continue to keep close tabs on what they perceive as the most active street gangs in Las Vegas, and provide us an overall picture of gang activity in the city (Table 6–2). Black gangs are concentrated in West Las Vegas, many operating out of public housing projects. Officers reported that black gangs dominate illicit drug markets in Las Vegas, particularly street-level sales of crack cocaine, PCP, and marijuana. They are said to be heavily armed with assault weapons and automatic weapons, and responsible for the majority of violent crime committed by gang members in the city.

Gang members identified by law enforcement nationally are overwhelmingly young, minority males.[49]

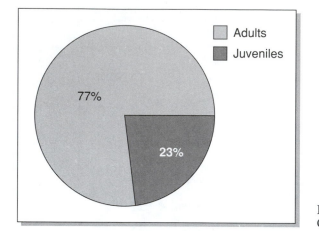

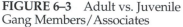

FIGURE 6–3   Adult vs. Juvenile Gang Members/Associates

Hispanic gangs are more dispersed, having migrated en masse to Las Vegas from Southern California after court rulings in the 1960s struck down discriminatory housing laws. Hispanic gangs, like black gangs, are reported to be fiercely territorial. Hispanic gangs in the area are also reported to be involved in the sale of narcotics, but the majority of their criminal activity is motivated by rivalries with other area Hispanic gangs. Members steal cars to use in drive-by shootings, burglarize gun shops to obtain weapons for use in gang warfare, and murder to avenge even trivial acts of disrespect.

There are also several Asian gangs in the area, GIS officers add, but unlike black and Hispanic gangs, Asian gang members do not normally claim a particular turf. Instead, they choose to hang out in casinos, pool halls, local malls, and video arcades. Many local Asian sects maintain ties to gangs in Southern California.

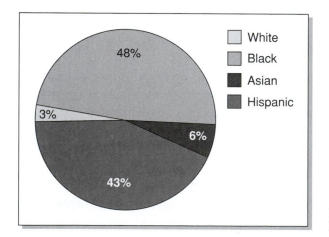

FIGURE 6–4   Race of Gang Members/Associates

TABLE 6–2   GIS Reported Active Las Vegas Gangs (number of members in parentheses)

Black Gangs	Hispanic Gangs
Donna Street Crips (350)	San Chucos (579)
Gerson Park Kingsmen (370)	28th Street (450)
Rolling 60s (244)	Lil Locos (310)
Playboy Bloods (670)	18th Street (225)
Piru Bloods (134)	Varrio Naked City (177)
West Coast Bloods (202)	White Fence (153)
East Coast Bloods (87)	
Anybody Murders (52)	
North Town Gangsters (83)	

Asian Gangs	White/Mixed Gangs
Flipside 29/Flipside Gangsters (150)	Reet Boys (82)
Pinoy Real (130)	Skinheads (60)
Horny Boys/Laos Boys (30)	Criminal Minded Mafia (21)
Bad Boy Pinoys (40)	
Kickboxers (60)	

According to one GIS officer, it is not uncommon for Asian gang members in California to commit a crime, then drive the short distance to Las Vegas to hide out until things cool down. The reverse also occurs, with Las Vegas Asian gangsters seeking refuge in the homes of their Californian counterparts. White/mixed-race gangs are small, less organized, and less criminally active.

GIS OFFICERS' CLAIMS REGARDING THE THREAT POSED BY LAS VEGAS GANGS

As a part of our study, we asked GIS officers to complete a survey that provided, among other information, their claims regarding the extent, nature, and trends of the gang problem in Las Vegas. All the GIS officers claimed that gang activity was a big problem in the area. About half stated that gang crime was the most serious problem facing law enforcement (Figure 6–5). Their claims about the gang problem in Las Vegas are not surprising, given the amount of crime they attribute to gang members: GIS officers reported that gangs were responsible for over half of all violent crime and two-thirds of all drug trafficking in the city.

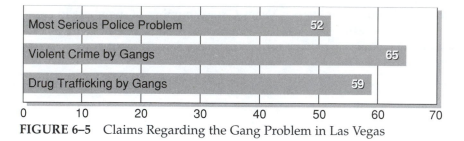

FIGURE 6–5   Claims Regarding the Gang Problem in Las Vegas

THE OBJECTIVE THREAT POSED
BY STREET GANGS IN LAS VEGAS

These kinds of claims have been made by law enforcement officials in Las Vegas since the "discovery" of the gang problem in the 1980s. But to what extent did such claims reflect the actual threat of street gangs to the Las Vegas community during those years? Were gangs, as police reported, responsible for most of the violent crime and drug dealing in the city? To answer these questions, we first obtained detailed information on all felony charges filed in Clark County District Courts for 1989 through 1995. Next, from GIS we obtained a list of all active gang members and associates. In instances where a gang member or associate had been arrested, the list noted a defendant identification number, used by the Clark County District Attorney's Office to monitor the flow of cases through the court system. By merging the two data sources, it was possible to document the level and trends of officially recorded gang crime during the period in which the gang panic occurred.

For violent offenses, overall the objective threat posed by gangs during this period was quite low and relatively constant (Figure 6–6). The proportion of all serious violent crime attributable to gangs increased from 3 percent in 1989 to a high of only 7 percent in both 1992 and 1993, and then declined to 5 percent in 1995. GIS officers, as noted earlier, claimed that gangs were responsible for more than half of all the city's violent crime and that gang-related violence had increased in recent years. This is not what the evidence shows. The proportion of homicides committed by known gang members and associates did jump from 1990 to 1993 (Figure 6–7). But throughout the years of the panic, gang members were never responsible for more than one out of five murders in the city.

During the years of the panic, and during our study, gang unit officers claimed that street gangs were major forces in local illegal drug markets. These claims also are not supported by official court records (Figures 6–8 and 6–9).

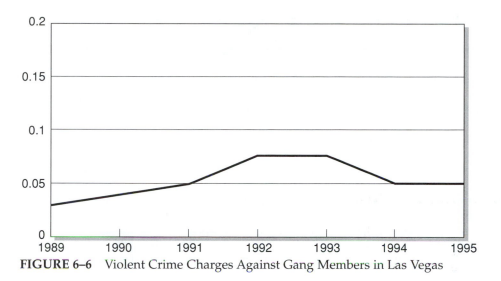

FIGURE 6–6   Violent Crime Charges Against Gang Members in Las Vegas

Though it does appear that gang involvement in drug sales and trafficking increased during this period, official records indicate that gangs were never more than minor players in illicit drug markets in the city. In 1995, when gangs were apparently most involved in retail-level sales, more than 90 percent of those charged with the sale of illegal drugs were neither gang members nor associates. Those arrested and charged with drug trafficking were even less likely to have their names listed in the gang file .

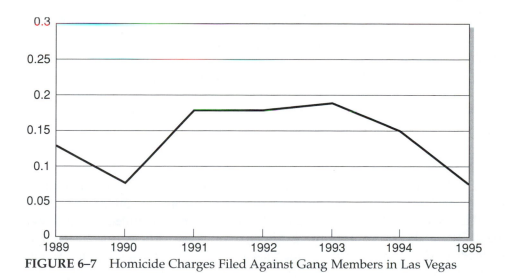

FIGURE 6–7   Homicide Charges Filed Against Gang Members in Las Vegas

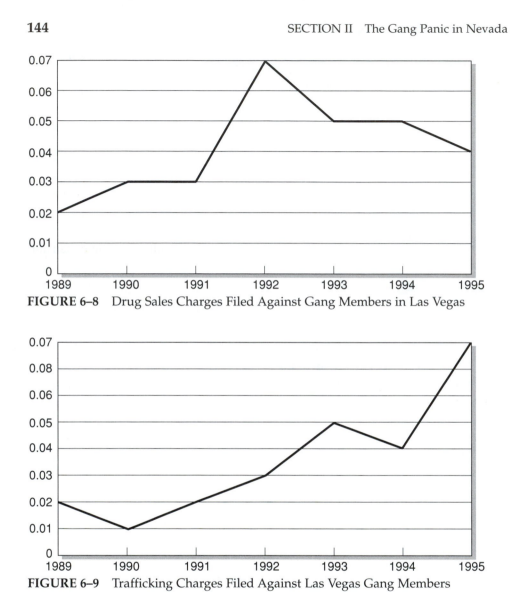

FIGURE 6–8   Drug Sales Charges Filed Against Gang Members in Las Vegas

FIGURE 6–9   Trafficking Charges Filed Against Las Vegas Gang Members

Conclusion

In the mid-1980s, the city of Las Vegas was told it had a relatively small problem with street gangs. Only a few short years later, law enforcement was reporting that the city was under seige by bands of ruthless thugs who killed for thrill and profit. Police claims of increasing gang activity, conveyed to the public through an eager media, sparked a widespread panic. Gangs became the defined as the central problem facing schools, neighborhoods, and the local economy. Law enforcement repeatedly warned city officials that Las Vegas was at risk of being overrun by street gangs, frequently drawing comparisons with the crisis in Los Angeles, and increased funding was provided to beef up gang units and subdue the gang threat.

Based on our examination of court records, the rhetoric surrounding gangs was clearly some distance from the reality of the problem during those years. To be sure, many abhorrent and irrational acts of violence were committed by offenders with gang affiliations And official records do suggest at least *some* increase in gang-related crime during those years. Nonetheless, it would be difficult to argue that the reaction was commensurate with the objective threat gangs posed to the city of Las Vegas. This was a moral panic, sparked by law enforcement claims, fueled by sensationalized media coverage, and resulting in the expansion of social control agencies.

Notes

1. D. Nerlander and J. Ferguson. 1990. *Street Gangs.* Unpublished manuscript, Research Division of the Legislative Counsel Bureau, Carson City, NV.
2. Nerlander and Ferguson, 1990.
3. Mike Hawkins. 1995. Lieutenant, Las Vegas Metropolitan Police Department. Personal communication. March 3.
4. *Las Vegas Sun.* 1984. "Teen Pleads Innocent in Gang Slaying." July 3.
5. *Las Vegas Sun.* 1985. "Special Police Units Probe Gangs in Southern Nevada." May 9.
6. *Las Vegas Sun.* 1985. "Special Police Units Probe Gangs in Southern Nevada." May 9.
7. *Las Vegas Sun.* 1985. "Gangs Holding 30,000 Hostage." August 22.
8. *Las Vegas Sun.* 1985. "Gangs Holding 30,000 Hostage." August 22.
9. *Las Vegas Sun.* 1985. "Westsiders Vow to Fight Gang Terror." August 22.
10. C. Ronald Huff. 1990. *Gangs in America* (ed). Second edition. Thousand Oaks: Sage Publications, 1996; Malcolm Klein. 1995. *The American Street Gang: Its Nature, Prevalence, and Control.* New York: Oxford University Press, 1995.
11. *Las Vegas Sun.* 1985. "County Official Says LV Gangs Gain Influence." May 14.
12. *Las Vegas Review Journal.* 1986. "Community Efforts to End Gangs Emerge." April 6.
13. *Las Vegas Sun.* 1985. "NLV Leaders Angry Over School Plan." May 14.
14. *Las Vegas Sun.* 1986. "Group Examines Las Vegas Gang Problem." March 13.
15. *Las Vegas Review Journal.* 1986. "Youth Gangs Divided Down Ethnic Lines." April 2.
16. *Las Vegas Sun.* 1986. "Group Examines Las Vegas Gang Problem." March 13.
17. *Las Vegas Review Journal.* 1988. "Shots Hurt Three at Roller Rink." February 16; *Las Vegas Sun.* 1988. "Search on for Rink Shooting Suspect." February 17.
18. *Las Vegas Sun.* 1988. "Rumble Reported." July 6.
19. *Las Vegas Sun.* 1988. "LV Gangs Fire Shots Near Dance." September 4.
20. *Las Vegas Sun.* 1988. "Gang Fight Terrorizes Little Leaguers." September 30.
21 *Las Vegas Sun.* 1988. "Gangs: Visibility to Invisibility." October 9.
22. *Las Vegas Review Journal.* 1987. "L.A. Street Gangs Flood to Las Vegas." October 11.
23. *Las Vegas Sun.* 1988. "Gangs in LV No Longer Fight Over Turf, But Right to Sell Drugs." May 30.

24. Randall Shelden, Sharon Tracy, and William Brown. *2001: Youth Gangs in American Society*. Belmont, CA: Wadworth.

25. *Las Vegas Sun*. 1988. "Typical Day Includes Putting on One's Colors, Drug Deals and Crime." October 9.

26. Lee Gates. Judge, Eighth District Court, Clark County, Nevada. Personal communication. 1995.

27. Center for Survey Research. 1989. Department of Sociology, University of Nevada/Las Vegas.

28. *Las Vegas Sun*. 1988. "Attack Forces School Security Review." September 9.

29. Susan R. Takata and Richard G. Zevitz. 1990. "Divergent perceptions of group delinquency in a midwestern community: Racine's gang problem." *Youth and Society*. Vol. 21 (3), pp. 282–305.

30. *Las Vegas Sun*. 1990. "Teachers' Union Calls for Tighter Security." September 15.

31. *Las Vegas Sun*. 1990. "Gangs to Affect School Zoning." May 15.

32. *Las Vegas Sun*. 1991. "Residents Gang Up." August 26.

33. *Las Vegas Sun*. 1988. "Gangs Create the Worst Problem LV has Faced in 30 Years." November 16.

34. *Las Vegas Sun*. 1988. "Metro Mobilizes Against LV Gangs." March 24.

35. *Las Vegas Sun*. 1988. "Metro Describes Gang Squad's Success." April 13.

36. *Las Vegas Review Journal*. 1988. "Gang Cash Flowing Through Airport." April 16.

37. *Las Vegas Sun*. 1988. "Gang Diversion Unit Called a Success." May 3.

38. *Las Vegas Sun*. 1989. "Two Vegans Killed in Street Shooting." March 11.

39. Jack Lazarotto. 1995. Chief of Security, Clark County School District, Nevada. Personal communication. September 29.

40. Lazzaroto, 1995.

41. *Las Vegas Review Journal*. 1990. "Eldorado Teen Gunned Down: Gunfire Erupts in Gang-Related Cafeteria Fight." August 27.

42. Vint Hartung and Lou Roberts. 1993. "Identification of Hispanic Gangs." *The Training Wheel* (November–December). Las Vegas Metropolitan Police publication.

43. U.S. Department of Education. 1998. *Students' Reports of School Crime: 1989 and 1995*. U.S. Department of Education, Office of Educational Research and Improvement, NCES 98-241; U.S. Department of Justice, Office of Justice Programs, NCJ-169607.

44. Bureau of Justice Statistics 1999. *Law Enforcement Management and Administrative Statistics, 1997*. Department of Justice. Washington, D.C.: Government Printing Office.

45. Las Vegas Metropolitan Police Department. 1995. *Gang Investigation Section Manual*. Mimeographed copy.

46. Las Vegas Metropolitan Police Department. 1995. *Gang Investigation Section Manual*, p. 1.

47. William Conger. 1997. Lieutenant, Las Vegas Metropolitan Police Department. Gang Investigation Section. Personal communication.

48. U.S. Department of Justice. 1997. *1996 National Youth Gang Survey*. Office of Justice Programs, Office of Juvenile Justice and Delinquency Prevention. National Youth Gang Center. Washington, D.C.: Government Printing Office.

49. U.S. Department of Justice. 1999. *1998 National Youth Gang Survey*. Office of Justice Programs, Office of Juvenile Justice and Delinquency Prevention. National Youth Gang Center. Washington, D.C.: Government Printing Office.

chapter 7

The Gang Panic in Reno

Approximately 400 miles northwest of Las Vegas lies the city of Reno, Nevada, the "Biggest Little City in the World." With a population of 170,000 in 1997, Reno is the state's second largest city. It is located on the banks of the Truckee River in Washoe County, a large valley blocked on the west and north by the Sierras and on the east and south by the Virginia Range of Comstock Lode fame. Like Las Vegas, the valley has experienced tremendous growth over the past two decades. Since 1980, the population of Washoe county has nearly doubled, a trend fueled by the growth of the casino industry. As in Las Vegas, the gang problem in Reno was discovered during a period of rapid population growth, racial diversification, and economic expansion.

EVOLUTION OF THE GANG PROBLEM IN RENO

The first hint of a gang problem in Washoe County appeared in 1982 when a group known as the SRPs surfaced in Reno, its members having been linked to a series of violent crimes and street-level narcotic sales. The SRPs, however, never represented more than a minor problem for area police. By 1985, the gang was no longer considered active. Concern about gangs resurfaced in the late 1980s following police reports of L.A. Crips gang members migrating to Reno in search of new drug markets. Crips gangsters were also reported to be responsible for the outbreak of graffiti, stabbings, burglaries, and drive-by shootings in the community.

In February 1988, a 16-year-old male was beaten to death with a lug wrench on the streets of Reno by alleged Crips gang members. Extensive media coverage of the crime included background information about Crips, as well as Bloods, gang culture and how both gangs "thrive on rock cocaine sales" and "kill indiscriminately to protect their turf."[1] The editorial pages of the Reno Gazette Journal, the largest newspaper in Washoe County, urged police to take immediate action to prevent street gangs from overrunning the city, portraying these criminal bands as well-oiled, entrepreneurial organizations driven by profit.

A move to control the growth and spread of street gangs can be successful if it attacks, in addition to other things, the profit motive. The Crips are not staking out strutting grounds like the affable little punks in "West Side Story." They're calculating entrepreneurs developing new markets in the very lucrative but competitive illegal drug market. The phrase "hostile takeover" acquires new meaning when the Crips are around.[2]

Concerned community leaders sought the help of outside experts to develop strategies that would reduce gang activity. In March, gang specialists from the Los Angeles and Sacramento police departments, along with officials from the California Youth Authority, presented workshops to Reno police, school officials, and juvenile parole and probation officers on gang culture, gang graffiti, and the gang–drug connection. Reno officials were warned that their city was an attractive target for gang activity because of the transient traffic and "money and people willing to buy dope," and advised massive action to prevent harm to the community and the local economy.[3] Reno police, however, were circumspect, stating they currently did not view area gangs as an overwhelming problem.

Less than a week after that assessment, a 13-year-old girl was beaten, robbed, and raped by four alleged Crips members operating in Reno. Area residents were shocked by the brazenness of the perpetrators, one quoted by a reporter that during the gang rape . . . "she (the victim) shed some tears . . . and then I waited until everybody had their turn."[4] The suspect also informed reporters that, like himself, most of the local Crip gang members had come from Los Angeles to Reno with the Job Corps program. The following day, the director of the Reno-based program denied the rape suspect's allegation that the federal program for training low-income youth was a breeding ground for criminal gangs, pointing out that only one of the four rape suspects had been enrolled in the Job Corps program. Nonetheless, over the coming weeks the director fielded dozens of abusive and threatening calls from angry Reno residents. Local businesses also called to cancel their commitments to train and hire the program's participants.

Growing concern led to the creation of the Northern Nevada Youth Gang Task Force in the summer of 1988, the first permanent organizational response to area gangs. Comprised of representatives from police, schools, and social agencies, the task force's objectives were to assess the threat, pool intelligence, and provide a base of information from which to develop gang suppression strategies. Reno police officials sat on the task force, though they remained unconvinced that the gang problem had reached levels that warranted the kind of alarm being sounded. One cautioned reporters at a press conference not to incite public fears, saying "By doing this (creating the Task Force), we're not saying gangs are here . . . but there are gang-related personnel present and activities that invite them."[5]

Though police were slow to acknowledge a gang problem in Reno, they were not unwilling to label particular crimes as gang related. In December 1989, for example, on a downtown street in an area lined with casinos and filled with tens of thousands of tourists, a knife fight between two groups of Hispanic males broke out. Police promptly reported the incident as gang related, explaining to reporters that some of those on one side were wearing red (the color identified with Bloods) and some on the other wore some article of blue clothing (the color identified with Crips). Police added that the crime was further evidence of the infiltration of L.A.-based gangs into the city, as was the graffiti increasingly seen on walls, benches, and structures throughout the community. In fact, it was at the request of police that the Reno city council enacted ordinances authorizing law enforcement to remove graffiti, even when it was on private property. More than a concern with aesthetics, police argued that the prompt removal of graffiti would reduce tensions between rival gangs by disrupting the primary means by which their threats were communicated.

Shortly after the outbreak of violence in downtown Reno, a disturbing twist was added to the gang problem. In the first drive-by shooting in Reno characterized as racially motivated, three members of a white supremacist group opened fire on a 27-year-old black male pedestrian, who staggered from the street and died on his sister's doorstep. Responding to death threats from local Skinheads, in January of 1989 black Reno bus drivers made their rounds accompanied by private security guards for their protection. While reporting that there were probably no more than 10 to 20 Skinheads in the area, Reno police confirmed that they were "taking the problem seriously."[6]

The gang problem was, fittingly, the theme of the annual National Council of Juvenile and Family Court Judges held in Reno in the spring of 1989. The director of the National Center for School Safety, a featured speaker at the conference, told an audience of 900 judges, prosecutors, and other juvenile justice officials that public schools had become magnets for street gangs seeking young recruits and expanded drug markets. Others on the platform provided lurid accounts of gang initiation rites, stating that some gangs even require kids to kill their parents to secure membership. Gangs were also said to be bringing increasingly sophisticated weaponry onto campus (as an illustration, one speaker presented a pocket pager than had been converted to a .22 caliber pistol). The most tragic part of the gang problem on campus, authorities added, was that about one-half of all victims of gang violence were innocent bystanders. The conference ended with a plea for a comprehensive approach to the gang problem and reminders of what might be the costs to children if such efforts were not realized.

The gang panic was further fueled by an outbreak of violence between what was reported as two rival Hispanic gangs in the spring of 1990. Sparked by a vicious attack upon a 17-year-old male by a band of baseball-bat wielding youth, the feuding continued throughout the summer at public parks, state fairs, and recreational centers, increasing the threat to innocent bystanders. Accounts of the most recent shooting or stabbing by warring factions became a common feature in local news reporting and typically included shots of Hispanic youth in gang garb and flashing gang signs. The editorial pages of the Reno Gazette–Journal reflected a city under seige from what many perceived as lawless bands of thugs.

> . . . we need to understand—all of us—that this is a war. We are under attack and we must respond forcefully and immediately, with every resource at our command. We must pledge to do whatever it takes to control this scourge. We must promise that our streets will not be overrun by thugs without a conscience, our schools will not be battlegrounds for teen-age hoodlums, our nights not punctuated by gunfire."[7]

The paper openly criticized the Reno police chief for his refusal to commit sufficient resources to the war on gangs. But while local media chastised the chief for his "denial," the Hispanic community grew increasingly critical of the media's portrayal of Hispanic youth. In a public forum in 1990, Hispanic leaders assailed news executives for their coverage of Hispanic youth crime, charging that the media had exaggerated and distorted the gang threat to sell papers and attract viewers. And as a result of this coverage, they argued, fear and prejudice toward Hispanic youth had increased, making it more difficult for them to succeed in school or find jobs in the community.[8]

Media coverage of local gangs (more often than not, involving Hispanic youth) had, in fact, exploded during the late 1980s (Figure 7–1). From 1983 to 1987, the Reno Gazette–Journal carried on average fewer than three gang-related stories each year. In 1988, the number of gang stories climbed to 56 and then jumped to a high of 164 in 1989.

THE POLICE GET TOUGH ON GANGS

Prodded by local media and public officials, the Reno Police Department beefed up its gang unit and adopted tougher zero-tolerance gang suppression policies. Suspected gang members were placed under constant scrutiny and arrested for any

"Public and institutional denial of the existence of gangs and a lack of proactive community measures are perhaps the greatest contributing factors in the alarming increase in the number, size, and strength of gangs."

National Alliance of Gang Investigators' Association, 1998.[9]

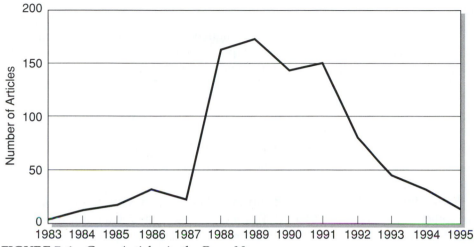

FIGURE 7–1   Gang Articles in the Reno Newspaper

and all violations of the law. While police reports suggested that these tactics were somewhat effective, the get-tough approach to gangs also produced several violent confrontations between police and Hispanic youth.[10] A backlash also occurred in the wider Hispanic community, angered by what it perceived as the department's indiscriminate labeling of Hispanic youth as gang members. In 1991 the police chief, under considerable pressure, resigned from office. His replacement publicly acknowledged the threat and promised to deal a harsh blow to area gangs. Needless to say, he was embraced by local media.

> Fortunately, the Reno Police Department is now admitting the problem up front, instead of glossing it over. The former police chief believed that publicizing gangs might glamorize and enlarge them. But the gangs grew anyway. Acting police Chief Dick Kirkland's new approach will help alert the community and convince it that the problem must be addressed with utmost energy.[11]

Confronted with a serious gang problem and widespread antipolice sentiment within the Hispanic community, the new police chief acted swiftly to restore public trust and also to reduce gang activity. His efforts were guided by the principles of community-based policing under a program he created known as COP+ (Community Oriented Policing Plus).[12] The initial step was the formation of Neighborhood Advisory Groups (NAGs) in high-crime areas. NAGs were designed to foster working relationships between police and residents in maintaining safe communities. They provided important feedback to the police on the most important issues faced by residents, as well as possible solutions. Using feedback provided by NAGs, the new chief decided to abandon the war against gangs in favor of

◆◆ ——

> The Office of Juvenile Justice and Delinquency Prevention argues that local law enforcement should concentrate primarily on the suppression of youth gang activity through the aggressive enforcement of laws.[13]

prevention and intervention strategies. A Community Action Team (CAT) was created that would work with families of at-risk youth or wannabees. Officers provided literature and counseling referral services to families, developed job internships programs with local businesses, and conducted a range of other youth outreach programs.[14]

For those hard-core gang members, other strategies were developed. In November 1992, the Violent Crime Task Force was created. Comprised of representatives from all law enforcement agencies in Washoe County, the task force was focused on the small number of gang members believed to be responsible for most of the serious crime in the area. It also began to collect regional intelligence on the movement of weapons and drugs between Reno and adjacent states. The Task Force's first major investigation was concluded in 1994 and produced nearly two dozen federal indictments for drug trafficking and the seizure of $100,000, numerous firearms, and eight pounds of cocaine.[15]

The advent of community-based policing did not end all friction between the police and the Hispanic community. In 1994, a 19-year-old Hispanic college student filed a class action suit against the Reno Police Department for discriminatory treatment. Denying that he had ever been a gang member, the plaintiff reported that he and other Hispanic youth had been repeatedly stopped and treated like violent criminal gang members by the police. That treatment included, he alleged, arbitrary detention, questioning, photographing, and inclusion in the "gang file."[16] Settling out of court, police officials agreed to no longer keep files on people only suspected of being gang members.

Nor did community-based policing end gang violence. Though reported gang crime continue to plague low-income minority communities, seemingly no part of the city was safe. For example: During the summer of 1995, a 13-year-old girl was shot to death in a public park just across the street from the home of the Washoe County District Attorney. Law enforcement officials, attempting to head off a full-scale public panic, presented police statistics showing that gangs were responsible for less than 2 percent of all serious crime in Reno.[17] At the same time, they modified the CAT unit and increased its staffing. The Special Targeting Enforcement Program (STEP) team was created, which would operate within CAT. STEP's primary goal was to identify, monitor, and arrest the most the most violent repeat gang offenders, as well as those involved in weapons violations. Over the following weeks, the intensity of the gang panic would subside, but not disappear.

INSTITUTIONALIZATION
OF THE GANG RESPONSE

We began our study of the gang problem in Reno the year following this tragic high-profile shooting. By that time, the staffing of the STEP/CAT unit had increased to 20 officers: fourteen police officers, two detectives, four sergeants, one lieutenant, and one deputy chief. As in Las Vegas, we were granted limited access to policy manuals and records, allowed to attend daily briefings, ride along on patrols, and interview gang officers.

STEP/CAT officers are guided by a detailed policy manual that includes criteria by which gang members and associates are identified (Table 7–1).[18] Arguably, the criteria for establishing gang membership are more rigid than those which guide gang identification in Las Vegas, no doubt due to the earlier court challenge.

As in Las Vegas, during field contacts we observed with criminal suspects, STEP/CAT officers collected identifying information (demographics, names, tattoos, monikers, vehicles, etc.), solicited admissions of gang membership, and took photographs. Unlike in Las Vegas, officers did not detain a suspected gang member unless the person had committed, or was about to commit, a crime, as prescribed by departmental policy. When information was collected, the unit supervisor was responsible for screening the field interview documents to ensure that person met the criteria for either criminal gang member or associate. Information on qualifying individuals is eventually entered into a computer database known as Intel-Trak. Another protection to persons not present in Las Vegas: Fifteen days prior to any information being entered into the database, STEP/CAT officers must notify the individual (or the parents of the person if a juvenile is involved) that they have been identified as a gang member/associate and this that information is going to be placed in their gang intelligence file. This notification procedure represents another modification to departmental policy as a result of the 1994 class action suit. After three years, policy also stipulates that the names of those no longer believed to be associated with gangs be purged from the database.

According to STEP/CAT officers, this database is the "most effective tool police presently have in recognizing, solving, and preventing gang related crime."[19] When gang-related crimes have occurred in the city, officers report they are able to enter any bits of information they may have regarding the perpetrator—monikers, tattoos, vehicles, etc.—into the computer and it will produce a list of potential suspects.

In 1996, a federally funded, national gang database was created with nearly 5,000 local, state, and Federal law enforcement agency members.[20]

TABLE 7–1   Special Targeting Enforcement Program Criteria for Gang Members and Associates

---

Criminal Gang Members   Persons who meet any of the following criteria:

1. When an individual admits to membership in a gang and there exists reason to believe that this information is accurate.

2. When a reliable informant identifies an individual as a criminal gang member. A reliable informant is an individual whose reliability has been previously tested successfully or a private person who is innocent of criminal involvement volunteers this information freely, openly, and does not demonstrate an alternative motive.

3. When an informant of previously untested reliability identifies an individual as a criminal gang member and the information he/she provides is corroborated by independent information.

4. When an individual has been arrested for an offense which is consistent with criminal gang activity and there is corroborating evidence of ongoing criminal gang-related activity.

5. When an individual has a criminal record which tends to establish a pattern of criminal gang activity.

Criminal Gang Associates   Persons who meet any of the following criteria:

1. Any person who individually or as part of a collective has engaged in criminal gang activity but is not a confirmed member of a criminal gang.

2. Any person who admits membership in a criminal gang but there exists reason to believe that this information is questionable.

3. When an individual is observed by law enforcement personnel to be engaged in conduct which reasonably indicates involvement or association with criminal gangs. Examples of such observations include but are not limited to the following:

    A. Tattoos, symbols, or body markings with gang names, signs and monikers, dress, or hand-signs which are reasonably related to current gang affiliation.

    B. Any written material or documents which can be reasonably determined to be an indicator of a criminal gang involvement or activity.

    C. Photos taken with current criminal connotations, such as insignia in the background or surroundings, or with a known criminal gang member(s).

Most of CAT's resources (as opposed to STEP officers'), however, are devoted to peripheral gang members or wannabes. For example, during our ride-alongs we observed CAT officers making contact (no questioning or photographing takes place) with younger adolescents who were in the company of known gang members, painting graffiti, or participating in minor offenses. In one case, the officer escorted the youth home and spoke directly with the parents. Families are informed of their child's activities and offered information about local service providers who can provide counseling or assistance. Because of the trust fostered by the community policing initiative in Reno, CAT officers stated that, after this kind of contact, these families often become invaluable sources of information regarding serious gang activity in their neighborhoods. Officers were also directly involved in intervention programs, referring and recruiting at-risk youth to a range of community-based programs developed specifically to combat the gang problem.

The police response to gangs in Reno is also distinguished by its media policy. Since the creation of CAT, procedures and policies were implemented to ensure accurate, nonsensationalized information regarding gangs and gang activity. For example, STEP/CAT officers are prohibited from releasing the names of individual gangs or gang members involved in suspected crimes. This standard is aimed at increasing victim/witness cooperation and reducing the likelihood of retaliatory violence by a rival gang. Giving specifics is also believed to glamorize gangs and foster gang cohesion and recruitment efforts.

STEP/CAT OFFICERS' CLAIMS REGARDING THE NUMBER OF GANGS AND GANG MEMBERS

As in Las Vegas, following the "discovery" of gangs, police estimates of the number of gang members in Reno regularly appeared in the local press (Figure 7–2). From the first count of 50 members in 1988, police reports of the number of gang members and associates grew steadily, to a high of 967 in 1994. According

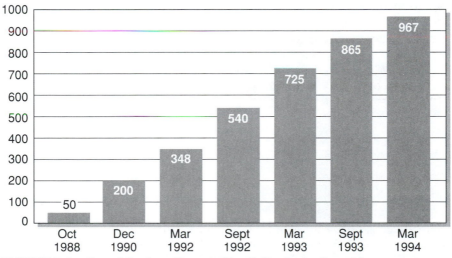

FIGURE 7–2   Gang Members Reported by Police in the Reno Newspaper

to STEP/CAT records reviewed for this study, in 1996 there were 828 active gang members and associates in the city This most recent figure suggests either an actual decline in numbers or a more restrictive application of the gang label to local youth.

Roughly one in five of those in the current gang file were juveniles, an even smaller proportion than discovered in Las Vegas (Figure 7–3). As was true in Las Vegas, those identified as gang members/associates were disproportionately minority (Figure 7–4). Most were Hispanic (about two-thirds), though nearly one in six was white (only 3 percent of those listed in the gang file in Las Vegas were white).

STEP/CAT officers closely follow the most active gangs in the area and freely offered us their perception of the problem (Table 7–2). Many of the gangs were said to be deeply involved with the trafficking and sale of illegal drugs: Well established drug routes have been identified as running between Southern California, Arizona, Las Vegas, and Reno. Though relatively fewer in number and size, as in Las Vegas black gangs in Reno reportedly dominate retail-level drug sales. The much larger number of Hispanic gang members, involved to a lesser degree in the drug business, were said to be much more involved in vehicular theft, residential and commercial burglary, and drive-by shootings.

Officers stated that in most gang violence, the victim is almost always a gang member, a pattern that has not changed over the years. Innocent bystanders have been victims, but such events were reported to be exceptionally rare. This is true despite the fact that gang violence is no longer confined simply to those neighborhoods where gang members reside; on occasion, gang violence erupts in even the "best" of neighborhoods.

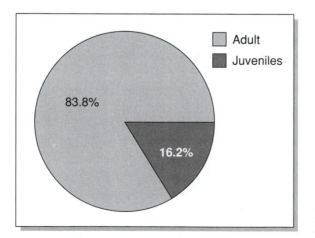

FIGURE 7–3   Adults vs. Juvenile Gang Members in Reno

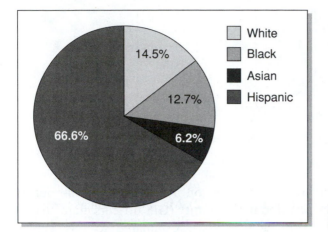

FIGURE 7–4   Race of Gang Members in Reno

STEP/CAT OFFICERS' CLAIMS REGARDING THE THREAT POSED BY RENO GANGS

Officers in the STEP/CAT unit were asked to report, via a self-administered survey, claims regarding the extent, nature, and trends of the gang problem in Reno (Figure 7–5). STEP/CAT officers generally rated the gang problem as less severe than gang officers had in Las Vegas. Only about one in three officers surveyed claimed gangs were a big problem in Reno , a marked contrast to perceptions held by Las Vegas gang officers (all GIS officers reported gangs were a big problem). Reno gang officers were also about half as likely to report that gang crime was the most serious law enforcement problem. They

TABLE 7–2   STEP/CAT Reported Active Gangs

Hispanic Gangs	*Asian Gangs*
Big Top Locos (19)	Flipside (Unknown)
Crazy Varrio Clique (17)	Pinoy Real (130)
Mara Villas (43)	*Black Gangs*
Montellos (93)	Bloods (misc. sets) (38)
South Side Locos (52)	Crips (misc. sets) (151)
Lewis Street (15)	*White/Mixed Gangs*
Mara Salvatruca (18)	East Wood Tokers (16)
Sunset Texas (32)	Skinheads (16)

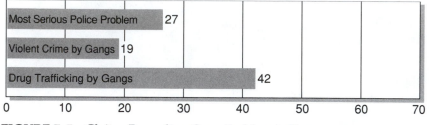

FIGURE 7–5   Claims Regarding Gang Problem in Reno

claimed that area gangs were responsible for, on average, about one out of every five violent crimes that occurred in the county (GIS officers claimed one out of two violent crimes were gang related). Compared to Las Vegas, STEP/CAT officers stated Reno gangs were far less involved in illicit drug trafficking, responsible for a third of all the drug trafficking in the area (compared to reports of two-thirds in Las Vegas).

THE OBJECTIVE THREAT POSED BY STREET GANGS IN RENO

Unfortunately, court monitoring data for Washoe County was not available in a format that lent itself to an examination of aggregate trends in gang and nongang crime, at least in the manner conducted in Clark County. As an alternative method, a list of all charges, defendants, and dispositional outcomes was obtained for all cases processed in Washoe County courts from 1989 through 1995. Supplied with a list of all known gang members and associates by STEP/CAT officials, we conducted a search to identify all gang members/associates processed through the courts in a particular year. To estimate the proportion of various categories of crime committed by gang members and associates, systematic sampling procedures were used to draw a comparison sample of nongang defendants. The process produced a sample comprised of all gang members subjected to court processing during 1989–1995 and a comparison group of roughly 400 to 475 nongang defendants for each of those years.

   In the analysis of those cases, we found that in Washoe County, much more so than in Clark County, there were sharp increases in the proportion of crimes committed by known gang members/ associates over the years of the panic (Figure 7–6).

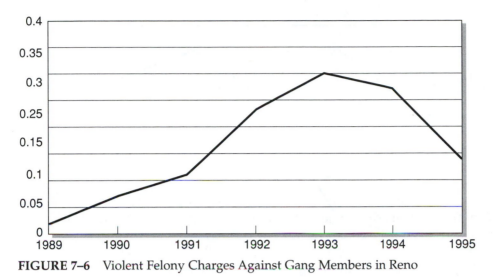

FIGURE 7–6   Violent Felony Charges Against Gang Members in Reno

For example, in 1989 only 2 percent of all violent felony charges in the sample were filed against gang members or their associates. By 1993, that figure had grown to nearly one in three. Similar increases were found for property and weapons offenses (Figure 7–7 and Figure 7–8), although the pattern for drug crimes is smaller and less consistent (Figure 7–9).

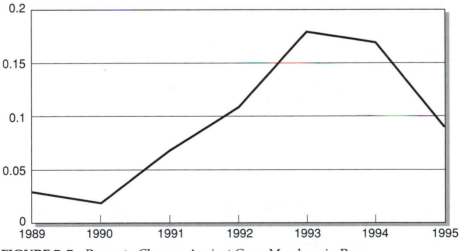

FIGURE 7–7   Property Charges Against Gang Members in Reno

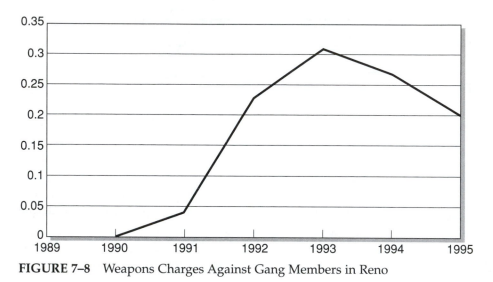

FIGURE 7–8   Weapons Charges Against Gang Members in Reno

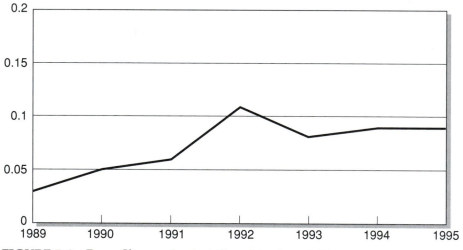

FIGURE 7–9   Drug Charges Against Gang Members in Reno

Conclusion

The response of law enforcement officials in Reno was significantly different from the response to gangs by Las Vegas police. Perhaps the most striking difference is in the manner in which gangs were "discovered" and the source of the panic itself. In Las Vegas, police directed and fueled public fears through repeated but unsubstantiated claims regarding the role of street gangs in violence and illegal drugs. Reno police, on the other hand, were accused by the community—particularly the news media—of being in a state of denial. The panic that swept the city was fueled not by police but primarily the local newspaper. Indeed, its executives were sharply criticized by the minority community for exaggerating and distorting the gang threat for profit.

Certainly, Reno law enforcement officials were aware of the presence of gangs, but rather than exploiting the problem to increase organizational resources, they initially chose to remain calm and provide a measured response to the problem. Official statistics were made public that showed very little of the city's overall crime problem was attributable to gangs. Instead of tough gang suppression tactics, Reno police chose to address the problem through innovative community-based policing practices that focused on prevention and intervention, not simply making arrests. Reno police officers currently assigned to gang duties clearly see gangs as a threat; they do not, however, believe gangs represent the most serious threat to the community.

As in Las Vegas, we concluded that a moral panic concerning gangs had occurred in Reno. But what is also clear is that moral panics can be ignited by the media even in situations where local law enforcement denies, at least initially, that there is a serious gang problem.

Notes

1. Reno Gazette–Journal. 1988. "Police Fear Growth Brings Drugs, Violence." February 21.
2. Reno Gazette–Journal. 1988. "Violent Gangs Worrisome but Can be Beaten." February 24, 1988.
3. Reno Gazette–Journal. 1988. "Local Officials Meet With Street Gang Experts." March 31.
4. Reno Gazette–Journal. 1988. "Jailed Suspect Tells of 13-Year-Old's Rape." April 3.
5. Reno Gazette–Journal. 1988. "City Officials Ponder Task Force to Fight Gang-Related Crime." June 19.
6. Reno Gazette–Journal 1989. "Racist Threats Against Citifare Drivers Alledged." January 5.
7. Reno Gazette–Journal. 1991. "Every Resources Must Be Used to Fight Growing Gang Menace." August 18.
8. Reno Gazette–Journal 1990. "Hispanic Community Critical of Gang Coverage." September 8, 1990.
9. National Alliance of Gang Investigators' Association. 1998. "National Gang Threat Assessment." http://www.nagia.org.
10. Jim Weston. 1993 "Community Policing: An Approach to Youth Gangs in a Medium-Sized City." *The Police Chief.* August. pp. 80–84.
11. Reno Gazette–Journal. 1991. "The Gangs Are Here For Sure; The Whole Community Must Respond." July 17.
12. Weston, 1993; Catherine Conley. 1993. *Street Gangs: Current Knowledge and Strategies.*

Department of Justice. Washington, D.C.: GPO.

13. Office of Juvenile Justice and Delinquency Prevention. 1994. Gang Suppression and Intervention: Community Models. *Research Summary*. Washington, D.C.: GPO.

14. Weston, 1993.

15. Reno Police Department. 1994. *Annual Report on the Status of Gangs in the City of Reno*. Public release version. Mimeographed copy.

16. Reno Gazette–Journal. 1994. "Suit Claims Cops Harass Hispanics." January 25.

17. Reno Gazette–Journal. 1995. "Weston: Only 2% of Reno Crime Committed by Gangs." March 17.

18. Reno Police Department. 1996. General Order No. 3/2226.000: *Criminal Youth Gang Intelligence Procedures*. Mimeographed copy, p. 2, p. 3.

19. Reno Police Department. 1995. *Annual Report on the Status of Gangs in the City of Reno*. Public release version. Mimeographed copy, p. 7.

20. Institute for Intergovernmental Research. 2000. Regional Information Sharing Systems (RISS) Project. Gang Investigation Coordination and Information Collection. http://www.iir.org/riss.

chapter 8

Gangs in the Legislature

The panic that swept through both cities eventually reached the state legislature, sparking heated debate and a frenzy of legislative activity. Without firsthand knowledge of gangs, Nevada law-makers were forced to rely on media accounts that distorted and exaggerated the threat. Moreover, the testimony provided by law enforcement officials during numerous committee hearings on street gangs only heightened their fears. Armed with charts, figures, and frightful anecdotes, in public hearings police portrayed gangs as a clear, present, and extreme danger to the community. Law-makers were outraged by police accounts of firefights between rival gangs, terror-stricken residents sleeping on floors to avoid gunfire, and wounded children. Many were shocked to hear of open-air drug bazaars where crack and other drugs were sold to customers from across the city. Warned that only heroic action would curb the escalating threat, law-makers moved swiftly to pass new laws. Some believed these new laws would, in fact, reduce the gang threat. Others signed on simply because they could not resist the political pressures that had been building during the panic to get tough on gangs.

Ten pieces of gang legislation were drafted, debated, and enacted during the 1989 and 1991 Nevada legislative sessions. Many others were introduced, but never made it out of committee. Through newspapers accounts, records from legislative hearings, and interviews with key state political figures, we were able to reconstruct the events surrounding the passage of legislation during the gang panic. As will be shown in this chapter, these new laws were based on the images of gangs and gang activity supplied by law enforcement and the media. In Chapter 9, we examine the extent to which these new laws corresponded to the reality of the gang problem facing Las Vegas and Reno.

To place what occurred in context, we begin with an overview of how state law-makers across the country have responded to the gang threat. Particular emphasis is placed on gang legislation developed in California, given that it was often the model used in other jurisdictions attempting to fight gangs through tougher laws. This was particularly true in Nevada.

GANG LEGISLATION NATIONALLY

Though gang crimes may sometimes have different motivations, the acts themselves are generally covered by existing criminal statutes. Consequently, very few states have enacted new substantive criminal offenses to deal with gang activity.[1] State codes, for example, typically contain provisions that provide criminal sanctions for those who aid and abet, even though an individual may have not been present at the time of the criminal act. Attempts and conspiracies to commit crimes are on the books in most jurisdictions. In most states traditional criminal statutes have been considered sufficient for local authorities to deal with the crimes committed by street gangs.

Prosecutors also have available federal, and often state, RICO statutes as a means of targeting organized criminal activity. Aimed primarily at the gang–drug connection, this legal strategy allows direct collaboration between local law enforcement and the FBI, DEA, and ATF. Most states have discovered, however, that street gangs generally lack the organization and hierarchical structure of traditional organized criminal groups. Consequently, although 31 states currently have RICO statutes, only 17 percent of large county prosecutors report actually having used them against gang members.[2]

Some states have found existing laws inadequate in the war against gangs. During the 1980s, several enacted gang suppression legislation, typically taking two forms.[3] Some states created *new substantive criminal offenses* to cover gang activity, in particular laws pertaining to random or drive-by shootings and defacing public property with graffiti. In certain jurisdictions, legislation has also targeted crack houses, crimes committed on school grounds, victim intimidation, assault weapons, juvenile waivers, and enhanced parental responsibility. Even though these laws do not specifically mention street gangs, they are intended directly or indirectly to respond to what are perceived as gang-related problems.[4]

The second approach to gang legislation has been the adoption of a *gang statute*, one that incorporates parts of existing codes by reference and provides enhanced penalties for gang-related activity. The prototype for this kind of comprehensive gang statute is California's Street Terrorism Enforcement and Prevention (STEP) Act. During the 1980s, rising concern about the role of gangs in street violence and drug distribution spurred a raft of gang legislation in the state.[5] The attention given to street gangs climbed to new levels in 1988 following a drug- and gang-related drive-by shooting in Westwood Village, Los Angeles— an upscale area frequented by tourists and adjacent to the University of California. Killed in the shooting was Karen Toshima, a young innocent female bystander. More than any other gang incident, her death forced the gang problem to the forefront of the public agenda in California.[6] In the weeks that followed, gangs became the subject of a media frenzy that led, in part, to a new round of legislative activity criminalizing street gangs.

◆◆ _____

Nevada's gang statute was modeled after California's STEP Act.

_____

Based on the RICO model, California's STEP Act made crime committed by street gang members a separate and distinctively punishable offense. As stipulated by the legislation:

> Any person who actively participates in a criminal street gang with knowledge that its members engage in or have engaged in a pattern of criminal activity, and who willfully promotes, furthers, or assists in any felonious criminal conduct by members of that gang, shall be punished in the county jail for a period of not to exceed one year, or by imprisonment in the state prison for one, two or three years (California Penal Code Section 186.22).

Under the statute, a "pattern of criminal gang activity" is defined as the solicitation, attempt, or commission of two or more specified offenses within a three-year period. The specified offenses include assault with a deadly weapon; robbery; unlawful homicide or manslaughter; the sale, possession for sale, transportation, manufacture, etc., of controlled substances; shooting at an inhabited dwelling or occupied motor vehicle; arson; victim or witness intimidation; and grand theft of a vehicle, trailer, or vessel. To avoid constitutional issues, STEP excluded the bulk of gang-related crimes committed for individual rather than gang purposes: almost all thefts, vandalism, minor assaults, weapon and drug possession, and minor assault. Gang members who are, however, convicted of one or more of the specified offenses are subject to one- , two- , or three-year penalty enhancements.

A critical and controversial component of California's STEP Act is the definition of a criminal street gang:

> . . . any ongoing organization, association, or group of three or more persons, whether formal or informal, having as one of its primary activities the commission of one or more of the criminal acts enumerated (above), which has a common name or common identifying sign or symbol, whose members individually or collectively engage in or have engaged in a pattern of criminal gang activity (California Penal Code Section 186.22, pp. 56–57).

To increase the deterrent effect of the statute, a gang is "STEPped": known gang members are notified in writing that they are being targeted and future offenses will be subject to the provisions of the law.[7] To date, four states—Florida, Georgia, Louisiana, and Illinois—have enacted STEP acts based directly on the California model. As will be seen below, other states, such as Nevada, have passed gang statutes that have been greatly influenced by the California legislation.

EVOLUTION OF GANG LEGISLATION IN NEVADA

By the beginning of the 1989 legislative year, concern about gangs in Nevada had reached levels that demanded strong action by elected officials. Las Vegas police were reporting sharp increases in the number of gangs and gang members. Random and drive-by shootings were reportedly on the rise and sensationalized accounts of gang crime were becoming increasingly common in the local press. Parents no longer felt their children were safe on school campuses. Graffiti marred walls, bridges, and billboards.

In January 1989 a Joint Meeting of the Senate and Assembly Committees on Judiciary Concerning Youth Gangs was held to discuss the scope of the problem and legislative alternatives. Law enforcement officials from Las Vegas and Reno provided testimony to lawmakers regarding the size, nature, and trend of gang activity in their respective jurisdictions. Gang members were described as "vicious, capitalistic, and entrepreneurial . . . contemptuous of authority, greedy, and indiscriminate in their actions."[8] According to testimony provided by police officials, Nevada's gangs were essentially an extension of Los Angeles gangs that had migrated to Las Vegas and Reno, lured by the huge potential profits in illicit drug markets. These street gangs were a corrupting force in the lives of Nevada youth, it was claimed, particularly the disadvantaged, who would likely view gang members as attractive role models. Gangs were also engaging in aggressive recruitment efforts; those youth who might resist risked certain injury or even death. These kinds of claims, not once publicly challenged during hearings, were instrumental in persuading law-makers of the need for tough new laws and increased penalties.

LEGISLATIVE RESPONSES TO GANGS IN 1989

As in California and other states, many of the statutes enacted by the Nevada Legislature during the 1989 session did not contain explicit references to gangs. The debate and substance of the legislation, however, was clearly directly toward what was perceived as a growing wave of street gang crime.

During the late 80s and early 90s, thirty-six states passed legislation making it easier to transfer juveniles to adult criminal courts.[9]

Juvenile Court Waivers

One of the problems associated with the prosecution of juvenile gang members is that such cases can frequently fall under the jurisdiction of both the juvenile and adult court systems. In Nevada, for example, juveniles charged with murder or attempted murder are automatically certified as adults and their cases transferred to adult court for prosecution. However, if the case also involves a rape or robbery, or some other offense, the juvenile court retains jurisdiction for the prosecution of those offenses. Consequently, the prosecution of the case would occur in two forums. To address this problem and facilitate the prosecution of gang cases, the Nevada Legislature amended Nevada Revised Statute (hereafter referred to as NRS) 62.060, which removed from the jurisdiction of juvenile court any crime committed by a juvenile arising out of the same set of facts as a murder or attempted murder.

Random and Drive-By Shootings

The 1989 legislature also addressed another problem related to gang prosecutions, one brought to their attention once again by law enforcement authorities. According to police officials, the targets of gang shootings—usually other gang members—refused to cooperate with law enforcement, preferring instead to wait and exact their own version of street justice on the shooter. In cases in which there was no injury to the target, current Nevada law provided for only a misdemeanor charge and, in the absence of a cooperative victim (or an officer who had personally witnessed the shooting), no arrest could be made. Consequently, the Legislature amended NRS 202.290 and increased the penalty for aiming a firearm at a person or discharging a firearm in a public place. Redefining these acts as gross misdemeanors also authorized police to make an arrest without a victim.

Similar arguments were also used to justify the creation of laws specifically designed to address drive-by shootings. According to police testimony at committee hearings, there were no good statistics on the number of these kinds of shootings, but several hundred a year was offered as a conservative estimate. A substantial number of these shootings were said to be drive-bys designed to intimidate or retaliate against rival gang members. Frequently, police added, these shootings occurred on crowded streets or public parks, posing a significant threat to innocent bystanders. The Nevada Legislature responded to these claims by enacting a drive-by shooting statute, adding a new criminal offense (Section 202.287) to the state criminal code. The legislation provided a prison term of one to six years and/or a fine of up to $5,000 for anyone convicted of discharging a firearm out of a motor vehicle in a populated area.

Crimes on School Grounds

Several pieces of legislation were also enacted in 1989 to cover what was reported as an increasing number of crimes committed on school grounds by gangs. Although law enforcement officials were present at hearings on school-related bills, school administrators provided the primary testimony in support of the proposed legislation. Public school officials testified about an alarming increase in the number of firearms confiscated from students on campus. School officials were frustrated because the only available sanction for students caught with a weapon on campus was expulsion, a penalty they believed was clearly not proportional to the offense. Moreover, nonstudents could come on campus with a weapon in plain sight and face no sanction whatsoever. In response, the Nevada Legislature created another new criminal code, making it a gross misdemeanor to carry weapons or firearms on public or private school grounds (NRS Section 202.265).

An existing statute (NRS 392.466) was also amended to strengthened expulsion sanctions against students found carrying weapons on school property, at school-sponsored events, or on school buses. For the first occurrence, the student had to be expelled for at least one year. A second violation brought a permanent expulsion, though a loophole was added allowing the student to be placed in an "alternative" school setting. Law-makers also doubled the prison sentences for anyone committing a felony on a school bus (Section 193.161). Penalties were also doubled for selling drugs on or nearby school grounds, bus stops, playgrounds, public swiming pools, recreation centers, and video arcades (Section 453.3345).

Using Minors in Drug Trafficking

According to school security police from Las Vegas and Reno, as well as representatives from law enforcement, there had been a proliferation of drug activity on school campuses during the late 1980s. Adult gang members were reportedly recruiting juveniles, some said to be as young as nine years old, to peddle illicit drugs to classmates. By letting juveniles control retail sales, these adult gang members reduced their operating risks while continuing to rake in enormous profits. After only brief debate, mainly as to how such legislation might affect state prison populations, the legislature doubled prison terms for anyone convicted of using a minor as an agent in the sale or distribution of illicit drugs (Section 453.3343).

A Center for Disease Control Study in 1990 found 1 in 20 high school students in the U.S. reported having carried a firearm to school in the past 30 days.[10]

Public Housing Evictions

Existing statutes were also amended to create a mechanism by which persons living in public housing and convicted of the manufacture, distribution, or sale of illegal drugs could be evicted. This action was necessary, according to testimony given by public housing authority officials, to address the "considerable" amount of drug activity taking place in low-income housing. Section 315.011 was subsequently amended to deal with "an intimidating minority of the residents of public housing . . . causing our public housing to become increasingly infested with violence, degeneracy and squalor. . . ." The statute provided authority to evict from public housing (or government-subsidized private housing) not only those who actively participated in unlawful activities, but also those resided with such persons.

There were additional bills proposed to the legislature that were, however, not enacted into law. For example, Assembly Bill 806 would have made it a misdemeanor to entice, procure, or induce any person under 21 years of age to become a member of a street gang. The bill, primarily affecting high schools, would also have mandated closed campuses for Nevada public schools. Students would no longer be permitted to leave the campus during the noon hour for lunch, or at other times of the day for work purposes: Once students arrived, they would not be permitted to leave. Such a measure was proposed by police officials, who stated that it would "reduce gang clashes" by preventing unauthorized persons from entering school grounds. This first section of the bill died in committee due to what were perceived as First Amendment infringements. The closed campus component was also rejected, in part because of the prohibitive expense of expanding school cafeterias to meet the increased demand.

1991 NEVADA LEGISLATIVE ACTIVITY

The "Gang-Buster" Tax

The escalation of gang activity in 1990 and 1991 reported by law enforcement strongly suggested that the efforts of the 1989 legislature had been inadequate and that even stronger measures were necessary to deal with gangs. In June 1991, a bill was introduced in the Nevada State Assembly which would have provided massive funding for a new State Task Force to combat street gangs. As introduced, A.B. 673 would have authorized the "imposition of property tax for prevention and suppression of criminal gang activities upon approval of voters." The bill defined criminal gangs as:

> . . . an association or group of three or more persons, organized formally or informally, with a common name or identifying symbol, whose members, individually or collectively, engage in criminal activity punishable as a felony (Nevada State Assembly Bill 673, Section 6).

This bill would have mandated county commissioners in counties of 100,000 or more to levy a tax of 3 cents on each $100 of assessed valuation of taxable property within the county. In counties of less than 100,000 residents, such a tax was permissible, but not required under the law. Only two counties—Clark (Las Vegas) and Washoe (Reno)—had populations that would have mandated the collection of this tax. Monies collected would be distributed quarterly among cities in the county in proportion to the total estimated number of criminal gang members for that county. Estimates of gang membership would be provided by the investigation division of the department of motor vehicles and public safety, the chief of that division being responsible for developing and operating a system of recording all information on persons with alleged connections with or who were members of criminal gangs.

The bill was debated in the Assembly Committee on Taxation in June 1991. Law enforcement officials from southern Nevada were present and provided testimony in support of the bill. One high-ranking police official testified that five years earlier, there had been no "extensive" gang problem in the community. He chastised law makers for not giving more attention and resources to the problem earlier; their inaction had placed the public at great risk. The police official warned legislators that the "longer the delay now, the worse the problem would grow." That prediction was echoed by another law enforcement official who, armed with an impressive array of charts, statistics, and color-coded maps, offered testimony that the problem was bad and growing worse. Though conceding it was "difficult to determine exactly what percentage of the city's total crime incidents are gang-related," he assured law makers that "in certain areas, the majority of activity is gang- and drug-related."[11]

Also testifying at the hearing was the head of Las Vegas Metropolitan Police Department's (LVMPD) gang unit. More numbers were presented ostensibly reflecting the extent and growth of gang activity in the city. Law-makers were reminded of the gang problem in Los Angeles, a city that, in his opinion, had "lost the war" against street gangs. He warned that unless sufficient resources were directed to the gang problem in Las Vegas, the city risked a similar fate. With the funds provided by this new tax, he assured law makers it would be possible to establish a credible police presence in gang-infested areas. In so doing, the police would become the intimidators and no longer the intimidated. Rising gang populations would be checked as the hanger-ons and wannabees would be deterred from full participation in gangs. The "hard-core, original gangster," he had concluded, would remain undaunted, but more gang officers on the street increased the likelihood that these incorrigibles would be arrested and removed from blighted neighborhoods.

There was no substantive debate as to the actual threat posed by street gangs. No one stepped forward to challenge law enforcement statistics or predictions. Police numbers and anecdotes were accepted as reflecting an underlying objective reality. Even a representative from the Nevada Taxpayers Association acquiesced to the need for a gang tax. Her primary concern was that rural cities within a county—those without a gang problem—would be taxed to pay for what was essentially an urban phenomenon.

The bill went through a number of revisions and was subsequently passed by the Assembly. It suffered a quick death, however, when sent to the Senate Committee on Taxation. With the state teetering on the edge of recession in the early 1990s, law-makers were reluctant to increase the taxes on Nevada residents.

THE GANG ENHANCEMENT STATUTE

In an impassioned speech the day following the cafeteria shooting in August 1990, the Governor of Nevada announced what he believed would be the coup de grace: a complete ban on gang membership. The statute, he promised, would be broadly written to ensure that "wearing gang colors, hanging around gangs, or even bragging about being in a gang" would be a criminal offense and subject to swift, severe sanctions.[12] The initial draft of his Gang Abolishment Act drew sharp criticism from local ACLU officials who claimed that, given the majority of identified gang members were minorities, the bill had disturbing racial overtones.[13] Veiled racism aside, the ACLU also maintained that such a law would be in clear violation of First Amendment guarantees to free association.

The initial draft consequently underwent major revisions, the charge of producing a workable gang bill principally falling to the LVMPD, the Clark County Prosecutor's Office as well. Redactors relied heavily on California's Street Terrorism and Enforcement and Prevention Act, a comprehensive piece of gang legislation that had withstood the scrutiny of California's appellate court.[14] Critical elements of the bill as drafted included a definition of criminal gang activity:

> Criminal gang activity is the commission, attempted commission, or solicitation of two or more of the following offenses, if at least one of the offenses occurred after the effective date of this act, the most recent of the offenses occurred within three years after an earlier offense and the offenses were committed on separate occasions or by two or more persons: (a) Murder (b) Manslaughter (c) Assault with a deadly weapon (d) Arson (e) Robbery (f) Theft of any vehicle (g) Shooting at an inhabited dwelling or occupied vehicle (h) Harassment (i) Any violation of NRS 453.326 to 453.338 inclusive.

In the initial versions of the bill, a criminal gang was specified as:

> . . . an association or group of three or more persons, organized formally or informally, with a common name or identifying sign or symbol, that has as one of its primary activities the commission of criminal gang activity and whose members, individually or collectively, engage in or have engaged in criminal gang activity.

◆◆
_____

> Law enforcement spokesmen have a special advantage over legislation given their access to government and their monopoly over crime information.[15]

_____

The language of the section on penalties similarly reflects the influence of the California model. S.B. 230 created no new separate offenses, but simply provided additional penalties for the primary offenses listed above.

> A person who is convicted of a felony committed for the benefit of, at the direction of, or in association with a criminal gang, with the specific intent to promote, further or assist any criminal conduct by a gang member, shall be punished by imprisonment in the state prison for a term of 3 years in addition to the term of imprisonment prescribed by statute for the crime. A person who is convicted of a misdemeanor committed for the benefit of, at the direction of, or in association with, a criminal gang, with the specific intent to promote, further or assist any criminal conduct by a gang, shall be punished: (a) By imprisonment in the county jail for a term not to exceed 1 year; or (b) By imprisonment in the state prison for a term not to exceed 3 years, in addition to the term of imprisonment prescribed by the statute for the crime.

As in California's STEP Act, a person convicted of a life felony would be required to serve a minimum of fifteen years before being eligible for parole. The language of S.B. 230 also permitted "double enhancements." For example, a person convicted of attempted battery in Nevada currently faced a penalty of one to three years. Under Nevada law, if that attempted battery involved the use of a deadly weapon, sentence enhancements would double the sanction, allowing for a prison term of up to six years. If that person were also convicted under the law proposed by S.B. 230, an additional three years could be tacked on to the sentence.

At a hearing of the Joint Senate and Assembly Nevada Committee on the Judiciary held in February of 1991, the proposed Gang Enhancement Statute took center stage. The meeting began with an overview of the gang problem in southern Nevada, provided by the ranking officer in LVMPD's gang unit.[16] Charts were presented depicting the growth, location, and criminal specializations of area street gangs. Testimony was given claiming that the number of street gangs and gang members over the past several years had "exploded." There were now gangs, he continued, in every geographical area of the city with at least one gang, sometimes several, in every Las Vegas high school. Gangs were now highly organized and ruthlessly driven to increase their profits from illegal drugs and crime.

Even more disturbing, he added, were the changes he had observed in gang members' attitudes and activities in recent years. Gangsters had become more brazen, increasingly involved in armed burglaries of occupied residences and carjackings. Law-makers were shocked by his vivid account of an incident in which a driver was shot in the face after refusing to give his keys to a "frenzied" gang member. He added that gang members displayed levels of contempt for authority previously unseen. As an illustration of gang disdain for the institutions of civil society, he reminded his audience of the bloody shootout between Blood and Crip members on the steps of City Hall. Another law enforcement officer, not assigned to the gang unit, also spoke to the more violent nature of gang members on the streets of Las Vegas.

> . . . it used to be they were fighting each other with sticks and baseball bats. That's no longer true. The weapons of choice are now 357 magnums, sawed-off shotguns, and automatic weapons . . . it used to be very seldom a police officer would stop a juvenile and find him carrying a weapon. That's no longer so . . . now when you stop a juvenile gang member, in all probability, he is carrying a weapon.[17]

Gangs were claimed by both officers to represent a clear and present danger to the community. But in what had become a common rhetorical device, emphasis was placed on the threat gangs posed to children. Area street gangs were said to be actively recruiting juveniles and using them as look-outs and runners in illicit drug sales and car thefts. Their recruitment efforts were said to be frequently successful because many at-risk kids "feel a need to belong . . . they come from broken homes, have low esteem . . . and the gang becomes their family."[18] In his concluding remarks, Lt. Hawkins offered a final admonition to legislators:

> Gangs are more than a passing fad . . . they are not going away; they're here to stay. We can look to southern California to see what they're experiencing and be forewarned about what we are in store for in Las Vegas. . . they're not going away because there are huge profits involved . . . the gang members portray an attractive role model to young kids . . . they aspire to be like them; they want to drive fancy cars, have a pocket full of money and wear a lot of jewelry. Of utmost importance, gangs are growing because they have not been held accountable for their actions . . . they know in a lot of cases they are not going to face prison time . . . we have to aggressively enforce the laws and to put them into prison, we need help in passing laws that will give those powers. A couple of months ago we indicted some kids on a racketeering drug charge, and during that trial we invited Sergeant Robert McBride of the Los Angeles Police Department to come as an expert witness. While Bob was up here he went into great detail as to what they are experiencing in southern California and readily admitted to us that they had written off and given up large neighborhoods in southern California . . . he said "You still have a chance in Las Vegas; you can still win it". . . I would submit to you, ladies and gentlemen, that we can.[19]

To remind law-makers of what could happen if swift actions was not taken, LVMPD brought in the head of Los Angeles's Hard Core Gang Unit, an office in the District Attorney's Office that dealt specifically with gang-related homicides in Watts, Compton, and South Central Los Angeles. He testified that . . .

. . . Los Angeles is a city under siege . . . it is a difficult place to exist in terms of prosecuting cases, in terms of law enforcement and for kids to go out at night in certain parts of Los Angeles. You have the opportunity here, based upon these hearings, to pass legislation early on . . . believe me, this area is attractive to gang members and its something you all need to be concerned about.[20]

Representatives from the district attorney's office were also present at the hearing. They contended that the proposed bill, if enacted into law, would be a preemptive strike against gangs. It would allow them to target gang leaders aggressively, since under the statute previously excluded evidence could, for the first time, be introduced at trial that would allow judges and juries to see the whole picture. School officials testified to the need for quick action, reminding legislators that while they "philosophize" about the gang problem, students are being "intimidated, injured, and killed" in local schools. The superintendent of the school district in Clark County argued:

I think now is the time for everybody to step forward. At some point we have to say enough is enough . . . if you assume it will get better you are in for a rude awakening. I am an educator and administrator, but we have what I think is a sacred obligation to young people today to protect them and make sure they are well educated. We have great difficulty doing that in the current climate. This is not an overreaction. This is not hysteria.[21]

This was not to be end of the debate on the proposed Gang Enhancement Statute. Subsequent hearings produced additional revisions to the bill, dropping the enhancements for misdemeanors, tightening the definition of gangs, and allowing judges some discretion in waiving enhanced sentences for defendants who aided in prosecution efforts. When submitted to a vote before the full Senate, the bill sailed through the Senate, attracting only four opponents, the most critical a black Senator who characterized the legislation as a "veiled effort to incarcerate more minorities."[22] In the minutes prior to the final vote on the bill in the Senate, Neal scolded his colleagues for avoiding the underlying issues and their desire for quick and easy solutions to the gang problem.

I rise in opposition to this bill, even though I understand the concern that the bill is attempting to reach. I've sat with members of the Judiciary Nevada Committee and listened to the testimony that was given in reference to why this bill should be needed. I heard the bigots, including the chairman of the Nevada Committee there, tell us about the five thousand or so gang members that were in the Las Vegas area. But, when it came time to demonstrate and show who the gang members were, we were only shown black members of gangs. So that raised a concern in my mind about this measure and what it would do. What we have seen that has happened in this country, in terms of arresting a black youth, we now have one out of four black youths between 16 and 24 that are part of the prison system in this country. I know that we feel good about pushing our green buttons here today and wipe our hands of this particular situation. As long as you have these social-economic conditions, you're going to continue to have gangs. I don't care what the penalties are. You'll have gangs. I see this measure, since you know the governor is part of my party, he pushed this measure. But he pushed this measure in the same context that Bush pushed the measure against Willie Horton.[23]

Following the 20-minute diatribe, most senators conceded the need for more prevention. Some even called for additional debate. However, another senator, the co-sponsor of the Gang Enhancement bill, then stood to remind fellow law-makers that "in the time it took for the Senator to deliver his remarks, three more people were killed in gang-related incidences around the country."[24] A vote was taken, and the bill was sent to the State Assembly. In an interview conducted in the course of this research, the chief sponsor of the bill conceded few law-makers had high expectations for the statute. Most, she had concluded, were simply swept along by the "political wave" that had been building for some time in the state to "really get tough" on gangs.[25] The same political pressures to act against the gang threat guaranteed smooth sailing in the Assembly. With far less debate than in the Senate, the Assembly passed the measure by a 39–3 vote. One dissenter, Wendell Williams, a black assemblyman from Las Vegas, made it clear why he had chosen not support the bill:

> . . . as long as we continue to ignore the causes and only address the symptoms, we'll continue to pass incriminating and discriminating laws that will only escalate the problem, and this is one. This bill will actually do nothing in the war against gangs as long as we continue to have a low-income housing fund with no funds in it . . . as long as we expect our children to come to school hungry from the night before . . . unless we begin to address one of the highest unemployment rates among teenagers in the nation.[26]

Elements of the Gang Enhancement Statute

Backers of the legislation were convinced that, these underlying problems aside, tougher penalties were critical to the battle against crime in general and gangs in particular. Nevertheless, the passage of the bill came only after major revisions were made. There were modifications, for example, in the definition of what constitutes a criminal gang. The definition became more inclusive, dropping the stipulation that only groups of three or more could be considered a gang. It was also was rewritten to be more consistent with existing RICO statutes, giving emphasis to what was believed to be the central feature of criminal organizations: permanence. The scope of the statute was narrowed, but toughened. The specific list of gang offenses (murder, harassment, robbery, etc.) was dropped, legislators hoping to exploit the deterrent effect of the statute by making the commission of any felony a trigger for the enhancement. Misdemeanors and gross misdemeanors were also excluded from the bill, largely as a result of pressure from minority legislators who hoped to lessen the blow of the statute to minority communities.[27]

> . . . "criminal gang" means any combination of persons, organized formally or informally, so constructed that the organization *will continue its operation even if individual members enter or leave the organization* (italics added), which:
>   (a) Has a common name or identifying symbol;
>   (b) Has particular conduct, status and customs indicative of it; and
>   (c) Has one of its common activities engaging in criminal activity punishable
>   as a felony, other than the conduct which constitutes the primary offense
> (Nevada Revised Statutes 193.168, Section 6)

But the most striking revision involved the penalty itself: from a 1–3 year enhancement to a doubling of the prison term for the primary offense—the toughest in the country.[28] Though legislators undoubtedly wanted to send a strong message to gang members, the passage of an even tougher law clearly reflected the ongoing politicalization of gangs in Nevada, the product of elected officials not wanting to appear soft on crime.

> . . . any person who is convicted of a felony committed knowingly for the benefit of, at the direction of, or in affiliation with, a criminal gang, with the specific intent to promote, further or assist the activities of the criminal gang, shall be punished by imprisonment in the state prison for a term equal to and in addition to the term of imprisonment prescribed by the statute for the crime. The sentence prescribed by this section must run consecutively with the sentence prescribed by statute for the crime (Nevada Revised Statutes 193.168, Section 1).

The determination as to whether a particular group constituted a gang, or an individual was a gang member, still would be based on the expert testimony of law enforcement personnel. That officer's testimony would also be allowed in court to establish that a crime was gang motivated and thus subject to the Gang Enhancement Statute.

> In any proceeding to determine whether an additional penalty may be imposed pursuant to this section, expert testimony is admissible to show particular conduct, status and customs indicative of criminal gangs, including, but not limited to:
>   (a) Characteristics of persons who are members of criminal gangs;
>   (b) Specific rivalries between criminal gangs;
>   (c) Common practices and operations of criminal gangs and the members of
>   those gangs;
>   (d) Social customs and behavior of members of criminal gangs;

(e) Terminology used by members of criminal gangs;

(f) Codes of conduct, including criminal conduct, of particular gangs, and

(g) The types of crimes that are likely to be committed by a particular criminal gang or by criminal gangs in general.

(Nevada Revised Statutes 193.168, Section 5)

The bill retained the provision that prohibited the court from granting probation to or suspending the sentence of any person convicted of a felony directed by or for the benefit of a criminal gang. An exception was carved out, allowing judges to suspend or reduce the sentence imposed on the primary offense in instances where the defendant renders "substantial assistance in the arrest and conviction of any other principals, accomplices, accessories or coconspirators" to gang-related crimes. Such a provision was included to give the prosecution a powerful plea-bargaining tool in gang cases involving multiple defendants. There is nothing in the existing statute that prohibits double enhancements, though case law forbids the practice.

In the past two legislative sessions (1993 and 1995), no new antigang legislation was enacted by law-makers. The panic that gripped the state during the late 1980s and early 1990s had subsided, though it had clearly left its mark on Nevada's criminal code.

Conclusion

During the late 1980s and early 1990s, Nevada passed a variety of new criminal codes and sentencing enhancements designed to address what was perceived as a rising tide of gang crime. Law enforcement personnel figured prominently in the legislative process, engaging in intense and sustained lobbying efforts during the period. At government hearings, police representatives offered testimony regarding the growing threat of street gangs, cultivating the perception that war-weary officers were outgunned and outmanned in street confrontations with gang-bangers. Police officials were also directly involved in the drafting of much of the legislation for which they lobbied. Undoubtedly, law enforcement officials believed that their efforts served the public interest; many abhorrent and irrational acts of violence were, in fact, being committed by offenders with gang affiliations. But the threat posed by such persons was subject to error and interpretation. No one stepped forward, however, to question the manner in which the gang problem had been defined or measured.

With these new or enhanced criminal codes, the legislature had provided local police and prosecutors with the weapons believed necessary to combat gang crime. In so doing, it shifted the responsibility for curbing gang violence to local law enforcement and court personnel. It would be in the trenches—on the streets and in the courtroom—where the battle against gangs would be won or lost.

Notes

1. Claire Johnson, Barbara Webster and Edward Connors. 1995 *Prosecuting Gangs: A National Assessment*. National Institute of Justice. Research in Brief. Washington, D.C.: GPO.
2. Johnson, Webster, and Connors, 1995.
3. Johnson, Webster, and Connors, 1995.
4. Johnson, Webster, and Connors, 1995.
5. Patrick Jackson and Cary Rudman. 1993. Moral panic and the response to gangs in California. In *Gangs: The Origin and Impact of Contemporary Youth Gangs in the United States*, S. Cummings and D. Monti (eds.). New York: SUNY Press.
6. Jackson and Rudman, 1993.
7. Malcolm W. Klein. 1995. *The American Street Gang: Its Nature, Prevalence, and Control*. New York: Oxford University Press.
8. Ken Elverum. 1989. Notes from Joint Meeting of the Senate and Assembly Committees on Judiciary Concerning Youth Gangs. State of Nevada Legislative Counsel Bureau. Carson City, Nevada. Mimeographed copy.
9. Office of Juvenile Justice and Delinquency Prevention. 1996. State Responses to Serious and Violent Juvenile Crime. *Research Report*. Washington, D.C.: Government Printing Office.
10. Center for Disease Control and Prevention. 1990. "Weapon Carrying Among High School Students." *Morbidity and Mortality Report*. Vol. 40, pp. 681–684.
11. Nevada Committee on Taxation. 1991. Minutes of the Assembly Committee on Taxation, Sixty-Sixth Session, June 6, p. 147. Mimeographed copy.
12. *Las Vegas Sun*. 1990. "Gov. Miller wants gangs outlawed." August 28.
13. Chad Kendrick. 1995. Director, American Civil Liberties Union, Clark County, Nevada Branch. Personal communication, July 18.
14. Nevada Committee on Judiciary. 1991. Minutes of the Joint Senate and Assembly Committee on Judiciary, Sixty-Sixth Session, February 13. Mimeographed copy.
15. Daniel Glaser. 1978. *Crime in Our Changing Society*. New York: Holt, Rinehart, and Winston.
16. Nevada Committee on Judiciary, 1991[a] (February 13), pp. 2–6.
17. Nevada Committee on Judiciary, 1991[a] (February 13), p. 8.
18. Nevada Committee on Judiciary, 1991[a] (February 13), p. 5.
19. Nevada Committee on Judiciary, 1991[a] (February 13), p. 6.
20. Nevada Committee on Judiciary, 1991[b] (February 13), p. 2.
21. Nevada Committee on Judiciary, 1991[b] (February 13), p. 8.
22. Joe Neal. 1995. Nevada State Senator. Personal communication, August 13.
23. Nevada Senate Daily Journal. 1991. Hearing on Senate Bill No. 230, p. 4–5. March 28.
24. Nevada Senate Daily Journal. 1991. Hearing on Senate Bill No. 230, p. 6. March 28.
25. Dina Titus. Nevada State Senator. Personal communication, October 12.
26. Nevada Assembly Daily Journal. 1991. Hearing on Senate Bill No. 230, p. 6. May 21.
27. Neal, 1995.
28. Johnson, Webster, and Connors, 1995.

chapter   9

Prosecuting Gangs

◆◆◆

Convinced it was impossible to effectively prosecute gangs using conventional strategies, prosecutors in Las Vegas and Reno created new organizational forms which promised to maximize conviction rates and increase prison sentences for gang members. Only through these specialized gang prosecution units, prosecutors would argue, could the statutory tools provided by the Nevada legislature be put to good account. In this chapter, we describe the events surrounding the creation of gang prosecution units in both cities. We also evaluate the claims made suggesting that gang crime and gang offenders were different from the run-of-the-mill, but much more common, cases and criminals processed in the justice system.

GANG PROSECUTION NATIONALLY

Gang cases can pose special problems for prosecutors.[1] Often they involve juveniles and adults working together and thus have to be prosecuted in different courts. Victims and witnesses are frequently other gang members who may be reluctant to testify. Prosecuting gang cases can mean placing the safety of victims and witnesses in jeopardy. The homes, families, and jobs of nongang witnesses and victims are often located in areas controlled by gangs, making them vulnerable to retaliatory violence. Jurors may also be subjected to intimidation tactics during court proceedings, from the defendant and also from fellow gang members who may be in attendance. In addition, effective prosecution of gang crime requires specialized knowledge of gang activities and the community context in which they occur. According to prosecutors assigned to Operation Hardcore, the Los Angeles gang prosecution unit:

> Gang cases are not easy to prosecute. Ten years ago the Los Angeles District Attorney's Office was losing a large percentage of them because gang members did not want to testify against rival gang members. Instead they preferred street "payback." Furthermore, if non-gang witnesses were at the scene, they were either too

frightened to cooperate or soon became so because of threats, actual physical intimidation or murder. There was another factor: gang members talked a language unique
to their culture. Attorneys did not maximize results because they did not know what
questions to ask or how to ask them.[2]

For decades prosecutors did not address the gang-related nature of many
crimes. Many believed that to identify a crime as gang-related ran the risk of
diverting the jury's attention away from the crime and toward the question of
gang affiliation.[3] This distraction was viewed by many prosecutors as counter-
productive, and thus to be avoided. In addition, many prosecutors did not have
enough information from law enforcement about the gang-related nature of
the crime. Many probably felt that their job was to prosecute offenders; who those
offenders were or to what groups they were affiliated was judged as irrelevant.
Crime was crime.

Some jurisdictions, however, decided gang crime was "different" and developed new approaches and organizational forms to prosecute gang members more
effectively. A survey of prosecutors' offices conducted in 1992 by the Institute for
Law and Justice found that 30 percent of prosecutors in large jurisdictions (counties
with populations over 250,000) and 5 percent in small jurisdictions (50,000 to
250,000) had formed specialized gang units.[4] In larger jurisdictions, these units
were typically staffed by two to four full-time attorneys.

Many of these gang units were modeled after Operation Hardcore, a program
developed in the Los Angeles County District Attorney's Office during the late
1970s. Operation Hardcore currently has a staff of 48 full-time, carefully selected
attorneys, a special investigative support team directly attached to the unit, and
low caseloads for both the attorneys and investigators. The unit emphasizes early
involvement in case preparation and investigation, widening the scope of search
warrants, pretrial detention through high bail requests, and the use of expert
witnesses who can establish gang membership and educate juries on gang culture,
practices, and rivalries. Special attention is also paid to witnesses. The unit
coordinates protection and relocation efforts, tapes witness statements, and
aggressively prosecutes witness intimidation.[5]

THE CLARK COUNTY
GANG PROSECUTION UNIT

Only a few weeks after its passage, local prosecutors concluded that the Gang
Enhancement statute was a necessary, but not sufficient, tool to fight gangs
effectively. In August 1991, the district attorney for Clark County suggested that
a specialized prosecution unit be created in response to what he now believed was

"an out of hand situation."[6] Even with the new legislation, according to the D.A.'s office, the complexities of gang cases made the application of the statute difficult.[7] Evidence required to support allegations of gang-sponsored crime was difficult to obtain, multiple defendants were the norm—often both juvenile and adult defendants, and critical witnesses were either afraid or other gang members who, for obvious reasons, made for reluctant witnesses. The author of the proposal to fund a gang prosecution unit in Clark County argued:

> In order for the criminal justice system to fulfill its goal of protection and deterrence, law enforcement and prosecutors must target those involved in gangs and those contemplating involvement in the gang and they must be put on notice that they will be swiftly and vigorously prosecuted if they are arrested for a gang related offense. However, the current system is not able to guarantee such a result because of the imbalance of resources. Although there is a special unit within the Las Vegas Metropolitan Police Department of 21 officers who investigate and gather information about gangs and gang members and probation officers who are involved solely with gang related cases, no such unit has been given budget approval at the District Attorney's Office in the future. As a consequence, without sufficient prosecutors the criminal justice system becomes nothing more than a revolving door through which arrested gang members are released within hours, to return to the streets to terrorize neighborhoods and intimidate and/or kill witnesses.[8]

As originally envisioned by the Clark County District Attorney's Office, the gang unit would be comprised of three prosecutors, each highly trained in the idiosyncrasies of gang prosecution cases and provided the time to develop rapport with witnesses. Small caseloads would permit the prosecution of gang cases, with a single prosecutor assigned to a case when a criminal complaint is filed and working that case until its final disposition.

In September 1991, the district attorney prepared to go before the Clark County Commission and request full funding for the gang unit, armed with a formal proposal outlining in detail the unit's objectives and the expected costs. Several days before the hearing, a call from the county manager reminded the district attorney of ongoing declines in local gaming and sales tax revenues, suggesting to the D.A. that a prosecution unit was, at this time, little more than a pipe dream.[9] The county manager suggested a gradual phase-in of the program.

Clark County Nevada's gang unit was modeled closely after Los Angeles's "Operation Hardcore."

The district attorney conceded and submitted a revised proposal to the Commission that requested funding only for an additional attorney to assist in prosecuting gang cases. Shortly into his presentation of the proposal at the hearing, two commissioners—aware of the D.A.'s original plan for a gang unit—began an emotional charge intent on convincing their elected colleagues of the danger posed by gangs. They reminded other commissioners of promises they each had made to increase public safety, promises that were partially responsible for their victories in the most recent election, and pressed them to provide full funding for the special unit in the district attorney's office.[10]

However, there was no proposal before the Commission for such a unit; to have provided support, without even a preliminary budget before them, would have been in violation of their own procedural rules. Confusion reigned. After several minutes of parliamentary bickering, calm returned to the chamber and the Commission, despite the procedural irregularity, voted 6–0 in support of the gang unit. Attempting to justify the rashness of the Commission's decision, one commissioner stated afterwards that "if one witness can be protected, if one gang member can be diverted from criminal activity, the action the board took tonight is well worth it."[11]

Objectives of the Gang Prosecution Unit

Clark County's Gang Prosecution Unit began operation in the Fall 1991. To have an impact on gang activity in the area, prosecutors assigned to the unit stated they would aggressively pursue a set of diverse and ambitious objectives.[12]

Gang-Tracking System Prosecutors lobbied hard for the development and operation of a centralized clearing house for information on gangs, gang membership, and gang-related criminal activities in Clark County. This information would come primarily from field investigation reports prepared by local law enforcement in general, and gang officers in particular. The database would be updated daily and would represent an on-line source of intelligence for local law enforcement, the courts, prosecution, and probation. One gang unit prosecutor, attempting to build support for the project, claimed that the kind of information maintained would not only allow more effective prosecution, but would also "allow us to more effectively assist in the rehabilitation of gang members."[13] Sentencing decisions would benefit, he explained, from knowing where a gang member lives, where he attends school, and who his friends are. Probation officers completing presentence investigations would also be able to ascertain the nature and extent of the gang problem in an offender's neighborhood, as well as degree of the offender's involvement in gangs. Such information, he suggested, might mean the difference between prison and probation.

Case Screening and Vertical Prosecution   Although the gang unit as proposed was to accept all gang-related cases coming into the system, in reality prosecutors would carefully screen and retain only those more problematic cases. All misdemeanor gang cases, and all but the most serious felony cases involving gang members or associates, were sent out for normal "track" prosecution. The unit also pledged to monitor the more active or violent gang members in the community and give them high prosecution priority should they be charged with a crime of any kind.[14]

Cases retained would be subjected to a vertical prosecution strategy, which, according to the lead gang unit prosecutor, was a "proven technique" that ensured "appropriate, swift, and sure punishment for the gang offender."[15] Bail motions, probable cause hearings, writs of habeas corpus, and other pretrial motions would all be handled by a gang unit deputy district attorney.

Victim Witness Protection   One of the primary duties of the investigators assigned to the Gang Unit would be to provide support for the management of victims and witnesses in gang cases. Investigators would be responsible for coordinating activities involving witness and victim case management with the Victim Witness Assistance Center. Investigators would be charged with insulating witnesses from potential threats and violence, including transporting them to and from the court, the courtroom, and being visible during the proceedings to deter intimidation from gang members. The Gang Unit would also be responsible for taking whatever steps were necessary to ensure the safety and protection of all parties against hostile gang members before, during, and after court.

Interagency Coordination   The District Attorney's Office recognized that gang prosecution alone is not the "sole solution to the problem of gangs, though it is an essential component."[16] Combating gangs required a team approach, one involving not only police and prosecutors but schools, churches, local service providers, and treatment centers. In the proposal, prosecutors pledged to provide leadership and coordination for public and private agencies in the community dedicated to curbing gang activity. The Gang Prosecution Unit would also be involved, through their input into presentence investigations, in diverting certain gang members to community-based alternative programs.

One-third of prosecutors in large jurisdictions have established gang units that use vertical prosecution strategies.[17]

Probation and Parole Monitoring   The Gang Prosecution Unit would have regular communication with parole and probation agencies with the goal of facilitating revocations in cases in which offenders continued to participate in gang activities. At sentencing, a recommendation could also be made to the judge that an offender be ordered to refrain from association with other known gang members. A violation of this specific condition, brought to the attention of probation officers by the Gang Prosecution Unit, would be grounds for a revocation hearing.

Joint State–Federal Task Force   The primary target of the Gang Prosecution Unit was the most dangerous hard-core gang members. Such persons, it was believed, were deeply involved in the sale and manufacture of illegal drugs. By working with federal, state, and local law enforcement agencies, prosecutors were convinced that the number of felony drug convictions against hard-core gang leaders would increase. Success would be assured, in part, because of access to the federal resources critical to intensive drug investigations (i.e., the cultivation of confidential informants, undercover stings, etc.). Furthermore, gang members netted through this joint action would be subject to the more severe sentences handed out by the federal courts. The Gang Prosecution Unit would provide the necessary coordination between local and state law enforcement and the United States District Attorney's Office, the Federal Bureau of Investigation, the Drug Enforcement Agency, and the Bureau of Alcohol, Tobacco, and Firearms.

Claims of Success   In early 1994, a report documenting the effectiveness of the Gang Prosecution Unit was submitted to Clark County Commissioners. According to the chief deputy district attorney within the unit, convictions were obtained in 92 percent of gang trials conducted in 1993. Nearly two-thirds of all felony defendants convicted had reportedly received a prison sentence, the average term being approximately eight years. These outcomes, the report went on to say, were "particularly significant in light of the fact that the overwhelming majority of these offenders are juveniles or are individuals with very limited prior criminal histories."[18] Overall, the Gang Prosecution Unit effort claimed it was responsible for incarcerating nearly 200 "prolifically violent gang offenders, many of whom would be otherwise free and criminally active upon the streets of the community."[19]

WASHOE COUNTY DANGEROUS YOUTHFUL OFFENDER TEAM

Though a gang prosecution unit was not formed until some years later, the district attorney of Washoe County actually declared a "war on gangs" in January of 1989. Following a series of high-profile acts of violence by alleged gang members in

Reno, he called for a mobilization of forces against what many perceived as a growing threat to local residents.

> It's unacceptable to me that people in this community are being intimidated . . . We cannot give up our homes to these damn people . . . We as a community have two choices: give up and let them take over our streets or fight back. We're going to fight back.[20]

Lane outlined a plan of action during a summit held with representatives from several local law enforcement agencies. Flanked by an assistant district attorney (who had just returned from a gang conference in Los Angeles), Lane made a pledge that no more plea bargains would be offered to those involved in gang-related crimes and high bails would be demanded by his office to make sure "these people" remained in custody and didn't have a chance to hurt or kill again. In response to those who were disturbed by the racial overtones beneath the new get-tough approach, the district attorney responded "I don't care if they're white, black, red, yellow, or any color . . . I'm not not going to stand for it any more."[21]

There is little indication that the prosecution of gang crimes changed substantially following the proclamation of war. The D.A. who declared the war was elected to the bench in 1990, and for a time the rhetoric subsided. Nonetheless, public concern about gangs remained high, and gangs were a central issue in the election of a new district attorney. Following through on campaign promises to get tough on crime and gangs, in March 1993 Washoe County's new district attorney created a specialized unit to prosecute gang crimes. At a press conference held on the courthouse steps, she announced the implementation of the Dangerous Youthful Offender (DYO) unit. She also supplied the justification for such a move:

> Our schools must remain safe havens for learning, not become armed camps full of warring factions. Our streets must remain safe for families and tourists to enjoy activities and the quality of life we offer here in Northern Nevada.[22]

Unlike her predecessor, the district attorney-elect scaled down the rhetoric surrounding gangs, pointing out that the DYO unit was not part of a war on gangs. The DYO unit was not, she stressed, concerned with gang membership as much as it was "the criminal apprehension and prosecution of that 15–20 percent of gangsters who are actively and repeatedly involved in criminal activity."[23] All but the hard-core gang members would be handled through normal prosecution processes, attempting—when possible—to divert those offenders to community-based agencies that would provide structure, treatment, and rehabilitation. Expressing confidence in the newly created unit, she affirmed that "an organized and consistent arrest and prosecution strategy will go far towards solving our criminal gang problem in this community."[24]

Five full-time attorneys were assigned to the DYO unit, assisted by one investigator and a secretary to manage caseloads. Heading the DYO unit was a hard-nosed prosecutor who had lost to Holmes in the race for the district attorney's office in 1990. Initially, the DYO unit failed to live up to its billing. According to the D.A., it "staggered a bit" in its first two years of operation, primarily because the unit's supervisor "did not buy into the concept and failed to follow the procedures and guidelines." That prosecutor was of the opinion that the threat posed by Washoe County gangs was exaggerated; he characterized the gang problem as little more than "a bunch of kids shooting each other up."[25] Not surprisingly, in July 1993, the prosecutor was fired (on the same day he announced he would run in the upcoming race for district attorney) and Holmes personally took over the supervision of the DYO unit. Holmes failed to win reelection that year. However, according to the lead prosecutor of the DYO unit, no substantive changes were made in the emphasis or process by which gang members were prosecuted in Washoe County with the election of a new D.A.

Objectives of the DYO Team

As in Clark County, the gang prosecution unit in Washoe County set for itself a diverse, though slightly less ambitious, set of goals. Unlike in Clark County, however, these objectives were never promulgated in government hearings or the local media. In fact, the implementation of the DYO unit generally received little attention from the media, probably because no additional public funds were requested for the DYO unit, as they had been for the Clark County Gang Prosecution Unit.

Intelligence/Dissemination   Though comprehensive gang files are maintained by the Reno Police Department's STEP/CAT unit, the DYO unit would also be responsible for maintaining records, gang histories, and other data necessary to stay abreast with the extent of gang crime committed by both adults and juveniles in the county. Weekly meetings would be held to assure that unit members were aware of current trends in gang activity and were familiar with all of the cases currently being prosecuted by other unit members. Officers from STEP/CAT unit would also participate in these sessions.

Notices that gang members had been convicted or sentenced were to be distributed to local schools and neighborhoods affected by gangs to deter others from gang activity. The DYO unit was also to provide the Washoe County School District with an annual report of the number and types of gang crime referred for prosecution from individual schools within the county.

Pretrial Release, Charging Practices, and Vertical Prosecution   The DYO unit would only handle cases in which the defendant was considered a threat to the community by virtue of the seriousness of his/her offense or criminal history. For those cases that met this criterion, DYO prosecutors were expected to vigorously oppose pretrial release and, if that should fail, advocate high bails to keep defendants in custody all criminal proceedings. While filing the highest provable charge against a defendants, unit attorneys would refrain from "stacking" charges (multiple charging) against defendants, a routine practice in general prosecution designed to gain leverage during plea bargaining negotiations (where charges or counts are dismissed in exchange for a guilty plea to a single charge). DYO prosecutors were instructed to avoid the practice since they "do not want gang members to think they had beat three to five felonies," having only been convicted of one.[26] Moreover, DYO guidelines specifically prohibited plea bargaining to reduce charges. There were nonetheless somewhat contradictory provisions contained within DYO guidelines that did allow for plea bargaining "if the circumstances of a prosecution become such that it appears some . . . concessions might have to be made . . ."[27]

Every effort would be made by DYO prosecutors to utilize the Gang Enhancement Statute, as well as the other statutory enhancements available under Nevada Revised Statutes (e.g., crimes committed with a weapon, crimes against the elderly, crimes on school grounds, etc.). Where Gang Enhancement is deemed inappropriate or cannot be legally substantiated, conspiracy charges were to be filed to establish joint participation in criminal or delinquent acts.

In Clark County, vertical plea bargaining was the ostensibly the *sine qua non* of the Gang Prosecution Unit; cases handled by the DYO unit, however, would be prosecuted vertically only "to the extent possible." Thus, the level of commitment to vertical prosecution in Washoe County appeared considerably lower than that stated by Clark County prosecutors.

Victim/Witness Compliance and Protection   Given the reluctance of many of the witnesses to or victims of gang crime, the DYO unit had a strong commitment to the use of material witness bonds or incarceration to ensure compliance and cooperation. As a matter of policy, any evidence that a witness or a victim had provided false testimony to law enforcement, or feigned cooperation with DYO prosecutors initially only to change their testimony during actual court proceedings, would result in charges being filed for false reporting or obstruction of justice. In addition, communication was to be maintained with victims throughout the case, notifying them of all court proceedings, results, and prospective releases of the offender from custody.

To reduce the incidence of witness/victim intimidation by gang members, grand jury procedures would be utilized to the fullest extent. Defendants who threatend or intimidated a witness/victim would be swiftly prosecuted to the fullest extent of the law.

WHAT IS DIFFERENT ABOUT GANG CRIMINALS AND GANG CRIME?

We have demonstrated that known gang members and associates were responsible only for a small amount of crime in both cities over the period in which the panic occurred. But in addition to claims of gang involvement in crime, in the media and before legislative committees, criminal justice officials consistently portrayed gang crime as "different." As a result of their repeated claims, gang crime nearly became synonymous with violence, automatic weapons, and illegal drug markets. Gangs were said to be capitalistic enterprises, highly organized and driven by profit. Crimes committed by gang members were purportedly done at the direction of gang leadership interested in protecting turf, expanding drug markets, and defending the gang's reputation.

To evaluate these claims, we collected information from all cases handled by the Clark County Gang Prosecution Unit (GPU) and Washoe County's Dangerous Youth Offender unit from their inception through 1994. During that period, 340 gang cases were handled by the Clark County Gang Prosecution Unit and 152 gang cases were processed by Washoe County's DYO unit. Preliminary analysis of these gang cases provided the basis for selecting a sample of comparable nongang cases handled by regular "track" prosecution channels within those counties. A total of 313 nongang cases from Clark County and 63 nongang cases from Washoe County were selected from prosecutor's files for the same time period, matching for the types of offenses found in the samples of gang cases. From the files on each case (gang and nongang), information was collected that included defendant characteristics, criminal history, current criminal charges, and offense characteristics.

Demographic and Criminal History Comparisons

The data was first examined to identify any differences in the characteristics of offenders prosecuted in the gang prosecution units and the normal "track" prosecution units in both counties. The demographic comparisons are presented in Table 9–1.

Gang defendants, in general, were younger and more likely to be minority males than nongang defendants. This is particularly true in Clark County, where gang defendants were, on average, nine years younger than nongang defendants and nearly four times as likely to be a minority. Compared to nongang defendants, at the time of their arrest gang defendants had actually lived in the community for longer periods of time. This pattern raises serious questions concerning the claims made that the gang problem in both communities was the result of an invasion of L.A. gang members. To the extent to which there was a gang problem, its origins were indigenous.

TABLE 9–1   Demographic Profile of Gang Members/Associates vs. Non–Gang Defendants

	Las Vegas		Reno	
	GPU	Track Units	DYO	Track Units
Age	20.9	29.4	20.8	22.1
Male	98.5	93.9	97.4	100.0
Race				
White	12.6	46.8	6.5	18.8
Black	50.9	39.5	22.2	3.1
Hispanic	25.9	11.5	62.1	68.8
Asian	10.3	1.9	2.6	4.7
Other	.3	.3	6.6	4.6
Residential Status				
Nonresident	4.4	6.8	1.3	0.0
1–12 mos.	4.4	7.1	7.8	7.8
Over 1 yr.	86.8	74.0	69.9	57.8
Unknown	4.4	12.2	34.6	34.4

We then compared the criminal histories of gang and nongang defendants (Figure 9–1). Gang defendants had much more contact with the juvenile justice system, with roughly three to four times as many juvenile adjudications. Some of this disparity, but certainly not all, may be simply a function of race; gang members were more likely to be minorities, and minorities are disproportionately involved in the justice system.

In the GPU, defendants had fewer arrests as adults. This is undoubtedly a function of age; gang defendants, at least those prosecuted in the GPU, were considerably younger and thus had fewer at-risk years as adults in the justice system. On the other hand, gang defendants in both counties were more likely to have been convicted of a prior violent felony (Figure 9–2).

In summary, gang offenders do differ from conventional criminals in several ways. Those prosecuted as gang members or associates were younger and much more likely to be black, Hispanic, or Asian. At the time of their alleged offense, they were hardly new kids on the block; most had been in their communities for at least a year, in many cases much longer. Compared to the run-of-the-mill defendant, gang defendants had many more brushes with the law. They were also much more likely to have been previously convicted of a serious violent crime. One clear difference between gang and nongang crimes in both jurisdictions was the number of offenders involved in the criminal acts.

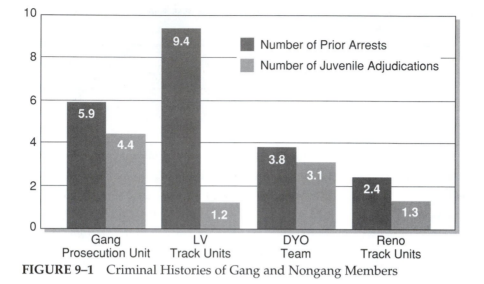

FIGURE 9–1   Criminal Histories of Gang and Nongang Members

Offense Comparisons

Is the nature of gang crime different from conventional crime? To address that question, we considered several characteristics of the crimes for which individuals—gang and nongang—had been charged (Table 9–2). Given the manner in which we constructed our sample of nongang defendants, only limited comparisons can be made. However, it is still instructive to note the type of charges filed against gang members in both the GPU and DYO. In Clark County's GPU, the most common charge was a weapons offense (carrying concealed weapon, possession of firearm by a felon, pointing a weapon at a person, etc.). In Washoe County, the most common charge filed against gang members was aggravated assault. Roughly half of all the charges filed against gang members were serious violent offenses.

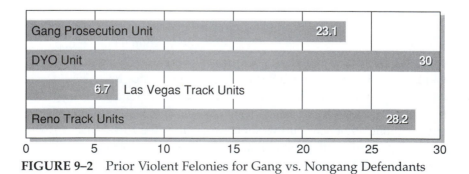

FIGURE 9–2   Prior Violent Felonies for Gang vs. Nongang Defendants

TABLE 9–2   Comparing the Characteristics of Gang and Nongang Violent Offenses

	Clark County		Washoe County	
	GPU	Track Units	DYO	Track Units
Number of offenders involved (%)				
One offender	33.1	69.1	32.9	64.1
Two offenders	22.9	21.7	30.3	9.4
Three or more offenders	44.0	9.2	36.8	26.6
Number of victims	1.92	1.39	2.13	1.30
Victim–offender relationship (%)				
Stranger	44.2	45.0	29.0	13.7
Family/relative	0.4	5.8	0.0	13.7
Acquaintance	18.1	35.8	22.6	66.7
Rival gang member	25.7	—	38.7	—
Unknown	11.6	13.4	9.7	5.9
Weapon used in crime (% yes)	91.0	79.4	93.5	90.9
Type of weapon used (%)				
Handgun	75.8	58.0	66.3	29.8
Shotgun	15.1	7.8	1.2	12.3
Knife	15.9	21.8	12.8	24.6
Other weapon	5.3	12.3	19.8	33.3
Extent of injury to victim				
Death	9.0	7.7	5.2	11.4
Hospitalization	13.3	12.7	19.5	15.9
Medical treatment	23.8	33.0	50.7	56.8
No injury	53.9	46.6	24.6	15.9

   The majority of offenses committed by nongang members involved a single perpetrator; in gang crimes, there were typically two or three offenders. Still, one-third of all gang-related crimes involved a single offender. There are also some interesting differences in the victims involved in both gang and nongang crime. For example, gang violence generally involved more victims than in nongang violent crime. Gang members were rarely charged with committing a violent crime against a family member (never, in Washoe County). Domestic violence was more common in nongang cases. In Las Vegas, strangers were often targets of gang violence, but no more frequently than in crimes in which offenders were affiliated with gangs. In Reno, gang members were actually more likely to target strangers.

> Though nearly all gang violence prosecuted in Las Vegas and Reno involved firearms, not a single incident involved an assault or automatic weapon.

The most common target of gang violence in both Las Vegas and Reno was a rival gang member. A good argument could be made against the distinction between "acquaintance" and "rival gang" member. An acquaintance is simply a person known to one, but not considered a close friend; rival gang members would certainly qualify under this definition. By merging the categories of rival gang member and acquaintance, the target of crimes by gang and nongang members are shown to be quite similar. In both cases, the typical victim was someone known by the offender.

In crimes of violence, gang members were more likely to have used firearms. In Las Vegas, over 90 percent of the alleged violent crimes by gang members involved a firearm of some sort, compared to roughly 80 percent of nongang offenders. In Reno, those differences existed but were negligible. However, and contrary to the claims of law enforcement and media portrayals, than there was not a single crime that involved an assault or automatic weapon of any kind. The guns of choice for the gang and nongang criminal alike were the medium-bore handgun and the shotgun. Though there were typically more victims in an incident of gang violence, when compared to the victims of nongang crime, the victims of gang crime were less likely to be seriously injured.

Use of Gang Legislation

In a previous chapter, we presented evidence that showed gangs in Las Vegas and Reno during the year of the panic never represented more than a minor threat to the community. The vast majority of crime, including violent and drug-related offenses, was committed by individuals who were not known to be gang members. In this chapter we have shown that gang members who were arrested for a crime were in *some ways* different from conventional criminals. They were younger, more likely than not to be black or Hispanic, and had more extensive juvenile records. Most of the time, but not always, they committed their crimes in pairs or small groups, a pattern consistent with youth offending in general. Gang members were often well armed, but they did not fit the Uzi-toting image presented by law enforcement and the media. But as is true for violent crime in general, the victims of gang crime were usually not innocent victims but persons they, to some degree, knew.

Under the assumption fostered by law enforcement and the media that gang crime was "different" from normal crime in its nature and motivation, new laws had been enacted to deal with the gang threat. As previously discussed, these statutes created new criminal offenses (e.g., drive-by shootings) and enhanced penalties for violations of existing criminal codes. Under the most sweeping of the new laws, the penalty for any crime judged to be gang motivated was automatically doubled. Law enforcement officials were instrumental in the design and passage of most gang legislation. Both the Gang Prosecution Unit and the Dangerous Youthful Offender Unit affirmed their commitment to the new laws, with formal policies stating that such statutes would be used wherever possible.

We reviewed the court records from Las Vegas and Reno, documenting the frequency of which these new gang statutes were filed, as well as the convictions obtained on those charges (Table 9–3). With only a couple of exceptions, most of the new laws were rarely, sometimes never, used. The most frequent charge under the new statutes was that targeting the random and reckless use of firearms (i.e., aiming a firearm at human being), typical of gang retaliatory crimes. From 1989 through 1995, nearly 1,800 such charges were filed against criminal defendants in Las Vegas alone. It should be remembered that these figures represent total number of charges filed; they are not separate criminal events in which the law was charged. It was not uncommon to find 15 or more charges under this law to be filed against a gunman who, for example, fired a single shot in the air near a crowd. And most of these charges, of course, would be dismissed during the process of negotiating a plea. This reality is confirmed by looking at the

TABLE 9–3   Use of Antigang Legislation in Reno and Las Vegas, 1989–1995

		Las Vegas	Reno
Gang Enhancement Statute: felony committed to promote activities of criminal gang	Charges filed	263	24
	Persons convicted	37	4
Aiming firearm at human being	Charges filed	1771	10
	Persons convicted	188	3
Discharge of firearm out of motor vehicle	Charges filed	199	26
	Persons convicted	22	1
Possession of dangerous weapon on property or in vehicle on school grounds	Charges filed	69	3
	Persons convicted	6	0
Soliciting a minor to commit crime	Charges filed	0	0
	Persons convicted	0	0
Crimes at or near school, school bus stop, or recreational facilities	Charges filed	0	0
	Persons convicted	0	0
Felony committed on a school bus	Charges filed	0	0

number of charges for which convictions were obtained. Of the charges filed in both jurisdictions, only 191 defendants were actually convicted of aiming a firearm.

Only 225 charges were filed against defendants for discharging a firearm from a motor vehicle (i.e., drive-by shootings); 23 defendants were convicted under the statute. Given claims that gang members were responsible for the proliferation of weapons on school campuses, it is surprising that only 72 charges were filed and only 6 persons convicted of having a dangerous weapon on school grounds. Even more surprising, three of the additional statutes targeting gang activity—soliciting a minor to commit a crime, committing a crime on school grounds, committing a felony on a school bus—were never once filed during all the years of the panic.

Furthermore, the Gang Enhancement Statute, touted by police and prosecutors alike as an absolute requirement in the battle against street gangs, was charged by prosecutors in both jurisdictions a total of 287 times in the four years following its enactment in 1991. However, the vast majority of those instances involved multiple counts against the same individual defendant. Only 41 gang members were actually convicted under the statute during those years. Given the purported scale of the threat posed by street gangs, Nevada residents might see these numbers as low.

Conclusion

Gang prosecution units were created in Las Vegas and Reno in the same frenzied social and political context in which specialized police gang units were formed. District attorneys are elected officials, and in the midst of great concern about gang crime the chief prosecutor in both jurisdictions moved to appease public fears. Specialized gang prosecution units were argued to be the next logical step in the war on gangs. With more tough gang laws and additional police gang officers to arrest gang members, proponents of gang prosecution units made persuasive arguments for beefing up prosecutorial efforts as well. Gang units were promoted as being able to deliver swifter justice, higher conviction rates, and longer prison

It seems as though much of the legislation that is being passed, particularly that which attempts to target gang activity, is done so without any real understanding of youth gangs.[28]

Randall Shelden, Sharon Tracy and William Brown, Youth Gangs in American Society, *2001.*

sentences. The gang expertise that would be developed in these units and the vertical prosecution strategies that would be employed would allow prosecutors to take full advantage of the antigang legislation that had become available.

But most of that legislation was actually used infrequently, if at all. For example, only 18 defendants were convicted under the Gang Enhancement Statute from 1991 to 1994. Given the magnitude and nature of the alleged threat posed by criminal street gangs, why was the law not utilized more frequently and effectively? According to criminal justice officials interviewed for this study, supporters of the statute made assumptions concerning gangs that simply proved to be false. Lawmakers had been greatly influenced by law enforcement reports and media stereotypes of gangs as highly organized, routinely violent, and dominating illicit markets in drugs and weapons. The language of the Gang Enhancement Statute specifically targeted this type of criminal organization. However, in the course of prosecuting gangs, prosecutors discovered that the reality of gangs was some distance from the stereotype. Gangs were not criminal enterprises, but loose and shifting confederations without stable leadership, role expectations, or collective goals. As in most cases processed, gang crime amounted to little more than the impulsive acts of marginal persons attempting to gain immediate, easy, and *individual* short-term pleasure.

Notes

1. Claire Johnson, Barbara Webster and Edward Connors. 1995. *Prosecuting Gangs: A National Assessment.* National Institute of Justice. Research in Brief. Washington, D.C.: Government Printing Office.
2. Michael Genelin and Loren Naimen. 1988. *Prosecuting Gang Homicides. Prosecutor's Notebook.* Volume X. California District Attorney's Association.
3. Irving A. Spergel. 1995. *The Youth Gang Problem: A Community Approach.* New York: Oxford University Press.
4. Institute for Law and Justice. 1993. *Gang Prosecution in the United States.* National Institute of Justice, Office of Justice Programs, U.S. Department of Justice.
5. Genelin and Naimen, 1988.
6. *Las Vegas Sun.* 1991. "DA wants unit to fight gangs." August 30.
7. Ron Lucherini. 1995. Chief Deputy Prosecutor, Clark County, Nevada. Personal communication. October.
8. Ron Lucherini. 1991. Chief Deputy Prosecutor, Clark County, Nevada. *Gang Unit Proposal.* Clark County District Attorney Office. Mimeographed copy.
9. Lucherini, 1995.
10. Clark County Comission. State of Nevada. 1991. Minutes from meeting of Clark County Commission. September 17.
11. *Las Vegas Sun.* 1991. "County puts money behind DA's gang unit." September 18.
12. Lucherini, 1991.
13. Lucherini, 1991, p. 16.

14. Lucherini, 1991.

15. Lucherini, 1991, p. 10.

16. Lucherini, 1991, p. 14.

17. Claire Johnson, Barbara Webster and Edward Connors. 1995. *Prosecuting Gangs: A National Assessment*. National Institute of Justice. *Research in Brief*. Washington, D.C.: Government Printing Office.

18. Chris Owens. 1994. Chief Deputy District Attorney, Gang Prosecution Unit. *Report of the Office of the Clark County District Attorney, Gang Unit*, p. 2. Mimeographed copy.

19. Owens, 1994, p. 2.

20. Reno Gazette–Journal. 1989. "Washoe DA declares war on gangs." January 18.

21. Reno Gazette–Journal. 1989. "Washoe DA declares war on gangs." January 18.

22. Reno Gazette–Journal. 1993. "Washoe DA forms team to battle youth violence." March 2.

23. Dorothy Nash Holmes. 1993 District Attorney of Washoe County, Nevada. Inter-office Memorandum. August 9. Mimeographed copy, p. 1.

24. Holmes, 1993, p. 3.

25. Dorothy Nash Holmes. 1994. Former District Attorney of Washoe County, Nevada. Personal communication. June 1.

26. Holmes, 1993, p. 4.

27. Holmes, 1993, p. 6.

28. Randall Sheldon, Sharon Tracy, and William Brown. 2001. *Youth Gangs in American Society*. Second edition. Belmont, CA: Wadworth.

SECTION III

Panic at the National Level

Our findings clearly demonstrated a sizeable gap between the rhetoric and the reality of street gangs in Nevada. But can this true in other parts of the country? The answer, we believe, is yes. There is no reason to believe that the processes of agenda-setting and policy-making in Nevada are substantively different from those in California, Florida, or any other state. As in Nevada, law enforcement bureaucracies elsewhere must compete for a finite pool of public dollars. This intense competition inevitably involves persuading policy-makers (and the public) of the urgency of the crime problem and the need for greater investments in law enforcement to contain the threat. Persuading others of that threat (i.e., claims making) will routinely involve symbolic representations that distort and dramatize either crime in general or, as is more likely the case, some particular aspect of the crime problem. Thus, there is every reason to question many of the claims made by law enforcement regarding street gangs in other parts of the country. We evaluate many of those claims in this final section.

At the national level, there is also a great deal of claims-making by members of the academic community; we look closely at some of their claims in this section as well. While not as important as law enforcement in discovering the gang problem, many criminologists have also had a hand in fueling the gang panic. As with law enforcement, there is much to be gained. Millions of dollars have been awarded to scholars over the past two decades to study the gang phenomenon for the purpose of informing public policy. But theoretical and ideological allegiances, rather than material rewards or careers, are the more likely explanation for renewed attention to gangs by scholars. Pointing to gangs as a major cause of crime, and gangs as a result of social and economic inequality, these scholars remain true to their convictions regarding human nature, the social causes of crime, and the public good.

c h a p t e r 1 0

A Nation in Panic?

The panic that swept across Las Vegas and Reno was sparked by several high-profile violent crimes by minority youth with alleged gang affiliations. These incidents were reported by police as evidence of the growing presence of street gangs, a problem that was potentially uncontrollable without a significant show of force by law enforcement. The public was soon inundated with news of the gang epidemic, the media creating and promoting images which suggested that both communities were under attack from warring tribes of heavily armed drug-dealing sociopaths. In the crusade against gangs that followed, thousands of (largely minority) males in Nevada were detained, tagged, and monitored by police. Most of them had committed no crimes and had no previous arrest records. Police gang units were created or beefed up, specialized prosecutorial teams formed, and new laws passed to deal with the threat posed by gangs.

That threat was less real than imagined. Though they did commit violent crimes, at the height of the panic gang members were responsible for only a fraction of either city's overall crime problem. Gang members did, in fact, sell and traffic illegal drugs, but they were never more than bit players in the cities' drug markets. The links among gangs, violence, and drugs drawn by law enforcement and hyped by the media simply didn't exist.

A CLOSER LOOK AT THE NATION'S GANG PROBLEM

As we mentioned in the introduction to this book, when we first began our research on gangs in Nevada, we more or less assumed that street gangs were ubiquitous, responsible for much of the violent crime in the country, that they dominated illegal drug markets, and generally were creating havoc on a unprecedented scale. We discovered this certainly wasn't the case in either Las Vegas or Reno. This made us question many of the popularly held beliefs about gangs in the country as a whole. Just how large a threat, we wondered, is the nation's gang problem?

THE HEAD COUNTS

Troubled by the lack of a uniform definition of gangs, Malcolm Klein rightly asks "How do you prevent or control a problem you can't identify?"[1] We agree, but would also ask how it is possible to *count* what you can't define. After all, what is considered a gang in one jurisdiction is often treated as no more than a group of trouble-makers in another. Moreover, whatever definition that is adopted is generally not based on any underlying reality but, as Irving Spergel argues, "local values, political considerations, statutory language, and public pressures . . . agency or organizational histories and predispositions, news media pressures, and intellectual fashions."[2] To illustrate the divergence of opinion, consider the definition of gangs found in the criminal codes of the following states.

> *Colorado:* "gang" means a group of three or more individuals with a common interest, bond, or activity characterized by criminal or delinquent conduct.[3]

> *Minnesota:* an "organized gang" means an association of five or more persons, with an established hierarchy, formed to encourage members of the association to perpetrate crimes or to provide support to members of the association who do commit crimes.[4]

> *Oregon:* An ongoing organization, association, or group of three or more persons, whether formal or informal, which has as a primary purpose the commission of a violent, street or drug-related crime . . . A criminal gang also has one or more of the following characteristics: (a) Conspires to commit, or commits, crimes against individuals or groups based on race, color, religion, sexual preference, national origin, or rival gang association; (b) Uses a gang name, a common identifying symbol, or has identifiable leadership; (c) Has a high rate of interaction among members to the exclusion of other groups; (d) Claims a neighborhood and/or other geographical territory; or (e) Whose members wear distinctive types of clothing or exhibit distinctive appearance or communicate in a peculiar or unique style.[5]

As these examples show, there are fundamental differences in the manner in which gangs are defined across the country. There is disagreement as to how large a group must be before it can be considered a gang. Tight organizational structure and clearly defined lines of authority are distinguishing characteristics of street

---

It is not possible to devise meaningful estimates of the exact or even the approximate number of youth gangs in the United States, partly because, as noted, there is no standard or national definition of "gang."[6]

Irving Spergel. The Youth Gang Problem, *1995.*

gangs in some jurisdictions; in others, a freewheeling knot of delinquents may be labeled a gang. Hate groups—such as the KKK or Skinheads—are recognized as gangs in some places, but not others.

How Do Police Define Gangs?

Given that police actually count gangs, their definition is particularly important. In the mid-1970s, Walter Miller surveyed police and youth service workers in six large cities reporting a "gang problem." One of the questions asked respondents was "How would you define a gang?"[7] Five criteria were most frequently mentioned:

1. Violent or criminal behavior as a major activity of group members
2. Group organization, with functional role division and chain of command
3. Identifiable leadership
4. Continuing and recurring interaction among group members
5. Claims of control over specific territory (Figure 10–1).

Ninety percent or more of respondents were in agreement on four of the five criteria. Miller combined these five elements to construct what has often been referred to as the "consensus-based"definition of gangs.

> A gang is a group of recurrently associating individuals with identifiable leadership and internal organization, identifying with or claiming control over territory in the community, and engaging either individually or collectively in violent or other forms of illegal behavior.[8]

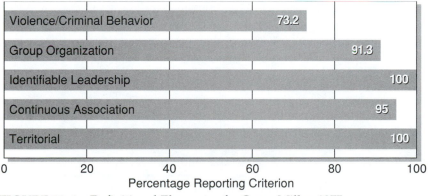

FIGURE 10–1   Definitional Elements of a Gang: Miller, 1975

Miller later expanded his survey to include police and youth service workers in 26 U.S. cities and metropolitan counties.[9] The findings led him to modify his definition, adding a sixth element stipulating that youth gangs also have a "specific purpose." This survey, as with that previous, found a high consensus among respondents across these six elements.

A similar study was conducted in the early 1980s by Jerome Needle and William Vaughan Stapleton.[10] Officials in police departments in 60 large urban areas were first asked "Do you have youth gangs in your community or jurisdiction?" Roughly one-half reported that they did. Those respondents were then asked "How does your department define a youth gang?" The definitional elements provided generally corresponded to those by respondents in Miller's study: violent behavior, organization, leadership, recurrent interaction, and territoriality (Figure 10–2). But in addition to the five criteria identified by Miller, their respondents also frequently mentioned dress, tattoos, and graffiti as distinguishing characteristics of gangs. Overall, however, Needle and Stapleton concluded that "many police departments define youth gangs according to Miller's criteria."[11]

Police Perceptions and Gang Realities

These surveys show that law enforcement generally views street gangs as cohesive, highly organized crime groups. But is this accurate? Among gang scholars we find two competing views.[12] In one camp are those who describe gangs in terms that generally correspond with law enforcement perceptions: Gangs are cohesive entities, analogous in many ways to Fortune 500 corporations, with a formal structure, stable and strong leadership, clearly defined roles for members, and organizational goals that include illegal acts.[13]

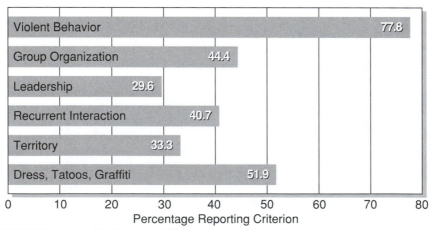

FIGURE 10–2   Definitional Elements of a Gang: Needle and Stapleton, 1983

The most extreme claims regarding the level of organization within gangs are offered by Martin Jankowski in his controversial book, *Islands in the Street*.[14] Jankowski claims there are three types of organizational structures found in gangs, two of which are characterized by high levels of organization. In the "vertical/horizontal" model, gang leadership is organized hierarchically, with three or four major offices such as president, vice-president, warlord, and treasurer. In the "horizontal/commission" model, leadership is not top-down but instead is arranged much like a city council where there is a number of officers with roughly equal authority. There is no formal leadership in gangs organized according to his "influential model." Leaders exist, but are selected on the basis of special skills or talents and affect group decision-making through charisma or force of will. Regardless of the type of organization, it is Jankowski's contention that gangs are cohesive, purposeful organizations.

> . . . a gang is an organized social system . . . one whose size and goals have necessitated that social interaction be governed by a leadership structure that has defined roles; where authority associated with these roles has been legitimized to the extent that social codes are operational to regulate the behavior of both the leadership and the rank and file; that plans and provides not only for the social and economic services of its members, but also for its own maintenance as an organization . . .[15]

At the other end of the organizational continuum is Leon Yablonsky, a venerable gang scholar who contends that not only are street gangs not organizations, they are not even groups, at least in the strict sociological sense. A group, he reminds us, "is an identifiable, coherent, and finite entity made up of people who relate to each other on the basis of defined norms and rules for interaction . . . the role of each member is clearly defined and entails certain rights, duties, and obligations . . . ."[16] Yablonsky suggests a more accurate categorization of a street gang is a "near-group," a collectivity that falls somewhere between a group and a mob (a spontaneous, short-lived crowd with no roles or membership status). Based on his research on gangs in New York, he concluded that violent street gangs were comprised largely of sociopathic personalities, with diffuse role definitions, shifting membership, very limited cohesion, and little normative consensus.

> . . . most gangs have an incoherent or inchoate form when compared to more socially approved groups. This is due in part to the emotionally unstable condition of most the youths and young men who participate in violent gangs. Gangs are often in a state of transition or flux. Their structure has a degree of coherence and some duration in time; however, they are not usually cohesive, clearly defined groups. Because of this inchoate nature of most gangs, membership in a gang is a concept that is different from membership in more normal groups. Although there are some member-defining factors—such as wearing a certain color (for instance, in Los Angeles, blue for Crips, red for Blood gangs)—and core members can usually

identify each other, more marginal members in most gangs are not clearly known to each other, and there is an impermanent quality about the structure of the violent gang.[17]

The vast majority of gang scholars today agree with Yablonsky that street gangs are not very well organized.[18] Malcolm Klein describes the typical LA gang as "a rather amorphous collection of subgroups, cliques, pairs, and loners" that are only loosely coupled.[19] Since interaction occurs primarily within cliques, gang members often even have trouble identifying other members of the gang.[20] Irving Spergel's work in Chicago has similarly led him to conclude that most gangs are far more like "'amoebic' social movements than rational business organizations."[21] In Milwaukee, John Hagedorn reported gangs were "a combination or coalition of age-graded groups," poorly organized and devoid of collective goals.[22] Scott Decker and Barrik Van Winkle's ethnographic study in St. Louis describes gangs as a "a loosely organized confederation of individuals bound together through common action, experiences, symbols, and allegiances."[23] These subgroups or cliques were the focus of illegal activities, not the gang as a whole; income-generating crime was rarely motivated or organized by the larger gang structure.

Other research has documented instability in gang membership, a trend which would preclude the degree of organization ascribed to gangs by Jankowski and others. For example, using data from the Denver Youth Survey, a longitudinal study of families and youth, Finn-Aage Esbensen and David Huizinga found that 67 percent of youths reported being a member of a gang for only few months.[24] Another long-term study of youth in Rochester by Terrence Thornberry and his colleagues produced similar findings, showing that most who join gangs remain members for only a year or so.[25] Given this turnover, it is difficult to imagine how gangs could sustain the rules, roles, and relationships that define formal organizations.

No doubt by now the reader has thought of at least one infamous street gang that does possess all the characteristics of formal organizations said to be absent or weak in gangs by these researchers. Examples of such gangs might be the Crips in Los Angeles or the Gangster Disciples in Chicago. But according to Spergel, "the idea of sophisticated gang organizations is still largely a product of the self- or organizational-interested musings of gang leaders, certain police officials, academic researchers, and media reporters."[26]

Contrary to police perception, most researchers have found street gangs to be disorganized, informal groups with high member turnover.

That assessment is confirmed by a recent study of two Chicago gangs generally believed to be highly structured criminal organizations: the Gangster Disciples (an African-American gang) and the Latin Kings (a Hispanic gang).[27] In that study, Scott Decker and his colleagues interviewed members of each gang and asked whether their gang had clearly defined roles and leaders, held regular meetings, had a set of written rules, or possessed other traits found in organized crime groups. The findings of their study suggested that the Gangster Disciples were more organized than the Latin Kings, having more defined leadership positions and a written set of simple, common-sense rules designed to maintain group cohesiveness and secrecy. However, aside from leadership positions, role differentiation within the gang was low and uncharacteristic of highly organized groups. The Disciples did hold meetings, but they were irregular, informal, and not dedicated to achieving any specific purpose. Though perhaps the most organized of any street gang in the country, Decker and his colleagues concluded the Disciples were not the sophisticated criminal enterprise portrayed by law enforcement and the media.

Territoriality

Another defining characteristic of gangs, according to law enforcement and other youth service workers, is their territorial nature or *turf* (an area under the gang's control). The image of gangs occupying and protecting neighborhoods has its origins in the "corner groups" of the 19th and early 20th centuries.[28] During this period, crowded and substandard living conditions in the tenements drove young ethnic males to the streets in search of relief and excitement. Boys from the same neighborhood or block drifted into groups, engaging in cafeteria-style delinquency and also fighting corner groups from other neighborhoods.

Many gangs today retain allegiance to their neighborhoods, and incursions by rival gangs are often responded to with violence. But modern transportation and other factors have weakened the relationship between gangs and neighborhoods. Youth almost always have access to automobiles, their own or a friend's, and where they may have once loitered on corners today "cruising" city streets holds more allure. As one gang scholar points out "Gangs are no longer confined to defending a turf where they live never going elsewhere."[29] The gang itself is changing, moving away from turf-oriented, traditional gangs to smaller, more independent forms that are less territorial than in the past.[30] The degree of territoriality displayed by gangs varies within and across cities, by how long it has been in existence, and also by ethnicity and race. Asian gangs, for example, are known to be extremely mobile and far less confined to or protective of any particular area.[31] For some African-American gangs, the neighborhood is no longer particularly valued or deemed worthy of defending.[32]

Dress and Graffiti

Gangs and gang members are also defined in terms of dress, tattoos, and hand signs. In both Las Vegas and Reno gang units, looking like a gang member, particularly in a "known" gang area (virtually all of which were low-income, minority neighborhoods), was enough to establish gang affiliation. The use of appearance to ascribe gang membership is common throughout the country. For example, the Chicago Police Department has several criteria for identifying gang members, one of which is "When an individual resides in or frequents a particular gang's area and affects their style of dress, use of hand signs, symbols, or tatoos."[33]

The use of dress, symbols, and mannerisms as criteria for gang membership is an extremely questionable practice, particularly given the diffusion of gang culture in America.[34] Though they may have their origins in gangs, the dress and mannerisms once peculiar to gangs are no longer confined to such groups. Movies and television dramas depicting inner city youth have infused American youth culture with many of the more stylistic elements of gang culture. "Gangster clothing"—the baggy pants, Pendleton-type wool shirts, starter jackets—is all the rage on junior and high school campuses across the country, mainstream retailers now offering a full line of "ghetto-wear" for those who seek the pretense of oppression. Using these kinds of markers to establish gang membership is bound to inflate gang rosters.[35] Often ghetto youth who only look and dress like gangsters are snatched up and labeled as such in police sweeps.[36] Indeed, some observers have suggested that the "so-called national spread of gang problems may be nothing more than another teenage fad—the 1990s version of the hula hoop or pet rock."[37]

Many police departments stipulate that appearance is relevant only when the individual in question "associates with known criminal street gang members."[38] This qualification, though, is meaningless given the other criteria for establishing membership. Many youth simply admit to police to being in a gang. But the mystique and status surrounding gangs today lead many youth to claim membership they don't really have.[39] Gang membership in some cities can also be assigned by police on the word of a "reliable informant," a vague standard that does not require police to demonstrate formally the informant's veracity or basis of knowledge. Depending on how they are dressed, many youth run the risk of being labeled gang members simply because they occasionally hang out with someone who either

---

Visual cues are important for cops. They drive around and see kids who look like gang members—or they see colors and graffiti—so it's easier to spot a "gang" problem."[40]

admitted to being a gang member to a police officer (when he in fact was not) or had been falsely identified as a gang member by another person due to ignorance or malice. Police tend to identify anyone interacting with a gang member as also being a gang member.[41]

The image of gangs produced by most empirical research stands in sharp contrast to that held by law enforcement. Gangs are generally poorly organized, purposeless, and without clear hierarchical leadership. Interaction is primarily confined to members of the same, age-graded cliques that are not integrated into the gang as a whole. Many gangs are, as police believe, territorial in nature. But territoriality is not a constant; a large and growing number of gangs is mobile and does not claim allegiance to any particular area.

Street Gangs or Law-Violating Groups?

In a previous chapter, we presented law enforcement reports on the number of gangs and gang members in the United States. Police counts from across the country in 1997 totaled 30,500 gangs and 816,000 gang members. Given the lack of correspondence between law enforcement's understanding of gangs and that derived from decades of research, the question forced upon us is: What exactly is being counted?

We suspect that some large proportion of those groups identified as gangs by police are actually what Walter Miller defines as *law-violating groups*. Several years after presenting his "consensus-based" definition of gangs, Miller became disenchanted with the term gang, contending it was "confused and connotatively contaminated."[42] He further argued that the term was too restrictive and that very few delinquent youth groups would qualify as gangs under the accepted definition (i.e., well organized, had identifiable leadership, claimed territory, etc.).

> The definitional finding thus indicates that the term gang, for most practitioners, refers to a group which . . . operates according to formal organizational procedures, has a well-developed hierarchical authority, and is specifically structured for the purpose of engaging in criminal activity. It is quite obvious that groups with such characteristics . . . must make up only a small proportion of all groups which posed serious crime problems."[43]

Though most youth crime is committed in groups, Miller stressed that the vast majority of these groups do not correspond to the image of gangs held by those in law enforcement. A broader concept was needed, he argued, that would encompass the full range of collective youth activity—the "law-violating youth group."

> A law-violating group is an association of three or more youths whose members engage recurrently in illegal activities with the cooperation and/or support of their companions.[44]

Unlike gangs, relationships between members in law-violating groups are often temporary and casual, leadership positions are generally undefined and shifting, and acts of delinquency and crime by members are not committed in any systematic fashion. Street gangs, as defined by law enforcement, exist but comprise only a very small subtype within this broader concept.

Using a series of extrapolations and assumptions, Miller estimated that in cities of 25,000 residents or more, for every street gang there were *eighty* law-violating youth groups.[45] Moreover, the ratio of law-violating group members to gang members was roughly 30 to 1. If police counts of gangs are actually enumerations of law-violating groups, applying Miller's ratios to recent law enforcement counts would perhaps give us a better idea of the actual number of street gangs (i.e., organized, hierarchically structured criminal organizations) in the country. The revised figures would be (for 1999) 325 or so street gangs (26,000 ÷ 80) and 28,000 gang members (840,500 ÷ 30). We are not suggesting these proportions are necessarily correct; the mix of law-violating youth groups to street gangs in police counts may be considerably lower. But we do know that most police departments cannot distinguish the concept of "groups" from "gangs" in a precise and systematic fashion.[46] But for that matter, neither can gang scholars.[47]

The absence of a clear and substantive definition of gangs and gang members may also serve to focus police attention on poor minority youth, who follow normative systems different from those held by a majority of police officers.[48] A cluster of young, white males on a suburban street corner will likely have a different connotation for most officers than that of several young African-American males clustered in front of a housing project.[49] Consciously or unconsciously, racism may be an important determinant in labeling gang members, particularly for African-American youth.[50]

Gang membership is further inflated by inadequate law enforcement record-keeping.[51] Information is often dated, and includes an unknown number of false positives (youth mislabeled as gang members). In most jurisdictions, there are policies for expunging the files of those identified as gang members if the person has not been involved in gang activity for some period (usually 3–5 years). The extent to which gang files are systematically monitored and purged is in question. Because these files are not routinely purged of former gang members, Irving Spergel argues, "police reports of gang membership lead to erroneous conclusions about the number of active gang members and the nature of the gang problem."[52]

The internalization of cultural stereotypes, specious definitions, racism, and shoddy record-keeping have undoubtedly inflated police reports on the number of gangs and gang members. These sources of error, of course, do not necessarily indicate a deliberate distortion of the gang problem by law enforcement. But we do know that government bureaucracies—including law enforcement—must compete

◆◆▸ _____

... it must be noted that since access to some federally funded law enforcement programs is more likely if a gang problem can be demonstrated in a community, some agencies may have vested interests in the "discovery" of gang activity.[53]

Robert J. Bursik and Harold G. Grasmick, Neighborhoods and Crime, _1993._

for public attention and resources, both finite commodities. And as is true for other bureaucracies, law enforcement claims-makers are often guilty of casting conditions in the most persuasive and dramatic terms. This frequently involves the manipulation of numbers to emphasize the severity of the problem.

Over the past two decades, a flood of federal dollars has been made available to law enforcement agencies if a gang problem can be demonstrated in their community. Economic considerations have been suggested as an explanation of the dramatic increase in the number of gang members reported by Phoenix police during the late 1970s.[54] Federal funds were also obtained by police in Springfield (MO) following reports that the number of gang-related crimes had jumped from 3 incidents in 1989 to nearly 400 in 1993.[55] Randall Shelden and his colleagues report in their research that one city (not named) formed a gang unit to compete for federal funds, though there was no evidence the city had any gangs.[56]

THE THREAT POSED BY STREET GANGS

Gangs have emerged as a major social problem because they have become nearly synonymous with violent crime. This close pairing of gangs and violence is a result of law enforcement reports and sensationalized portrayals of gangs in the news and entertainment media. The link has also been confirmed by the vast majority of gang researchers over the past two decades.[57] Regardless of study design or research methodology, virtually all studies have demonstrated that gang members are more likely than nongang youth to commit crimes—especially violent crimes—and to do so with greater frequency. In accounting for this relationship gang scholars minimize individual and familial variables and ascribe causal significance to the normative structures and group dynamics within the gang. Broader interpretations of their findings draw heavily from William Wilson's "underclass" concept, explaining gang formation in the context of changing urban economies.[58]

While most of what we know about gangs comes from field studies, many of which were discussed earlier, survey research has generally been used to examine the unique role of gang membership in the production of criminal behavior. One the earliest was conducted in Philadelphia by Paul Tracy, who found major differences in official arrest rates between police-identified gang members and other arrestees.[59] Among juveniles, there were three gang arrests for every nongang arrest. The differences among adults in the sample were even greater: five gang arrests for every nongang arrest. Similar ratios were also found using self-reported crime, though the offending rates were considerably higher. Official and self-reported data were also used in a study by David Curry and Irving Spergel using a sample of adolescent Hispanic and African-American males drawn from Chicago inner city schools.[60] Findings suggested that gang involvement was a significant predictor of delinquency, though the authors could not rule out the possibility that gangs may have recruited members from adolescents who were already delinquent, or at least had already demonstrated a potential for trouble-making.

A recent study by C. Ronald Huff also explored differences in delinquency between gang and nongang members in Cleveland, Ohio.[61] Huff attempted to further isolate the effects of gang membership by selecting a control group of nongang members from environments similar to those of gang members and referred by schools and social services agencies as being at risk for joining gangs. Self-reported gang members were significantly more likely than the at-risk youth to report having committed certain violent offenses, including homicide, drive-by shootings, intimidating or assaulting victims, and carrying concealed weapons.

Though these cross-sectional studies suggest gang membership has significant and powerful effects on offending, they cannot rule out a reverse causal order (more serious, chronic offenders being recruited into gangs). Longitudinal studies are needed to clarify the temporary ordering of gang membership and criminal behavior. Several such studies have been conducted, all confirming a higher prevalence and frequency of serious and violent offending among gang youth.

Two such studies involving large samples of high-risk, inner city youth were conducted in Denver and Rochester. Using data from the Denver Youth Survey (DYS), Finn-Aage Esbensen and his colleagues found self-reported gang members reported committing nearly three times as many serious and violent offenses as nongang youth.[62] Confirming the influence of the gang, the findings showed that youth committed more serious and violent crimes while they were gang members, with lower rates of offending both before they joined the gang and after they left the gang. The authors of the study also report a trend toward increasing delinquency among gang members for at least two years before they joined the gang. Rather than a serious consideration of the role of individual traits or propensities to account for this tendency, the researchers suggested that "gang membership is but a more formalized form of co-offending that was initiated within a delinquent peer group in prior years."[63]

The dynamics of gang membership were also explored by Terrence Thornberry and his colleagues (1993) with data from the Rochester Youth Development Study.[64] Particularly interested in why gang members are more likely to be involved in serious and violent crime, the researchers tested three alternative explanations. The *selection* or a "kind of person" model posits that gangs recruit adolescents for membership who are already delinquent. In the *social facilitation* or a "kind of group" model, gang members are no more delinquent than nongang youth, but the normative structure and group processes in the gangs result in high rates of crime. The *enhancement model* is a combination of the two. Here gangs recruit adolescents who are already delinquent and the gang milieu encourages offending.

The greatest support was found for the social facilitation model. Unlike in the Denver study, gang members did not have higher rates of offending before joining the gang. But once they became members, their rate of offending increased substantially, and fell once they left the gang. The authors of the study concluded that "being in the gang is generative of violent behavior."[65]

Some Nagging Inconsistencies

These studies, particularly those using longitudinal designs, provide strong support for a gang–crime link. Still, some of the findings are perplexing. For example there is the prevalence and rate of violence reported by gang members, particularly since the respondents were typically quite young (12–15 years old). In one of the studies, nearly one in six gang members reported having committed a homicide in the previous year![66] These kinds of findings contrast sharply with arrest data showing serious gang violence is heavily concentrated among older gang members.[67] Moreover, the survey results suggest that most gang crime is violent crime and that gang violence is a common occurrence. But scholars who have spent the better part of their careers on the street actually observing street gangs have concluded that violence is the least prevalent gang-specific behavior.[68]

Have gang members in these survey accurately reported their involvement in violent crime, or have they simply told researchers what they thought they wanted to hear? In most surveys, no attempt was made to verify respondent answers. While studies have generally confirmed the validity of self-report surveys, their validity has been shown to vary according to the criminality of respondents (the higher the criminality, the lower the validity of the crime measure).[69] From his research on Los Angles gangs, Malcolm Klein warns us that one certain way to overstate gang violence is to rely on the reports of gang members.

> Gang members talk violence a great deal; they do far less . . . Street gangs through the years have done nothing more often than they have done something exciting. Their most customary activities are sleeping, eating, and hanging around. Criminal

212 SECTION III Panic at the National Level

acts are a minority of the activities they engage in, and violent acts are a minority of those. We must remember that despite the drama and lethality of gang violence, its prevalence does not deserve using the label *violent gang*. This only feeds a stereotype that needs no help from scholars. To repeat, most gang members' behavior is not criminal, and most gang members' crimes are not violent. And of course, most violent people are not gang members . . .[70]

The levels of serious crime reported by gang members in these studies also seems inconsistent with police reports of gang-related crime. In a national survey conducted in the early 1990s, for example, law enforcement officials reported more than five times as many gang members as gang-related incidents.[71] True, much crime in the country does go unrecorded, but this is less true for the kinds of serious violent offending (homicide, robbery, etc.) reported by gang youth in these studies.

Our confidence in the findings from these studies is also undermined by a number of serious methodological problems that will not be discussed here.[72] Nonetheless, it seems reasonable to conclude that *some* gang members in *some* gangs do commit more violent crimes than youths not in gangs, though the extent and nature of, and reasons for, those differences remain unclear.

PUTTING THE GANG THREAT IN PERSPECTIVE

However, what is the most troubling about the gang-violence studies discussed here is the failure of researchers to contextualize their findings. In other words, assuming gang members do commit more serious crimes, just how great is that threat in relation to the overall crime problem?

To put the gang threat in perspective, first we need to keep in mind that relatively few youth belong to gangs. In the Denver Youth Study previously discussed, less than 7 percent of youth reported gang membership.[73] In a recent survey of some 6,000 eighth graders from 42 schools in 11 cities, only 9 percent reporting they currently belonged to a gang.[74] One notable (and highly disputable) outlier comes from Los Angeles, where according to police estimates, almost half of all black males between the ages of 21 and 24 are known gang members.[75]

A rough estimate can also be calculated through figures provided by law enforcement in the 1998 National Youth Gang Survey.[76] That year, police reported 780,000 gang members. Using a rule of thumb provided by Walter Miller during the first national survey of gang problems,[77] let's assume that 90 percent (702,000) of these gang members were males. According to Bureau of Census statistics for that year, there were nearly 29 million males in the country between the ages of 10 and 24 (the general age range for gang membership).[78] Thus in 1998, roughly 2½ percent of all adolescent and young adult males in the United States had been identified by law enforcement as gang members.

Not only are relatively few youth involved in gangs, gang crime represents only a small proportion of all serious crime that occurs in schools, cities, or other settings.[79] Herbert Covey and his colleagues estimate that between 5 and 15 percent of all crime in the U.S. is committed by youth gang members, though they add the "the true percentage is probably closer to 5 than 15."[80] As with the definition of a gang, the definition of a "gang-related" crime also varies; consequently, estimates are bound to vary. Chicago, for example, uses a restrictive "motive"-based definition of gang crime (crime that is a function of gang membership or motivated by gang goals). Using that definition, Lawrence Bobrowski found that less than 1 percent of all Part I (index or serious) crimes in Chicago during the late 1980s was "gang-related."[81] Spergel reports that in Chicago in 1987, gang-motivated homicides accounted for only 7 percent of all murders in the city, less than 5 percent of all felonious assaults, and under 1 percent of all robberies.[82]

On the other hand, Los Angeles police use a more liberal "member-based" definition of gang crime (any crime committed by a known gang member, regardless of motivation). It should not be surprising, particularly since half of all young African-American males in the city have been labeled gang members, that gang crime in LA constitutes a larger share of all crime. In 1987, one-fourth of all homicides, 11 percent of serious assaults, and just under 7 percent of all robberies in the city were recorded as "gang-related."[83]

A perspective on gang violence also comes from the findings of the 1994 National Institute of Justice Gang Survey.[84] Law enforcement officials across the country were asked if they had a gang problem in their jurisdiction and, if so, to provide data on the amount of gang-related crime in the previous year. For those cities that reported a gang crime problem, but had no supporting data (i.e., no statistics on gang-related crime were recorded), researchers assigned estimates based on similarly sized cities. From the data researchers calculated a "conservative" total of 437,066 gang crimes in 1993. A more "reasonable" estimate of 580,331 gang crimes was also computed. These are both rather large numbers, to be sure, but consider that in 1993 there were approximately 14.1 million Part I (serious, Index) crimes recorded by police.[85] Thus, that year (using the higher, more "reasonable" estimate) gang members accounted for only about 4 percent of all arrests for serious street crime. If we look at those who are not only arrested but also convicted and imprisoned, we find a very similar proportion. Only 6 percent of state prison inmates in 1991 reported having been a gang member prior to incarceration.[86]

One final vantage point from which to assess the relative contribution of gang crime is provided by victimization surveys. National Crime Victimization Survey (NCVS) data for 1991 show that just 6 percent of all serious violent offenses involved two or more juveniles (a liberal definition of a gang).[87] In 1997, survey victims were specifically asked whether one or more of their offenders were gang members. Less than 5 percent of all violent incidents reported by victims that year involved gang members.[88]

Viewed in these ways, the problem of gang crime actually appears rather insignificant, particularly when considering the attention it has received from gang scholars. One might also ask those researchers to account for the declining rates of crime (violent and property) in the U.S. over the past eight consecutive years, at a time when, by all accounts, the number of gangs and gang members in the country has exploded.

THE GANG–GUN CONNECTION

There is a furor currently raging nationally over gun control, and we have no desire to throw ourselves into the fray by suggesting that guns—particularly in the hands of youth—are not a serious problem. Clearly, they are. Of the over 15,000 murders committed in the U.S. during 1999, nearly 7 out of 10 involved firearms—more often than not, a handgun.[89] Gun homicides do not affect the population uniformly: Offenders and victims are disproportionately young, male, African-American, and inner city residents. Perhaps the most disturbing of all crime statistics, since the late 1960s the leading cause of death for African-American males between the ages of 15 and 24 has been firearm-related homicide.[90]

Many scholars attribute the increase in serious gang violence over the past two decades (though there is little evidence documenting such an increase[91]) to the greater availability and lethality of firearms among gang members.[92] Research has consistently shown that gang members are more likely than nongang members to own guns.[93] In the largest study to date, Scott Decker and his colleagues examined firearm availability and use in a sample of 7,000 booked arrestees in 11 major U.S. cities.[94] While 14 percent of arrestees reported carrying a weapon all or most of the time, and 20 percent of nongang juveniles did so, almost one-third (31 percent) of youth gang members claimed to carry a weapon regularly.

The prevalence of gun ownership among the nation's youth (and it appears, particularly among gang youth) is sufficiently disturbing without the caricaturization of the problem by some who study, police, or prosecute gangs. More specifically, gangs are routinely linked by many to the most sophisticated and lethal weapons available: AK-47s, Uzis, MAC-10s, Tech-9s, and other assault weapons. But in Las Vegas and Reno, none of the several hundred gang incidents we examined involved either an assault rifle or automatic weapon. Our finding is consistent with reports from jurisdictions across the country, though sometimes it is necessary to delve beneath the hype. During the early 1980s in Los Angeles, for example, police and the media began reporting an epidemic of drive-by shootings between rival gang members involving assault weapons.[95] Pressed for documentation by some in the community, L.A. police admitted that though they had "heard" about local gangs buying Uzis and other weapons, the only guns they had actually confiscated were shotguns and handguns. Record searches document that assault weapons are, in fact, rarely used by gangs in drive-by shootings or gang homicides.[96]

During the late 1980s, a time when increased gang violence was being reported in many cities, less than 3 percent of all guns seized by police in the U.S. were assault weapons.[97] In an effort to combat drug dealing by street gangs, in the 1980s Chicago police seized hundreds of firearms during drug warrant executions and arrests. Only three Uzis and three MAC IIs (semiautomatic weapons) were confiscated; none of the weapons had been converted to automatic fire.[98] And the suggestion that semiautomatics are routinely converted to fully automatic weapons is pure Hollywood. Over 4,000 guns were confiscated by L.A. police during a one-year period in Los Angeles; only 6 had been converted from semi- to fully automatic weapons.[99]

Moreover, there is evidence to suggest that gang members are actually less likely to own these semiautomatic weapons than the general population of gun owners.[100] In 1991, 31 percent of the handguns used in drive-by shootings in Los Angeles were semiautomatic pistols. Yet 62 percent of the handguns produced and sold by U.S. manufacturers (the source of 85 percent of all new guns) were semiautomatic pistols. Since violent gang members in Los Angeles were only half as likely to use semiautomatic pistols as one would expect based on recent handgun sales, it appears that gang members actually "disprefer" the semiautomatic weapons.

THE GANG–DRUG CONNECTION

In addition to violent crime and guns, street gangs have come to be closely associated with illegal drug sales and trafficking, particularly crack cocaine. Malcolm Klein is convinced that the "connection has been blown way out of proportion by some zealous police officials, federal enforcement leaders, issue-hungry politicians, and headline-hunting media reporters . . . " and also by "academic writers who play to the dramatic aspects of the purported connections."[101] One of the academics Klein has in mind is undoubtedly Jerome Skolnick, a police scholar whose research has done much to promote the gang–drug stereotype.

Skolnick's conclusions are based on interviews conducted during the late 1980s with 39 inmates in four California state prisons and 42 police and corrections officials.[102] He found that gangs in Northern California and African-American gangs in Los Angeles were highly structured, "organized solely for the purposes of distributing drugs, " and controlled illegal drug markets.[103] While the northern gangs were geographically stable, Skolnick reported that L.A. Crips and Bloods gangs were migrating to cities across the country, motivated by the increasing violence in local drug markets, declining prices, and intensified law enforcement efforts.

Two recent works provide the strongest support for the concept of the "entrepreneurial" gang. From a 10-year study of 37 gangs in three cities, Martin Sanchez Jankowski concluded that gangs were highly structured organizations that serve both individual and collective interests through a variety of illegal activities.[104] By far the most profitable money-maker, however, was illegal drugs and he reports that virtually all gangs are active in the market. Most youth join gangs to sell drugs, simple as that. The gang offers higher earning potential, safer working conditions, and financial security during the unexpected pitfalls of life (injury, arrest, etc.). According to Jankowski, most of the drug profits are kept by members, but some are earmarked for the gang itself in order to purchase legitimate businesses or expand drug markets.

Carol Taylor's research on drug dealing gangs in Detroit paints a similar picture.[105] "Corporate gangs," according to Taylor, were well-oiled, money-making machines with all the characteristics of any good corporation: strong leadership, commitment to organizational goals, and powerful incentives to employees.

The evidence to support such claims is weak and largely anecdotal. In fact, shortly after Skolnick's report was issued, the Los Angeles County District Attorney's Office began its own study examining the role of gangs in local drug markets.[106] Authors of the study found the involvement of street gangs in the sale of illegal drugs was minimal, episodic, and completely disorganized. Similar findings were reported in a study of the gang–crack link in Los Angeles.[107] All arrests for crack sales for 1983 through 1985 (the height of the crack epidemic) from five L.A. police stations were examined to determine the extent of gang involvement. The records demonstrated that 75 percent of those arrested for selling crack were not gang members, and the researchers concluded that "the world of crack in Los Angeles belonged principally to the regular drug dealers, not to street gangs."[108]

In St. Louis, Decker and Van Winkle found that nearly all gang members interviewed claimed to have sold drugs—usually crack cocaine—at some point in their lives.[109] However, few reported joining a gang to sell drugs or that profits from sales were used to further gang objectives. Gangs did not run most of the

---

Though some gang members sell drugs, few control drug trafficking operations and there is little evidence that gangs migrate to other areas of the country specifically to set up drug operations.

crack houses in the area and most drug dealers were not gang members. They argued that gang members did not, and could not, control the illegal drug market in St. Louis since they "lacked the skills or commitment to organize for a long-range profit-making venture."[110]

There is also little evidence of a massive migration of street gangs to other cities in order to set up new drug operations, as Skolnick claimed.[111] There are probably some big-city gang members that do move to the suburbs or smaller towns, recruit local youth, and establish gang franchises. However, the vast majority of gang members move because of family reasons.[112]

Another stereotype shattered by research concerns the link between gangs, drug trafficking, and violence. Studies have shown, for example, that gangs engage in violence of whether or not they are selling drugs.[113] While some acts of gang violence are drug related, the vast majority are the result of status or turf conflicts. In Chicago, Carolyn Block and her colleagues found that of the 1,984 gang-related homicides that occurred between 1965 and 1994, only 43 (2.2 %) involved a drug motive.[114] Drug motives are actually more common in nongang violence than gang violence.[115]

Conclusion

Have we experienced a moral panic concerning gangs at a national level? We can, of course, only speak with confidence about what we observed and recorded in Nevada. But there are enough inconsistencies between the hype and the facts to at least make one wonder. Even if not on a scale of a full moral panic, there seems little question that gang members have been portrayed as modern day "folk devils" in order to sell papers, attract viewers, increase police payrolls, secure federal funds, and win elections.

Notes

1. Malcolm Klein. 1995. *The American Street Gang: Its Nature, Prevalence, and Control.* New York : Oxford University Press, p. 209.
2. Irving Spergel. 1995. *The Youth Gang Problem.* New York: Oxford University Press.
3. Institute for Law and Justice. 1993. *Gang Prosecution in the United States.* Mimeographed copy. Alexandria, VA. September. pp. 3–6.
4. Institute for Law and Justice, 1993, p. 3–7.
5. Institute for Law and Justice, 1993, p. A-25 (Appendix).
6. Spergel, 1995, p. 27.
7. Walter Miller. 1980. "Gangs, groups, and serious youth crime." In D. Schichor and D. Kelly (eds.), *Critical Issues in Juvenile Delinquency.* Lexington, MA: D. C. Heath & Co., pp. 115–138; Walter Miller. 1975. *Violence by Youth Gangs and Youth Groups as a Crime Problem in*

American Cities. Office of Juvenile Justice and Delinquency Prevention, U.S. Department of Justice. Washington, D.C.: Government Printing Office.

8. Miller, 1975, p. 9.

9. Walter Miller. 1992. *Crime by Youth Gangs and Groups in the United States*. Office of Juvenile Justice and Delinquency Prevention. U.S. Department of Justice.

10. Jerome Needle and William Stapleton. 1983. *Police Handling of Youth Gangs*. Office of Juvenile Justice and Delinquency Prevention, U.S. Department of Justice. Washington, D.C.: Government Printing Office.

11. Needle and Stapleton, 1983, p. 8.

12. G. David Curry and Scott Decker. 1998. *Confronting Gangs: Crime and Community*. Los Angeles: Roxbury Publishing.

13. Jerome Skolnick, T. Correl, E. Navarro, and R. Rabb. 1988. *The Social Structure of Street Drug Dealing*. Sacramento: Office of the Attorney General of the State of California; Felix Padilla. 1992. *The Gang as an American Enterprise*. New Brunswick, NJ: Rutgers University Press; Carl Taylor. 1990. *Dangerous Society*. East Lansing, MI: Michigan State University Press.

14. Martin Sanchez Jankowski. 1991. *Islands in the Street: Gangs and American Urban Society*. Berkeley: University of California Press.

15. Jankowski, 1991, pp. 28–29.

16. Lewis Yablonsky. 1997. *Gangsters: Fifty Years of Madness, Drugs, and Death on the Streets of America*. New York: New York University Press, p. 191.

17. Yablonsky, 1997, p. 58.

18. See Curry and Decker, 1998 for a review.

19. Malcolm Klein. 1995. *The American Street Gang: Its Nature, Prevalence, and Control*. New York: Oxford University Press, p. 61.

20. Malcolm Klein. 1971. *Street Gangs and Street Workers*. Englewood Cliffs, NJ: Prentice-Hall; Mark Fleisher. 1995. *Beggars and Thieves: Lives of Urban Street Criminals*. Madison, WI: University of Wisconsin Press.

21. Irving A. Spergel. 1995 *The Youth Gang Problem: A Community Approach*. New York: Oxford University Press, p. 18.

22. John M. Hagedorn. 1988. *People and Folks: Gangs, Crime and the Underclass in a Rustbelt City*. Chicago: Lake View Press, p. 90.

23. Scott Decker and Barrik Van Winkle. 1996. *Life in the Gang*. New York: Cambridge University Press, pp. 271–272.

24. Finn-Aage Esbensen, David Huizinga, and Anne W. Weiher. 1993. "Gang and non-gang youth: Differences in explanatory factors." *Journal of Contemporary Criminal Justice*. Vol. 9, pp. 94–116.

25. Terrence P. Thornberry, Marvin D. Krohn, Alan J. Lizotte, and Deborah Chard-Wierschem. 1993. "The role of juvenile gangs in facilitating delinquent behavior." *Journal of Research in Crime and Delinquency*. Vol. 30, pp. 55–87.

26. Spergel, 1995, pp. 79–80.

27. Scott Decker, Tim Bynum, and Deborah Weisel. 1998. "A tale of two cities: Gangs as organized crime groups." *Justice Quarterly*. Vol. 15, pp. 395–425.

28. Hagedorn, 1988.

29. Hagedorn, 1988, p. 135.

30. Klein, 1995.

31. Ko-Lin Chin. 1990. "Chinese gangs and extortion." In R. Huff (ed.), *Gangs in America*. Newbury Park, CA: Sage, pp. 129–145; Spergel, 1995; Klein, 1995.

32. Hagedorn, 1988.

33. Deborah Weisel and Ellen Painter. 1997. *The Police Response to Gangs: Case Studies of Five Cities*. Washington, D.C.: Police Executive Research Forum, p.22.
34. Klein, 1995.
35. Robert Bursik and Harold Grasmick. 1993. *Neighborhoods and Crime: The Dimensions of Effective Community Control*. Lexington, MA: Lexington Books.
36. Klein, 1995.
37. Douglas Clay and Frank Quila. 1994. "'Spitting the lit'—fact or fad? Gangs and America's schools." *Phi Delta Kappan*. Vol. 76, p. 65.
38. Weisel and Painter, 1997, p. 15.
39. Klein, 1995.
40. Mark Fleisher. 2000. Cited in "The Youth Gang Epidemic That Was—or Wasn't," *Youth Today*. Vol. 9(8), p. 48.
41. Jeffrey Rush. 1996. "The police role in dealing with gangs." In J. Mitchell and J. Rush (eds.), *Gangs: A Criminal Justice Approach*. Cincinnati, OH: Anderson Publishing, pp. 85–92.
42. Miller, 1992, p. 17.
43. Miller, 1980, p. 121.
44. Miller, 1992, p. 18.
45. Miller, 1980.
46. Needle and Stapleton, 1983; Miller, 1992.
47. For a discussion of the issues and problems surrounding scholarly definitions of gangs and gang members, see Irving Spergel. 1990. "Youth gangs: Continuity and change." In M. Tonry and N. Morris (eds.), *Crime and Justice: A Review of the Research*. Vol. 12; Richard Ball and G. David Curry. 1995. "The logic of definition in criminology: Purposes and methods for defining gangs." *Criminology*. Vol. 33, pp. 225–246; Ruth Horowitz. 1990. "Sociological perspectives of gangs: Conflicting definitions and concepts." In R. Huff (ed.), *Gangs in America*. Beverly Hills, CA: Sage, pp. 37–54.
48. James Quinn and William Downs. 1993. "Police perceptions of the severity of local gangs problems: An analysis of noncriminal predicators." *Sociological Spectrum*. Vol. 13, pp. 209–226.
49. James F. Short, Jr. 1997. *Poverty, Ethnicity, and Violent Crime*. Boulder, CO: Westview Press; Hagedorn, 1988.
50. Spergel, 1995.
51. Ira Sharkansky. 1996. "The policy analysis of gang violence." In J. Mitchell and J. Rush (eds.), *Gangs: A Criminal Justice Approach*. Cincinnati, OH: Anderson Publishing, pp. 143–160.
52. Spergel, 1995, p. 197.
53. Bursik and Grasmick, 1993, p. 116.
54. Majorie Zatz. 1987. "Chicago youth gangs and crime: The creation of a moral panic." *Contemporary Crisis*. Vol. 11, pp. 129–158.
55. A.L. Marsteller. 1996. "A social construction of a gang problem." Paper delivered at the Academy of Criminal Justice Science. Las Vegas. Mimeographed copy.
56. Randall Shelden, Sharon Tracy, and William Brown. *Youth Gangs in American Society*. Belmont, CA: Wadsworth.
57. For a review of this literature, see James C. Howell. 1998. *Youth Gangs: An Overview*. Office of Juvenile Justice and Delinquency Prevention. National Institute of Justice. Washington, D.C.: Government Printing Office; Curry and Decker, 1998.
58. Bursik and Grasmick, 1993; Spergel, 1995.
59. Paul Tracy. 1982. "Gang membership and violent offenders: Preliminary results from the 1958 Cohort Study." Cited in Spergel, 1995.

60. G. David Curry and Irving A. Spergel. 1992. "Gang involvement and delinquency among Hispanic and African-American adolescent males." *Journal of Research in Crime and Delinquency.* Vol. 29, pp. 273–291.

61. C. Ronald Huff. 1998. *Comparing the Criminal Behavior of Youth Gangs and At-Risk Youths.* Research in Brief. National Institute of Justice. Washington, D.C.: Government Printing Office, October.

62. Esbensen et al., 1993.

63. Esbensen et al., 1993, p. 583.

64. Thornberry et al., 1993.

65. Thornberry et al., 1993, p. 81.

66. Huff, 1998. See Exhibit 2, p. 4.

67. Klein, 1995; Spergel, 1995.

68. Jeffrey Fagan. 1989. "The social organization of drug use and drug dealing among urban gangs." *Criminology.* Vol. 27, pp. 633–666; Klein, 1995; Miller, 1975.

69. Michael Hindelang, Travis Hirschi, and Joseph Weiss. 1981. *Measuring Delinquency.* Beverly Hills, CA: Sage.

70. Klein, 1995, p. 29, p. 70.

71. G. David Curry, Richard Ball, and R.J. Fox. 1994. *Gang Crime and Law Enforcement Recordkeeping.* Washington, D.C.: National Institute of Justice.

72. See Bursik and Grasmick, 1993; Michael Gottfredson and Travis Hirschi. 1990. *A General Theory of Crime.* Stanford University Press; Michael Gottfredson and Travis Hirschi. 1987. "The methodological adequacy of longitudinal research on crime." *Criminology.* Vol. 25, pp. 581–614; Merry Morash. 1983. "Gangs, groups, and delinquency." *British Journal of Criminology.* Vol. 23, pp. 309–331.

73. Esbensen et al., 1993.

74. Finn-Aage Esbensen and D. Wayne Osgood. 1997. *National Evaluation of G.R.E.A.T.* Research in Brief. National Institute of Justice. Washington, D.C.: Government Printing Office.

75. Ira Reiner. 1992. District Attorney, City of Los Angeles. *Gangs, Crime and Violence in Los Angeles: Findings and Proposals from the District Attorney's Office.* National Youth Gang Information Center, NYGIC Document D0049.

76. U.S. Department of Justice. 2000. *1998 National Youth Gang Survey.* Office of Justice Programs, Office of Juvenile Justice and Delinquency Prevention. National Youth Gang Center. Washington, D.C.: Government Printing Office.

77. Miller, 1975; Curry and Decker, 1998.

78. United States Census Bureau. 1999. Population Estimates Program, Population Division. Washington, D.C.: Government Printing Office.

79. Spergel, 1995.

80. Herbert C. Covey, Scott Menard, and Robert J. Franzere. 1997. *Juvenile Gangs.* Second edition. Springfield, IL: Charles C Thomas Publishers, p. 44.

81. Lawrence Bobrowski. 1988. "Collecting, Organizing, and Reporting Street Gang Crime." Cited in Spergel, 1995.

82. Spergel, 1990.

83. Spergel, 1990.

84. G. David Curry, Richard A. Ball, and Scott H. Decker. 1996. "Estimating the national scope of gang crime from law enforcement data." *Research in Brief.* U.S. Department of Justice. National Institute of Justice. Office of Justice Programs. Washington, D.C., August.

85. Kathleen Maguire, Ann Pastore, and Timothy Flanagan. 1997. *Sourcebook of Criminal Justice Statistics, 1997.* Washington, D.C.: Bureau of Justice Statistics.

86. Bureau of Justice Statistics. 1991. *Survey of State Prison Inmates*. National Institute of Justice. Washington, D.C.: Government Printing Office.

87. H. N. Snyder and M. Sickmund. 1995. *Juvenile Offenders and Victims: A National Report*. Office of Juvenile Justice and Delinquency Prevention, U.S. Department of Justice. Washington, D.C.: Government Printing Office.

88. Bureau of Justice Statistics. *National Crime Victimization Survey, 1992–1997*. National Institute of Justice. Interuniversity Consortium for Political and Social Research. Ann Arbor, MI.

89. Federal Bureau of Investigation. *Uniform Crime Reports, 1999*. National Institute of Justice. Washington, D.C.: Government Printing Office.

90. Center for Disease Control and Prevention. National Center for Health Statistics. 1999. *National Vital Statistics Reports*. Vol. 47. Washington, D.C.: Government Printing Office; Herbert C. Covey, Scott Menard, and Robert J. Franzere. 1997. *Juvenile Gangs*. Second edition. Springfield, IL: Charles C Thomas Publishers; The Department of the Treasury and the Department of Justice. 1999. *Gun Crime in the Age Group 18–20*. Washington, D.C.: Government Printing Office. June.

91. "Beyond the unsystematic collection of anecdotal reports, there is little solid evidence to support the assertion of an increase in gang violence over the last decade or two." Klein, 1995, p. 116.

92. Carolyn Block, Rebecca Block, and Richard Block. 1993. *Street Gang Crime in Chicago. Research in Brief*. National Institute of Justice, Office of Justice Programs, U.S. Department of Justice. Washington, D.C.: Government Printing Office; Spergel, 1995; Miller, 1975; Hagedorn, 1998.

93. See Howell, 1998 for a review.

94. Scott Decker, Susan Pennell, and Amy Caldwell. 1997. *Illegal Firearms: Access and Use by Arrestees. Research in Brief*. National Institute of Justice. Washington, D.C.: Government Printing Office.

95. Reported in Gary Kleck. 1997. *Targeting Guns: Firearms and Their Control*. Hawthorne, NY: Aldine de Gruyter.

96. H. Range Hutson, Deirdre Anglin, and Michael Pratts. 1994. "Adolescents and children killed or injured in drive-by shootings in Los Angeles." *New England Journal of Medicine*. Vol. 330, pp. 324–327; H. Range Hutson, Deirdre Anglin, Demetrious Kyriacou, Joel Hart, and Kelvin Spears. 1995. "The epidemic of gang-related homicides in Los Angeles County from 1979 through 1994." *Journal of the American Medical Association*. Vol. 274, pp. 1031–1036.

97. Kleck, 1997.

98. Kleck, 1997.

99. Kleck, 1997.

100. Kleck, 1997; Russ Thurman. 1994. "Shooting industry's firearm business analysis." *Shooting Industry*. Vol. 39, pp. 107–112, p. 118.

101. Klein, 1995, p. 40, p. 120.

102. Jerome Skolnick. 1990. "The social structure of street level drug dealing." *American Journal of Police*. Vol. 9, pp. 1–41.

103. Skolnick, 1990, p. 4.

104. Jankowski, 1991.

105. Taylor, 1990.

106. Reiner, 1992.

107. Malcolm Klein. Cheryl Maxson, and Lea Cunningham. 1991. "'Crack': Street gangs and violence." *Criminology*. Vol. 29, pp. 623–650.

108. Klein et al, 1991, p. 647.

109. Decker and Van Winkle, 1996.

110. Decker and Van Winkle, 1996, p. 159.

111. Hagedorn, 1988; Howell and Decker, 1998; Klein, 1995; Cheryl Maxson, Kristi Woods, and Malcolm Klein. 1996. "Street gang migration: How big a threat?" *National Institute of Justice Journal*. Issue 230. National Institute of Justice. Washington, D.C.: Government Printing Office, pp. 26–31.
112. R. Zevitz and S. Takata. 1992. "Metropolitan gang influence and the emergence of group delinquency in a regional community." *Journal of Criminal Justice*. Vol. 20, pp. 93–106.
113. Fagan, 1989.
114. Carolyn Rebecca Block, Antigone Christakos, Ayad Jacob, and Roger Przbylski. 1996. Street Gangs and Crime: Patterns and Trends in Chicago. Research Bulletin. Chicago, IL: Illinois Criminal Justice Information Authority.
115. James C. Howell. In press. "Youth gangs homicides: A literature review." *Crime and Delinquency*.

Index